D0935437

THEOLOGICAL INVESTIGATIONS

Volume XIX

THEOLOGICAL INVESTIGATIONS

VOLUME I
GOD, CHRIST, MARY AND GRACE

VOLUME II
MAN IN THE CHURCH

VOLUME III
THEOLOGY OF THE SPIRITUAL LIFE

VOLUME IV
MORE RECENT WRITINGS

VOLUME V
LATER WRITINGS

VOLUME VI
CONCERNING VATICAN COUNCIL II

VOLUME VII
FURTHER THEOLOGY OF THE SPIRITUAL LIFE 1

VOLUME VIII
FURTHER THEOLOGY OF THE SPIRITUAL LIFE 2

VOLUME IX
WRITINGS OF 1965–1967 1

VOLUME X
WRITINGS OF 1965–1967 2

VOLUME XI
CONFRONTATIONS 1

VOLUME XII
CONFRONTATIONS 2

VOLUME XIII
THEOLOGY, ANTHROPOLOGY, CHRISTOLOGY

VOLUME XIV
ECCLESIOLOGY, QUESTIONS OF THE CHURCH,
THE CHURCH IN THE WORLD

VOLUME XV
PENANCE IN THE EARLY CHURCH

VOLUME XVI
EXPERIENCE OF THE SPIRIT: SOURCE OF THEOLOGY

VOLUME XVII
JESUS, MAN, AND THE CHURCH

VOLUME XVIII
GOD AND REVELATION

VOLUME XIX
FAITH AND MINISTRY

VOLUME XX
CONCERN FOR THE CHURCH

THEOLOGICAL INVESTIGATIONS

VOLUME XIX
FAITH AND MINISTRY

by
KARL RAHNER

Translated by Edward Quinn

CROSSROAD · NEW YORK

1983

The Crossroad Publishing Company
575 Lexington Avenue, New York, N.Y. 10022

A translation of portions of
SCHRIFTEN ZUR THEOLOGIE, XIII and XIV
published by Verlagsanstalt Benziger & Co. A. G., Einsiedeln

Library of Congress Catalog Card Number: 61-8189
ISBN: 0-8245-0522-7

Printed in the U.S.A.

CONTENTS

PART ONE

Faith and the Church

1

FOUNDATIONS OF CHRISTIAN FAITH

I hope it will not seem presumptuous on my part to offer some introductory observations on the purpose and content of my book *Grundkurs des Glaubens: Einführung des Christentums*.* In West Germany eleven printings, comprising more than forty thousand copies, have appeared. It has also appeared in the German Democratic Republic. Dutch, Italian, Spanish, French, Anglo-American, and even Japanese editions have been published, all of which would seem to justify these comments.

It is not a question of commending the work or defining its place in modern theological literature. Nor does the author want to praise the book, but to explain quite straightforwardly his purpose in writing it and to describe its contents. It is obvious that this can be done only in a fragmentary fashion. I cannot deal, for instance, with the many reviews and criticisms that have appeared since the book was published. But perhaps I may be permitted to quote the conclusion of the longest review that I have seen up to the time of writing. Joseph Ratzinger, now Cardinal Archbishop of Munich and a well-known German theologian, writes:

> A large book always provokes discussion. Rahner's basic course is a large book. It is sustained by the same passion for knowledge as that which led Anselm of Canterbury to attempt to deduce Christianity *rationibus necessariis*. Even someone who is not disposed to accept in its entirety the 'idea of Christianity' elaborated by Rahner will find here a presentation of the Christian reality which

* Freiburg im Breisgau, 1976; 11th printing 1979. English trans. *Foundations of Christian Faith: An Introduction to the Idea of Christianity,* trans. William V. Dych (New York: Crossroad/London: Darton, Longman and Todd, 1978).

> he cannot positively or negatively refuse to consider. We cannot but be grateful to Rahner for producing now, as the fruit of all his past efforts, this impressive synthesis, which will remain a source of inspiration long after much of modern theological work has been forgotten.[1]

That is *Cardinal Ratzinger's* opinion, not mine. But it certainly provides me with a moral justification for saying a few words about my own work.

First of all, the title of the book. For my own part, I would have liked to call it simply *Einführung in den Begriff des Christentums* ('Introduction to the Idea of Christianity'). The publisher wanted the title *Grundkurs des Glaubens* ('Basic Course of Faith'). This title is not wrong, but it could be misleading if it were taken to mean a popular presentation, a kind of catechism, of Christian doctrine in its traditional form for everyone. But this is not what the book was meant to be. Certainly it is to be hoped that the content of the book, when translated and popularized (by others, of course), may form part of the Christian proclamation to *all*; but the book itself is intended as a scholarly work, to be understood only as a result of what Hegel called the 'exertion of the idea.' As the subtitle indicates, it is presented as an introduction to the *idea* of Christianity; there is no question of repeating in their traditional formulations particular statements of Christianity about God and salvation history, but rather (so far as this is possible in view of the historicity of salvation history and of God's freedom) of bringing Christianity as a whole under one *idea,* of reflecting on the ultimate unity and the essential coherence of everything that Christianity proclaims. It is true, of course, that such a study, properly understood, amounts to a basic course of Christianity in the sense of a quest for the ultimate grounds of faith; but it is not a popular catechism for the multitude.

Despite the endeavour to establish a comprehensive idea of Christianity (as is made clear again in the book's closing remarks on brief formularies of faith) and despite the academic level which the book attempts to maintain, its distinctive feature really lies not in its conceptual presentation or its scholarly character but in the firm determination it expresses to pursue the question of the essence of

[1] Joseph Cardinal Ratzinger, 'Vom Verstehen des Glaubens: Anmerkungen zu Rahners Grundkurs des Glaubens' in *Theologische Revue* 74 (1978): 177–86.

Christianity on what I would describe as a 'primary plane of reflection'. What does this mean? Certainly not that I intend to get involved in deep and serious problems of a theory of knowledge. The term 'primary plane of reflection' means something quite simple, but it also involves the explicit and resolute acceptance of all the consequences. What is the position of the Christian today who wants honestly to justify his faith to himself and others, and to make really clear to himself up to a point what as a Christian he accepts as true and how he must live?

The normal Christian and even the professional theologian (who can really be an expert only in a tiny sector of theology as a whole) are faced today by a philosophy and theology to which there appear to be no limits. It was possible for Francis Suarez (1548–1619), for example, to assume rightly that he could have present in his subjective consciousness more or less everything that might be important for the justification of Christian faith at his time and in his situation (I mean, explicitly and reflectively present). This has become simply impossible for any individual today. No one can know and write everything that would be necessary for the justification of faith 'as such' in the light of the requirements of scholarly reflection (requirements of reflective knowledge, philosophy, and its modern divisions and problems; exegesis and its assumptions; history of dogma that is not adapted from the outset to school use; general linguistics and epistemology, and all the questions about the assumptions derived from the history of ideas and sociology behind religious statements as a whole). No individual can present and justify his Christian faith today in the way that traditional fundamental and dogmatic theology formerly assumed to be possible. If I wanted today to justify the primacy of the pope in the light of a traditional scholarly reflection on Matthew 16:18, I would need to have studied exegesis all my life, to know from the sources the theology of Judaism at the time of Jesus, and to write some hundreds of pages about this problem. But even then I would certainly not know enough about philosophy, epistemology, about the history of the Church, of law, of dogma, to defend in the traditional fashion the legitimacy of the papal primacy—which is certainly not to be found simply and literally in Matthew. Another example: I once had a clever student who wrote a dissertation on the question of how, in the light of the problems of modern philosophy as a whole, we must methodically set to work epistemologically and philosophically merely to raise at all the question of the personal character of God.

When all is said and done, no one today, entirely on his own, can present his Christian faith as substantiated by fundamental theology and in its dogmatic content in the way that really ought to have been possible and was in fact pursued according to the scholarly ideals of former fundamental and dogmatic theologies. (Nor, of course, can someone who interprets himself from the standpoint of unbelief claim support for his opinions in science as understood according to the ideals of the nineteenth century.) Merely incidentally, it is really obvious that it is impossible to get out of this difficulty with the aid of teamwork, since in *this* matter each individual ought to test the conclusions of the other person's scholarship for their soundness: in these disciplines it is not possible as it is in the natural sciences to rely on the conclusions of other scholars.

Nevertheless, since we can realize Christian faith only as freely responsible subjects, we must be able to justify it rationally and understand its statements. Consequently there must be a way of justifying and understanding Christian faith that does not emerge as a conclusion and synthesis from the study of all the individual theological disciplines. In this respect, in the last resort, it is irrelevant whether or not we describe as a science this justification and understanding of the meaning of Christian faith, which does *not* emerge from the individual theological disciplines (unmanageable for one person in their present-day complexity) but is prior to all such studies. It is also obvious that such efforts by individuals will be made in very different ways and in varying degrees and in varying planes of reflection, dependent on the character of the person involved and the mental climate and the existential situation in which he is placed. If then we speak of a primary plane of reflection, this does not mean that the primary plane is the same for all or that it does not exhibit substantial variations: the term 'primary plane of reflection' is meant to contrast with that scholarly reflection on the Christian faith which is made up of all the methods, considerations, investigations, and conclusions of the many individual historical and philosophical sciences which on the one hand must find expression on this 'secondary' plane of reflection and on the other cannot today be mastered in their entirety by any one person. Consequently the task envisaged in my book was simply to explain how a normal Christian (who cannot be an expert on all the relevant disciplines) can justify the legitimacy and meaning of his faith to himself and to others, without at the same time attempting in a little book to investigate in all their complexity the problems and conclusions of all the individual philosophical and theological disciplines.

Of course, modern works on dogmatics and fundamental theology nowhere actually manage to carry out the abstractly conceivable and scientifically exact study of all the individual disciplines on which they objectively depend; they do not, however, admit expressly and precisely this impossibility, but they are presented as if they were the result of a critical appraisal of all the disciplines they presuppose. A short book of *that kind* on the totality of Christian belief cannot be written today by any one person. That is why I make the explicit claim that this book belongs merely to a primary plane of reflection, that it is not meant to be a learned work, but is itself based on scholarship (if we may use these terms) in its own right and its unavoidability. From what was said about the nature of the primary plane of reflection in the field of existentially important knowledge and decisions it is immediately obvious that a book of this kind must nevertheless be written (as far as one individual can do this) with a view as wide and clear as possible of the problems of the disciplines relevant to theology, that even this work is arduous and perhaps could not be directly accomplished by many people, that it is the sort of book that might be written quite differently. It is impossible to explain here at greater length how and why, even on this primary plane, in practice reflection partly goes on as theology hitherto proceeded (on a plane of higher scholarly reflection), but partly also is compelled to proceed by other ways. Hence, for example, it is impossible on this primary plane of reflection and in a book like this to examine the question of why a person should be a Catholic and not a Protestant precisely in the way in which traditional fundamental theology discussed it with the aid of an immense amount of historical research; this task is today quite beyond the resources of any one individual, if these reflections are to be exact, based on the sources, and without bias. In a word, this book is meant to be a study on a primary plane of reflection, giving an account of the meaning and credibility of Catholic belief precisely in the way that is possible for one person, for one theologian. The absence of 'scholarship' is admitted and intentional, but, I think, is itself existentially-ontologically and theologically justified; it is a question of an explicitly and deliberately accepted lack of scholarship.

In addition to its form, it seems to me that the contents of the book have their own special characteristics. In what follows, I may be permitted to draw attention to some of these.

My theology has often been described as transcendental. I have nothing against this description as long as it is correctly understood and is not meant to suggest that my theology as a whole can quite clearly and unambiguously be characterized in this way. As I understand the term, it simply means that, with reference to all statements of faith and theology (if they are to be justified) the question must be asked how and why man, in virtue of his own nature (which is concrete anyway and thus from the outset irrevocably under the influence of the grace of God's self-communication), is the one with whom these statements can and must actually be concerned. The description does not mean that in my theology man is a subject of faith and religion only in his abstract transcendentality and not in his historicity and his history. For me, he is a subject of faith as a historical being in his concrete history. This, however, is the very thing that is not obvious but must be shown to be possible in a transcendental reflection. It must be shown that history can really be significant for salvation to the intellectual subject, who is always more than space and time. In the last resort it must be shown that man's history is *not* something in which he is involved *over and above* his transcendentality to God as the absolute being and mystery, but that it is only *as* history of this transcendality in freedom that history is actually history in which salvation can come about.

It is typical and important for this book that grace in its first impact and ultimate meaning is always understood strictly as God's *self*-communication and consequently that a proper understanding of the Catholic doctrine of grace and a real understanding of the 'supernatural' can be attained only in the light mainly of 'uncreated grace', although this does not mean the denial of the traditional teaching on created grace as (simultaneously) precondition and consequence of uncreated grace. The dimension of the supernatural and also of revelation is primarily established by God's self-communication, in which God with his own nature, albeit as unmerited grace, becomes an actual internal principle of man: that is, when God represents in regard to man not only the principle of efficient causality, but also the principle of a quasi-formal causality by which the finite becomes really capable of the infinite. But this self-communication of God may not be understood, as in Jesuit baroque scholasticism, merely as entitative objectivity, outside the scope of consciousness; it always means essentially also the *a priori* dynamism of man's knowledge and freedom towards the immediacy of God himself. Man's mental transcendentality as knowledge and freedom is the real and original point at which the grace of God's self-communication is received. This grace is originally a transcendental and not a categorial factor in man's existence.

This gracious self-communication of God as the radical orientation of human transcendentality to the immediacy of God (so that this transcendentality does not always merely point to God, while forever remaining at a distance, but also actually attains him in himself) is not something that happens to man as an isolated event in space and time. It is a permanent existential of man, present always and everywhere, even though in man as inarticulate it takes the form merely of an offer and a precondition for his freedom and in man as historically mature in the form of free acceptance or in the form of free rejection.

Insofar as this self-communication of God present everywhere in history as an existential of man involves a radical orientation of man's transcendentality to the immediacy of God, there is also present a genuine, supernatural, personal revelation of God, even though the latter as the radical orientation of man's transcendentality has not yet been consciously considered and objectified, or at any rate not clearly or perhaps badly. Consequently the history of mind co-exists with the history of revelation. What we usually call history of revelation (what is known as primitive revelation, revelation from Abraham and Moses to Jesus Christ) is therefore not the history of revelation as such, but only a particular, selected part of the history of revelation generally and as a whole, which is established by God's self-communication as an existential of man and as occurring everywhere on very diverse planes of reflection in the history of mankind. Hence the history of religion, even outside explicit, verbalized, and institutionalized Christianity, together with the Old Testament, is not merely the vain attempt of *man* with the aid of his natural transcendentality to establish from below a relationship to God, but is also always and everywhere from the outset a history of revelation and salvation coming from above, even though this history of grace is *really* history: that is, a slowly increasing articulation of this grace in man's consciousness which can take on a variety of forms and even be terribly debased.

It is in this light also that the meaning of anonymous Christianity and anonymous Christians must be understood. The term as such is not important. Anyone who thinks it implies a depreciation of explicit and institutionalized Christianity need not use it. The thing itself, however, cannot be disputed, at least after Vatican II, since it is taught there that always and everywhere in the world anyone who is faithful to this consciousness is living in the grace of God and united to the paschal mystery of Christ. In such a view of the co-existence and co-extensiveness of the history of humanity's mental existence, of the history of salvation and revelation, the absolute necessity of Jesus Christ must not be obscured; but it is permissible to approach Christology from a universal pneumatology and not only to proceed in the opposite direction, so that Jesus Christ appears as the unsurpassable peak of a universal history of grace as God's self-communication to the world as a whole, a peak at which this universal history of salvation is no longer merely at the stage of an open offer of grace to man's freedom, but where this offer from God has been established victoriously and irreversibly, as far as mankind as a whole is concerned.

Something must now be said about the treatment of Christology in this book. Compared to the total content of the book, Christology occupies a very large space. This is because the fact that Christianity after all is about Christ must not be obscured, even though the most fundamental idea of Christianity as presented here is that of the gracious self-communication of God in himself. It is a Christology which must, of course, make use of historical statements and which cannot be a merely speculative development of a 'Christ-idea' (even though a transcendental Christology is legitimate and has its part in this book), insofar as the history of man's transcendentality and its radicalizing by grace is shown to be directed unquestionably toward a point at which it is established as irreversibly victorious and there appears as historically tangible. The fact remains, however, that in principle (and consequently in this book) there must be a place for an *a posteriori* Christology based on historical experience of Jesus as the Christ: that is, the question must be answered as to where in the concrete course of history it is legitimate to find that God-man toward whom a transcendental Christology is directed as to the irreversible culmination of universal salvation history. A Christology 'from below', an 'ascending Christology', is therefore legitimate and necessary.

All this was understood by traditional theology when it included as part of its fundamental theology a treatise *De Christo legato divino*. In this sense the Christology of the present book is meant to be and is in fact traditional, since it asks in the first place who this Jesus was, what he proclaimed, and what account he gave of himself. But traditional Christology considered Jesus within the scope of fundamental theology only in the light of the formal, abstract idea of a divinely attested prophet and then went on to assume that testimony of the God-manhood, the incarnation, and the hypostatic union was to be found, not only in Johannine and Pauline theology, but also expressly and directly in Jesus' own statements about himself in the Synoptics. According to this traditional theology, the divinely attested prophet Jesus himself proclaims directly and explicitly his divine sonship in the sense of Chalcedonian Christology.

On this point the author of the present book felt it necessary to proceed more cautiously if the conclusions of modern exegesis were to be honestly respected. There is no attempt here (at least, no systematic attempt) to find in Jesus' own words a statement about himself which is directly and formally identical with the teaching even of Johannine and Pauline Christology and its further development in the dogma of Chalcedon. This does not mean breaking or denying a genuine, legitimate, and necessary connection between the historically demonstrable self-interpretation of Jesus and the Church's dogma. With reference to this question the basic thesis of the book is that Jesus proclaims that in him—in his person and his teaching—the kingdom of God (that is, God's gracious self-communication) is not merely always present as an offer to man's freedom, but has reached us victoriously and irreversibly, has been actually victoriously established by God, and that the last, definitive word of grace has been irrevocably spoken in history: a word that in Jesus' resurrection, where he is definitively accepted in his solidarity with other human beings, has become the unsurpassable and definitive word of God in history. From this standpoint, the view is maintained in the book that this historically tangible self-interpretation of Jesus as the definitive, unsurpassable prophet, as the definitive word of God's self-promise to the world in its history, also contains implicitly the Chalcedonian Christology and simultaneously offers a critical norm to make sure that the Church's ecclesial Christology, in itself absolutely true and binding, is not misunderstood in a monophysite sense (a misunderstanding that undoubtedly always represents a serious danger in Christendom and psychologically is the reason why the Church's Christology is rejected by many as mythological). In these brief reflections of course it is impossible to bring out in detail the content of the historically demonstrable self-interpretation of Jesus as the last of the prophets and the final bringer of salvation and the connection of this content with the Church's Christology; even in the book itself these themes are only incompletely explained. Here we must be content with having at least indicated the specific nature of the Christology of this book. Nor can we enter more closely here into the book's teaching on Jesus' resurrection. This teaching also has what we may describe as a certain transcendental approach, based not on a Platonic anthropology but on the correctly interpreted unity of spirit and matter in man (which does not mean a monotonous sameness), in its view that man's final achievement of salvation and fulfillment with God itself implies what is really meant by man's resurrection and consummation.

We must pass over the treatment of ecclesiology and eschatology in the sections *after* that of Christology. At the end there is a discussion of a number of 'brief formularies' of faith. These brief credal statements are not meant, of course, to replace or suppress the Apostles' Creed or other official creeds of the Church. But they can help to make clear the fact that Christianity, despite its historicity, can be condensed up to a point in a brief 'compendium' and that there are many ways of acquiring a general understanding of the Christian faith which perhaps have been too much neglected in the traditional forms of proclamation.

Any book by a theologian has its flaws and deficiencies. The most important of these are bound to escape the author's attention, otherwise they would have been avoided. All this is obviously true of the present book. The most important flaws and deficiencies in regard to the themes will have escaped this author's attention, even though he is not to be blamed for the absence of anything which cannot be part of his theme in the light of his method and basic approach. But the author is also aware of deficiencies and faults which might perhaps have been avoided. The treatment of the doctrine of the Trinity, for instance, has turned out to be perhaps briefer than it might have been in the light of the book's aim and structure. I think however that the charge of modalism in my treatment of the doctrine of the Trinity, made by a German theologian, is unjustified. It has been refuted in fact by a lengthy Roman dissertation of a Brazilian theologian[2] and Cardinal Ratzinger did not notice any such modalism. Unlike some other modern theologians, however, I readily admit that I fear the danger of modalism less than that of an implicit tritheism, which cannot easily be avoided. For the rest, I must point to what I said about the Trinity in the large work of dogmatic theology *Mysterium Salutis*.[3]

Another theme perhaps inadequately considered in my book is that of 'evil' in the world and its compatibility with faith in an infinitely holy and purely good God. The book does not put forward any theory of an apocatastasis, but stresses the importance of a legitimate *hope* of an eschatological universal reconciliation, even though man in his still open history of freedom must always and incessantly allow for the possibility of final perdition. But perhaps the theology of evil is not outlined vividly enough in this book. Nevertheless, it seems to me that a Christian with a humble and universal hope that knows no bounds does more credit to God's holy goodness than one who even now wants to know precisely that evil, even though condemned by God, has a certain finality in this world.

There is nothing in this book about angels or devils. Whatever its theological importance, it does not seem to me absolutely necessary to deal with this doctrine in a book mainly concerned with the ultimate basic idea of Christianity. Anyone interested in my views of the subject will find them in the essay 'On Angels' in this volume.[4]

[2] M. de França Miranda, *O mistério de Deus en nova vida: A doutrina trinitária de Karl Rahner* (Fé e realidade 1; São Paulo, 1975).

[3] *Mysterium Salutis: Grundriß heilsgeschichtlicher Dogmatik*, vol. 2 (Zurich, [3]1978), pp. 517–40. English trans. (as a separate volume) *The Trinity* (London/New York, 1970).

[4] It originally appeared in *Schriften zur Theologie*, vol. 13 (Zurich, 1978), pp. 381–428.

My friend Herbert Vorgrimler[5] has rightly drawn my attention to the omission in the chapter on ecclesiology of any reference to a theme on which I have elsewhere written comparatively freshly and insistently—the theme of the Church of sinners, of the sinful Church—although an impartial consideration of this theme could be of great importance particularly at the present time to enable people to adopt an uninhibited attitude towards the Church. As I said, Vorgrimler is right in this respect. The ecclesiology of this book has turned out to be perhaps too innocuous, even somewhat triumphalist.

Finally, I can see and expressly admit the limitations of the book insofar as it represents a certain individualistic approach to theological problems as a whole. Political theology and the theology of liberation are not expressly represented here. This does not mean that I simply reject these theologies: that would contradict much that I have said about them elsewhere. There are completely orthodox and legitimate political theologies and theologies of liberation, even though we need not for that reason approve them in *all* their forms. There are theologies which rightly bring man's sociality to bear on all theology from the very outset and consequently are not to be identified with the particular discipline of Christian social science. It would be possible therefore, even in an introduction to the idea of Christianity, to work from the outset with the basic conceptions of a political theology and a theology of liberation without for that reason betraying the orthodoxy of an ecclesial theology or reducing theology, contrary to its true nature, to themes which do not cover its entire scope. But I think it is also possible to justify the admitted absence of political theology and the theology of liberation from this book. For one thing, in a comparatively small book in which an attempt is made to consider all the traditional themes of dogmatic and fundamental theology, the limitations of space make it almost impossible to integrate also these theologies, particularly since, as they now exist or continue to exist, they have not shown very clearly or in detail that it is possible in the light of their approach to cope with all that is binding dogma in all its parts. If they are to be justified and to cover the whole of dogma, these theologies, too,

[5] Cf. H. Vorgrimler, 'Nachdenken über Jesus und seine kirchlichen Nachfolger' in *Deutsches Allgemeines Sonntagsblatt*, no. 38, 19 September 1976.

need transcendental-speculative reflections and historical material; they must not only proclaim passionately their formal nature, but also engage in a theological activity which they have in common with traditional theology. These theologies anyway are also in danger of becoming so enthusiastic about the novelty and urgency of their task that they are liable to forget difficult and absolutely imperative theological problems and tasks. I agree that my book suffers from a certain one-sidedness, but this may serve to correct the fashionable and misleading exuberance on the part of these theologies which is also possible and actually exists here and there. My book is to be read, not in an exclusive, but in a positive sense. Then, I think, it can be approved even by a defender of a political theology or a theology of liberation.

I would not like this book to be regarded as a systematic, all-integrating presentation of my theology. For this, too many problems with which I have been occupied for some forty years are disregarded here. But on the primary plane of reflection it offers a survey of Christian doctrine as a whole. This is difficult and involves many more risks than are involved in a theological study, however exact, within a particular field. The greater the task, the more likely is it that the result will fall short of complete fulfillment. But we must have the courage to make the attempt, even though the accomplishment of the task remains almost hopelessly inadequate.

2

ON THE RELATIONSHIP BETWEEN NATURAL SCIENCE AND THEOLOGY

In the light of its own ultimate intention and its understanding of itself, theology is likely in the first place to adopt an attitude of tacit mistrust towards the natural sciences. Regarded objectively and historically, this is not at all surprising. Directly or indirectly, all natural sciences involve anthropology; they all say something abut man. Examined closely and in the end result, what they say is never the expression of a precisely definable material understanding *about* something *in* man; it defines or influences the idea of man *as one and whole*, even when the particular science tries to avoid exceeding the limits of its method or of its content. At this point, however, the theologian almost inevitably begins to feel irritated, since he regards the doctrine of man revealed in the Christian faith (which is the object of his reflections) as the proper, true, and unsurpassable self-understanding of man. He can hardly fail to regard the anthropology of natural science in its method and conclusions as a threat to his own theological anthropology. There is a theological uneasiness in regard to natural science: an uneasiness in principle and (as the history of the last centuries shows) also in practice. Even at the point where no insuperable contradictions can be seen between a theological and a scientific anthropology, where both exercise a wise self-restraint and restrict themselves closely to their own field (being prepared thus to make concessions), this uneasiness continues and, in fact, on both sides (there is always someone on whom no regulations can be imposed and who nevertheless can interfere in the other's business).

In the light of his own self-understanding, the theologian must recognize this situation as legitimate, must admit that his own business does not permit or enable him to abolish the situation, that (to be exact) there is a scientific anthropology existing in its own right which must be acknowledged by the theologian and which in virtue of its contents and in a critical spirit can and may in principle always have something to tell the theologian about his own anthropology. Of course it is true that there can be no absolutely contradictory opposition between faith and knowledge, between theological and scientific anthropology; in the last resort a 'double truth' is nonsense. Of course it is true that very many conflicts between the two anthropologies can be cleared up by a closer reflection on the nature of the methods of each, by a more exact definition and demarcation of their particular subject matter, etc. It is also true that in the course of the history of theology and of the empirical sciences the attempt has repeatedly been made so to define the respective fields of theology and the natural sciences that they could be seen not to border on one another and that conflicts could not only be solved up to a point but were impossible from the outset. But such an oversimplified clarification of the frontiers is not possible.

The natural scientist cannot from the outset always and unambiguously restrict himself only to those anthropological statements which by their very nature and unequivocally are irrelevant for the theologian and in no way touch on the latter's field of study. An unequivocally and radically materialistic biology, materialistic not only in its method, not only considering its object merely insofar as the latter is accessible to its method, but also declaring that there is no reality beyond the reality investigated in this way—a natural science claiming thus to be science purely and simply would be a natural science which could not co-exist with a Christian faith in one person. Consequently it is impossible for natural science and theology to accept a clarification of frontiers which would prevent them from the very outset from coming into conflict. They must co-exist, they must exist alongside one another, without being absorbed into one another; they cannot assume from the outset that they have nothing to do with each other; hence they inevitably threaten and disturb each other.

This obvious and yet uneasy situation could, of course, be much more fully clarified and more deeply investigated in principle and historically. In this question, too, differences of opinion in the light of controversial theology must be noted between individual theologians of the different Christian churches. If, for example, Catholic teaching states that God can be known by the light of natural reason or if the typical Catholic understanding of fundamental theology is considered, it can also be seen that specifically Catholic teaching in principle allows for a larger field of conflict than does a Protestant theology, which in general has a notion of faith that of its nature is placed at a greater distance from secular science.

However odd it sounds at first, it can nevertheless be said that the relationship between theology and natural science can be defined theologically perhaps most clearly in the light of the theological notion of concupiscence. The assumption behind this at first apparently strange thesis is merely that the understanding of man which finds expression in the notion of concupiscence holds equally for the dimension of knowledge and for that of the will and freedom. This assumption is really obvious in view of man's original unity, in view of the mutual dependence of his individual dimensions and realities, in view of the interconnection of his dimensions. Knowledge is itself one act, even though a specific act, of freedom, and consequently carries with it also all the peculiarities of creaturely and specifically human freedom. Concupiscence in the theological sense means that despite an original unity of man there is a pluralism of his faculties and impulses which in practice can never be integrated into an absolute unity surveyable and controllable from a single point. Concupiscence also means that man nevertheless has the task and obligation of working asymptotically toward such a unity, even though it can never be established completely in man's individual and collective history and within the course of that history; it means finally that this pluralism, which can never adequately be integrated, although not really sinful in itself, can always lead to essentially destructive sin and is in any case the reason for the agonistic character of human existence. This nonintegrated pluralism of human existence known as concupiscence, having always a complete integration before it as a task, leading to sin, unavoidably involving conflict, is a peculiarity also of man's gnoseological dimension. From this standpoint and in the very light of theology as such, it is possible to make something out of the relationship of theology to the natural sciences.

From this standpoint it must be said first of all that man, particularly as a Christian, has to allow for an irreversible pluralism of sciences. These sciences do not originate at a fixed point of unity under man's control and power, from which their multiplicity could be maintained indisputably and harmoniously in unity from the very outset. The sciences exist in a plurality as alien to one another; they arise in the course of man's history without looking for mutual recognition from the outset; subsequently it may perhaps be possible with a great effort for scientific systematology and theory to work out a system of the sciences, but in the last resort this system does not permit the individual sciences to be brought under control, with each of them being assigned its own task and method. Theology, too, must live with and find its place in this insuperable pluralism of the sciences. Theology deals with the one all-embracing and sustaining source of all reality and with the one all-integrating and reconciling goal of all history that we call God. But, insofar as theology acknowledges this God precisely as the incomprehensible mystery and declares man to be eternally distinct from this God of original unity, the singular uniqueness and dignity of theology in principle simply does *not* provide the means and the way to overcome this pluralism of the sciences. Theology (together with metaphysics), known as the supreme science, is not a kind of sovereign ruler reducing the other sciences to acting as its instruments and carrying out its plans; it is *one* science among others, with the special task of providing a living example of the fact that the pluralism of the sciences does not permit any dominion that could be exercised by man in a kind of theological totalitarianism.

The traditional teaching of Christianity on concupiscence states also that there is an insuperable pluralism of the sciences which cannot be completely reduced to a humanly comprehensible system, but must be endured with a prudent restraint and the humility befitting the creature. It is therefore the task of theology both constantly to unmask the claim of an individual science to an ideological totalitarianism as an arrogant falsification of reality and also to return itself to the attitude of modesty which permits all sciences to be subject to God but not to itself. In this sense also all the unease which the sciences mutually generate today and all the uneasiness felt by theology in regard to the natural sciences, because of the threat which these present to it, can never mislead theology into denying their autonomy and meaningfulness. Theology is accustomed to declare that in a case of conflict it possesses ultimately the competence to decide between true and false, since it can appeal to divine revelation. This traditional statement of its claims by theology may in principle and formally be completely correct. But, fundamentally and in the light of historical experience, in such cases of conflict between theology and natural science, theology is equally and frequently compelled to reexamine itself, to understand itself better, to give way to natural science. Even in a case like this the revision of theology may certainly consist in a return to a better understanding of its own principles. But this in no way alters the fact that this return to its own principles is in practice caused and necessitated by the conclusions of the natural sciences. In practice, therefore, there is an open relationship between natural science and theology: possible situations of conflict, even though they can be solved in principle, are not *a priori* avoidable. As reflection on divine revelation, theology does not dissolve the pluralism of the sciences in which it is a modest individual science and is not itself the power of a manageable unity.

Seen in the light of the notion of concupiscence, this pluralism of the sciences, including also theology, is not a static reality remaining always the same, but takes the form of a task demanding a truly historical even though asymptotic trend toward an integration and a unity. Pluralism of the sciences does not exist merely in the one human being, whose original unity would not need to have anything to do with man's actual history. Achieving man's unity in the integration of everything with which he is involved and thus also the unity of his sciences is a wholly existential task. Interdisciplinary discussion (as it is described today) is not merely a game or a diversion to be taken up or abandoned at will. If the individual sciences were separate territories without any common frontiers, the striving for unity of the sciences, interdisciplinary discussion, and a general course of studies could be left to the choice of the individual person. But since every science (because of the unity of the one God, of a unity of man, of the *one* human being, in origin, nature, and goal), without detriment to its own character, its specific method, and its formulation of the question, etc., can properly sort itself out only (paradoxical as it sounds) by transcending its own nature; since the individual sciences in each case reach a complete understanding of themselves only when they know more than themselves, the continually fresh, albeit asymptotic, attempt at an integration of the different sciences, including theology, is a task and a moral obligation imposed on man.

There must be universities of knowledge which are more than organized collections of different faculties. This task of integrating the individual sciences (including, that is, the natural and the mental sciences) into a unity will continually achieve positive results; people will continually perceive (at least, bit by bit) how things hitherto merely juxtaposed in consciousness fit in with each other. But there will never be a single, all-inclusive, universal formula in this history of knowledge; and the ultimate unity to be granted to man seeking knowledge pluralistically—already present and yet remaining also a task that is continually new—is the surrender of all knowledge in a *docta ignorantia* to the eternally abiding mystery of God and his underivable will. This unity also, granted and not produced in the entrusting of all plurality to the only radically one God, is part of the task of integrating the pluralism of our knowledge into a unity.

Christian teaching on the concupiscent plurality of our unintegrated impulses states that this plurality, although not necessarily and always itself sin and guilt, can lead to sin and in any case causes an agonistic situation in man. The fact that the mirror of our consciousness as such does not reflect all reality as one and entire in unity but has in a certain sense been shattered into a thousand fragments each of which reproduces only a part of reality that is never completely understandable, all this is not yet necessarily sin in man, even though it is interpreted in Christian anthropology as the consequence of a sin at the primordial beginning of the mental history of mankind. But it can lead to sin and in fact continually leads to sin in individual and collective history because this gnoseological pluralism is not endured in patience or continually, freshly, and asymptotically integrated towards greater unity but is simply accepted uneasily and lazily as a matter of course or is supposed to be abolished by an illegitimate claim of an individual science to dominate the others. The indifferences of a particular science and of individual scientists toward other sciences and their representatives, what is known as one-track specialization, the narrow-minded selfishness with which individual scientists or institutions attempt to claim for themselves as much as possible of the limited resources of the state; the attempts (sometimes truly ridiculous) to rig up out of the categories of an individual science a universal formula meant to explain everything without exception; the inclination too often implicitly to refuse to acknowledge as scientific other efforts to acquire knowledge with other methods, as a result of the desire presumptuously to reserve the predicate 'scientific' to one's own field of scholarship—these and similar phenomena in the field of the sciences (whether they are peculiarities of the individual scientist or are institutionalized) are occurrences or evidences of the sin that arises out of the concupiscent pluralism of our knowledge.

A theory of the actual sinfulness of our knowledge and its institutions ought sometime to be developed. Science is not a paradise of innocence. And who knows if the greatest lapses have not already taken place in this area? If—and this is a serious problem—there could be a moral obligation to be content to leave unknown something which, as we are aware proleptically, could be studied and known, there might be moral problems in the field of knowledge which we are presumably completely disregarding today. But in any case, there exists also in the field of knowledge the agonistic situation which is involved permanently and irremoveably in man's concupiscent state. If the representatives of the different sciences arrogantly make excessive claims for their own special fields, if we regard with amusement or irritation the wrangling of the scientists and their institutions for social esteem and for endowments as large as possible, in the last resort these things are not incidents that could be eliminated with a little wisdom and decisiveness, but tokens of an agonistic situation which could not simply be removed, where the sciences and scientists struggle with one another in conflicts never to be definitively resolved, since there is no earthly authority able to create from the outset a situation in the society of science and scientists in which conflicts simply cannot arise. Knowledge of the agonistic situation even of the sciences (rightly understood) provides no excuse for as much selfish conflict as possible among sciences and scientists, but serves as a reminder humbly to allow for conflicts that are never wholly avoidable even in the field of the sciences and thus to strive for as much peace and integration as possible.

The agonistic situation even in the field of knowledge is one that exists also in the mind and heart of each individual scientist. He wonders which task of knowledge among the many possible tasks open to him should have priority. The older scientist may perhaps wonder in some anxiety whether he should continue his intensive investigation of a single problem within his science or (in the light of the basic problems of his science) become a metaphysical philosopher or a universal guide, if his limited resources and brief lifetime do not permit him to do everything together and at one and the same time. For the individual scholar, who even as scientist never can or even should wholly exclude his own existence, the agonistic state of his existence as a scholar has another aspect. In the last resort his struggle ends in a defeat which only the believer knows to be possibly his greatest victory. He grows older, his powers fail, interest in his special field becomes faint and feeble, his achievements are surpassed by his colleagues in that field, he dies. At the same time in the last resort it is no consolation if the contribution he has made to knowledge by his scientific work lives on in the heads of a future generation. For that generation is likewise doomed to death, the death that renders all actual science itself mortal.

In conclusion it may be said once more that the right to existence of the natural sciences cannot be questioned, even by theology, despite the unease which they cause. Faith and theology do not really give the natural sciences their right to exist, but find them already existing and thus see that their validity must be recognized even in the light of the very nature of the understanding of man produced by faith; they see that they must live together with these sciences in an open dialogue the concrete outcome of which cannot exactly be foreseen by either side. At the same time, theology also admittedly has the task of rejecting the arrogance (always present as a temptation) of every science as it tries to establish a monopoly and a totalitarian claim to be the complete solution to all the riddles of the universe. Absurd as such an attempt may seem to us human beings of the present time with our weary scepticism, it has constantly been made from the period of the Englightenment onward, and even today the danger persists that this arrogance of the empirical sciences will be upheld with the aid of the powers of the state.

3

THE CHURCH'S REDEMPTIVE HISTORICAL PROVENANCE FROM THE DEATH AND RESURRECTION OF JESUS[1]

I would like first of all to attempt to say something about the problem raised here and about the solution traditionally offered in Catholic textbook theology in the last centuries, together with the problems in turn raised by this traditional but not officially defined solution. After that, I would like to suggest that the same question of the origin of the Church from Jesus Christ can now perhaps be understood and interpreted somewhat differently, so that this possible solution can be more easily and more simply reconciled with the conclusions of modern historical science.

The question before us (which I can consider here only as a systematic theologian, with the opportunities at my disposal, distinct as such from those of an exegete) really amounts simply to the problem of whether we can speak of an institution of the Church by Jesus Christ. When the problem is raised in this way today, in the first place we must ask the question whether Jesus of Nazareth of the pre-Easter period, as historically palpable (perhaps only with difficulty), or the risen Christ is meant.

In practice this distinction does not appear in traditional textbook theology, in traditional ecclesiology, or in fundamental theology. If

[1] With reference to the theory of *ius divinum* in the Church's constitutional law as presented here, the reader should also consult the author's 'Reflection on the Concept of "Ius Divinum" in Catholic Thought', *Theological Investigations*, vol. 5 (London/Baltimore, 1966), pp. 221–42.

something connected with the Church is put into the mouth of Jesus, in the Synoptics or in John, whether it is the Jesus of the pre-Easter period or the risen Jesus creates no difficulties for traditional textbook theology. But when the question is raised today, this distinction must obviously be considered. The fact that the approach to a solution as outlined in the second part of my exposition again carries with it a special problem is something that must emerge from our reflections in that second part.

What then does traditional textbook ecclesiology say, as it existed especially in the post-Tridentine period and mainly under the aegis of St. Robert Bellarmine, the Doctor of the Church, with his notion of the Church, and as I heard and learned it myself when I was studying theology forty or more years ago?

It might perhaps be said (I am concentrating the problem, of course, on the questions that are of interest here) that in traditional textbook theology the Church is regarded as instituted by Jesus (of the pre-Easter or post-Easter period) insofar as and because this institution is ascribed to explicit, propositional statements of Jesus, interpreted more or less juridically even at that stage.

The traditional conception is of Jesus appointing Peter to be the first pope, gathering around himself a group of apostles who formed the first college of bishops; and he gives to what I might describe as this society juridically established on the basis of the explicit words of institution, understood in this sense, quite definite powers, which he can give precisely because it is he whom Christian faith perceives in Jesus of Nazareth.

The crucial point of this sort of ecclesiology then is that these ideas of the Church's institution belong *a priori* to a propositional, juridical plane. This ecclesiology is conceived in terms of the institution of a specific society. Consequently, even for Bellarmine's ecclesiology (which, up to Pius XII's *Mystici Corporis,* was, I might say, not the sole and not the complete but certainly the dominant ecclesiology) the idea of the Church up to the present century was that of the *societas perfecta,* the perfect society, a juridical organization of sociological character. Of course it was always known that this Church is something more than a secular society, a secular state or some other secular combination of human beings, but (and here we come closer to our real problem) it cannot be denied that the institution of this society by properly and explicitly juridical statutes can be associated only with difficulty with Jesus as Redeemer, the Crucified and Risen. I said earlier that for this traditional ecclesiology it is basically irrelevant whether Jesus said any of these words of institution as the pre-Easter Jesus (who, for us today, did not from the outset expect the failure of the cross) or as the Risen One. The conception of the Church in fundamental theology as, we might say, a sociological factor, established by Jesus' words of institution, understood juridically, and an ecclesiology which, in Paul's words, regards the Church as the mystical body of Christ, or (as we might express it today) as the basic sacrament of salvation, or (as we could also say) as the enduring presence of the salvific deed of Jesus Christ: these two conceptions (that is, the sociological ecclesiology of fundamental theology and the properly soteriological dogmatic ecclesiology) were formerly not expressly separated, but in fact existed side by side, basically unreconciled and unconsidered in their duality.

Today an ecclesiology of this kind as a part of fundamental theology (as I have just attempted to explain it, if only very briefly) of course presents extraordinarily serious difficulties. It was in fact simply taken for granted in classical fundamental theology up to the 1950s, as we can see by looking up H. Dieckmann or other fundamental theologians. The problems arising from this approach to Jesus' institution of the Church became clear as such sixty or seventy years ago, in the modernist period. But, as things go, it is not surprising that it takes some time and occasionally too long before such problems are faced and not simply pushed aside in a premature conservative reaction, but really admitted, worked out, and surmounted. Hence (at least it seems so to me) we can say in all modesty and cautiously that Catholic ecclesiology needed fifty or sixty years to master to some degree the ecclesiological problems in Catholicism (we are leaving Protestantism aside at present for practical reasons) as they were brought to light by modernism.

What, then, were the difficulties brought to light here? An important fundamental theological problem which, as I said, was so to speak swept under the carpet and not really faced at the time of Pius X by *Lamentabili* and *Pascendi* was, of course, Jesus' imminent expectation. Jesus, it was said, expected (without indicating a precise time) the early advent of the eschatological, definitive kingdom of God in his own generation, and in view of this imminent expectation could not have intended to institute a Church. With the world coming to an end in a few years, who would begin to organize a Church which would be pointless and without any function? All that remained was the early approach of the Last Day, the kingdom of God, the judgment, perhaps the salvific and redeeming judgment of God's mercy. But since, as it was claimed, Jesus was mistaken in his imminent expectation, the Church did come into existence, not however from him, not by his intention. What happened was that this imminent expectation gradually waned and from the community of disciples who believed in him as the Risen One there developed in practice slowly in the course of history what came to be called the Church. Whether this happened more quickly or slowly in one place than in another was regarded as a secondary question and not urgent here and now.

The first problem, then, raised by historical-critical exegesis in regard to the traditional understanding of the Church as instituted by Jesus is that of his expectation of the imminent end of the world. A second problem, among others which could certainly be mentioned but which I am leaving aside at present, is the fact that the Church in New Testament times in Judaistic and Hellenistic areas or elsewhere does not present the image of something absolutely fully constructed as it is described in traditional ecclesiology as the institution of Jesus. Thus it is said that in the early Church, in addition to Paul, there might perhaps be discovered somewhere a Peter, but not a pope; that in the first Church of Pauline times there were apparently the most diverse possibilities of a community organization existing alongside one another and formed in accordance with the different sociological conditions present in the Judaistic or Hellenistic areas or elsewhere. It is said that Catholic ecclesiology is episcopal and papal in character and this episcopal and papal structure is explained as a structure instituted by Jesus Christ himself, permanent and unchangeable by divine right—that is how we Catholics expressed it at the time. But within New Testament times it is possible to discover any structure of this kind at most only in its quite modest beginnings. Can we then (and this is the problem) speak at all of Jesus 'instituting' a Church?

Before attempting to answer these questions, I would like to say that I have no doubt that with the pre-Easter Jesus and the group of disciples gathered around him there were already the rudiments of a certain sociality, of a sociological organization, that Peter had already been given a prominent position by Jesus, and so on; that Jesus and his group of disciples did not secede as a Church from Israel and its covenant, but nevertheless had already something of a sociological structure. Of course, I have no wish to obscure or deny these things in the second part of the present essay, but they could be dealt with more precisely only by an exegete or a biblical theologian and I neither can nor will play that role here. The problem facing us in the light of Jesus' imminent expectation and of the appearance of the communities in New Testament times is that Jesus does not seem to have instituted a Church. Despite the Church's radical opposition to modernistic ecclesiology at the time of Pius X and even subsequently, the situation today is such that, for example, Hans Küng can uninhibitedly and, I would like to say, with a sincerity which cannot now be denied or concealed declare that Jesus did not institute a Church. The fact that Küng nevertheless regards the Church as meaningful, necessary, etc., is a different question which must not be obscured by my reference to his statement that Jesus did not institute a Church.

What could I recommend here (without claiming any special competence) as a suitable approach to a solution of this question of the institution of the Church? Again, it is possible only to make a few suggestions.

First of all it is of course obvious that, although the theme attracts me, I cannot here and now in this connection deal with the problem of Jesus' imminent expectation as such. If Jesus expected the advent of God's eschatological kingdom, was he 'mistaken' or can this qualification of his opinion and teaching be rightly avoided? What remains concretely that is absolutely right, still radically important and valid even today, about such an imminent expectation, when we must now obviously admit without hesitation that two thousand years have passed since Jesus' time and the world has not yet been transformed in the fire of God's anger into God's eternal kingdom? These again are of course questions into which I cannot enter here. I mean that (obviously unlike what happened in the time of Pius X) we must admit impartially, sincerely, realistically, and clearly that with Jesus there was a chronological imminent expectation which, as he 'imagined' it and expressed it in words, was not fulfilled. But this is far from saying (I cannot now develop this point) that we ought for this reason to admit that within his horizon of understanding, etc., he was mistaken. If however someone were to say just this, it would not be heresy, but essentially a wrong expression which (without wanting to leave anything obscure) can and should be completely avoided, since behind it is an existentially false notion of truth. But I cannot now discuss this further. And obviously it is of decisive importance (from the nature of the case we shall return to this question anyway with our actual offer of a solution) that there is certainly contained in this imminent expectation of Jesus something that is absolutely essential and enduring, something that even today is of absolute importance for faith for all of us.

Our real problem, however, and our real theme is the question: What can we say and how can we speak of an institution of the Church by Jesus or its provenance from him, if and although he proclaimed this imminence of the kingdom of God? Although Hans Küng might perhaps charge me with the dubious tactic of coming to an arrangement, I would like to ask now if there are circumstances in which I can do without the term 'institution' and yet see what is meant by this traditional term and what it is intended to maintain as a matter of faith better and more straightforwardly and nevertheless honestly in the term 'provenance'? The term 'institution', if understood in its varied and possibly analogous usage, need not be synonymous with the description of the juridical organization of a society. Admittedly, the latter is the kind of institution of which we generally and instinctively think when it is said that Jesus instituted the Church, although it is not a conception that could easily be upheld today in face of the critique of historical-critical biblical scholarship. In order, therefore, to maintain what the Church has always said and taught (in asserting that the Church was instituted by Jesus), it is sufficient, I would say, not to replace this term, but at least to interpret it in the sense of 'provenance'.

If something originates from something else in a really understandably practicable way, if reality *a* necessarily involves reality *b* (this must of course be shown to be the case), it can be said either that *b* is 'instituted' by *a* or that *b* quite clearly 'comes from' *a*. This however is merely a preliminary terminological observation.

After this terminological observation, I now come directly to what is implied in the title of this article. The Church comes from the death and resurrection of Jesus as part of the eschatological permanence of the Crucified and Rise One. This is more or less the thesis I am now trying to make to some degree intelligible.

To speak about the redemptive historical, eschatological meaning of the death and resurrection of Jesus is, of course, to touch on a theme that in itself is extraordinarily difficult, mysterious, profound, differentiated (more so than can be made clear here). Nor can I at this point deal with questions like those of whether Jesus actually rose or how he himself, the historical Jesus, interpreted his own death, etc. Here, where we are attempting to reflect on the provenance of the Church from Jesus, crucified and risen, we assume the Christian-Catholic dogma and the conviction of the New Testament of the redemptive, historical, universal, and eschatological significance of Jesus Christ himself.

But if, in connection of course with our intention in these reflections, it is asked how we can state quite briefly what came about by Jesus' death and resurrection, this is what we can say: Through Jesus Christ, crucified and risen, the victorious self-communication of God, established by God himself, has been manifested as victorious, as eschatological, as definitively final.

The fact that God loves the world from the very beginning despite all sin, that this God with his grace is always from the beginning and everywhere in the history of the world and humanity the innermost dynamism, the innermost entelechy of this world, driving on this whole, perhaps two-million-year-old history of humanity toward that immediacy of God which we call the beatific vision—all this was really something not known so clearly before the time of Jesus, but even then was the internal structure and dynamism of this world history. From the very outset God himself with his own glory had always been established in the world as power, source, and goal, in the form of an offer to the world's freedom. In relation to the world, God is not merely Creator in the sense of placing as it were something different from himself in the empty space of nothingness surrounding God, not merely keeping this distinct reality, as we might say, at an absolute distance, although he remains Creator and Legislator; but God takes this other world, creatively produced by him, in what we call grace and glory, into his own splendour. He gives us, his creatures, not only something he creates as distinct from himself; but he gives himself to this creature, at least he offers himself as gift to the history of freedom of this humanity. But, in the light of this self-offering of God to man's freedom and in the light of the ambivalence of all creaturely freedom, the fate of mankind, the end of history, always remains open; the concrete outcome remains uncertain.

Whether this tremendous offer (in which God gives, not something, but himself) is accepted or rejected, remains for the time being an open question. And all the terror of world history, all the sense that an Augustine had of this *massa damnata* of a world history—none of this seems to suggest from the outset that this tremendous, final, unsurpassable height of the history of humanity which plunges into the glory of God himself is actually scaled by man as one and whole. Where, then, does Jesus Christ come in? What we call the preaching of the kingdom of God, what with Paul we know as justification not by the works of the law but by grace, what is proclaimed in John as the descent of the light into the darkness of this world, really means nothing other than this: that through the death and resurrection of Jesus this actually ambivalent salvation history in acceptance *or* rejection of God's self-offering does in fact have a definitively *good* outcome.

All this of course is far from making anything clear about the fate of each individual, but what it does imply is something wholly unparalleled, something not at all obvious, which is actually left to God's freedom and man's: that this appalling, terrible history, always, as it were, hurtling down into the abyss of death and sin, nevertheless, by the power of God's grace, has in fact a positive outcome. Jesus (if I may put it in this way) enters into solidarity on the one hand unambiguously with God and is aware of himself in an indestructible unity with him whom he calls his Father and this same Jesus enters into solidarity on the other hand unambiguously and indisputably with human beings, with sinners, with wastrels, and hence, as from the outset (sustaining his conviction even throughout his failure), he can scarcely do anything but reject an alternative of deciding either for God or for men and must say: No, this pitiful humanity is victorious, not only by way of offer but by way of real success, it is a humanity victoriously saved by God, loved into God's own glory.

This is then definitively sealed by what we call the resurrection. This Jesus, crucified and risen, is therefore the permanent promise of God himself to the world, not merely in the offer, but in factually definitive victory. This the crucified and risen Jesus can be only if and insofar as this so victorious self-offering of God is permanently present in the world.

From this standpoint we can perhaps even say in a completely positive, albeit not in an exclusive sense, with the exegete Willi Marxsen, that Jesus must rise into the faith of those who believe in him. Not in the sense that he exists only in that faith; but if and insofar as there is not a community of faith, believing in Jesus as crucified and risen, as vindicated Son of God, as the eschatologically unsurpassable, definitive prophet (or however it is expressed), if there is not such a community of faith as permanent presence of this self-communication of God present in history and now victorious over the world, then this very Jesus does not exist at all as God's self-promise to the world.

The Church as eschatologically definitive and nevertheless historical, as a community of faith, is the permanent presence precisely of this eschatological and eschatologically victorious self-promise of God to the world in Jesus Christ. And he is what he is only if this community of faith is always there in the world, to make sure that he remains historically as God's eschatological promise to the world. In what numbers the Church exists or will exist is quite another question. In the last resort, the Church as 'sacrament' of the world's salvation, as the 'primordial baptism' of the world, is not tied to any particular size or sociological power.

All this of course is only by way of suggestion. But at least the implication is clear that from Jesus, crucified and risen, there is a provenance of the Church, which as such a community of faith is itself constitutive of the reality of Jesus and is consequently necessary as such. He would not be what he is if there were no such Church. His proclamation that God's salvation is now irreversibly present in the world would not exist at all if the Church were not present as the enduring community always upholding this proclamation in the world. If Jesus is not reduced to a preacher of morality or a revivalist, doing no more than making statements which might perhaps not have been made without him but which anyway can easily be approved and understood; if Jesus is not regarded as a preacher of morality or a revivalist talking about a kind of humanitarianism that depends for its realization on man's freedom and arbitrary choice; if we believe in God and know who God is, and are convinced by faith that this absolute God in his absoluteness, unapproachability, and incomprehensibility has promised himself as himself definitively to the world as its very own salvation, then I think it is clear that this has happened only in Jesus, crucified and risen, and that consequently the Church really exists even now as the permanence of this historically perceptible, eschatologically irreversible self-promise of God.

It might be claimed that what I have just said is all very fine, that a normal Christian, at any rate a devout Protestant who believes in Christ, would not deny it; in this respect at least Catholics and Protestants could certainly agree. But, it might be said, the concrete structure of this eschatologically invincible, enduring community of faith is still not clear. It might be said that if the Crucified and Risen One exists historically as God's irreversible self-promise in the world this promise must obviously remain and there must be a community of faith; but how this is canonically organized is quite a different question; things do not have to proceed (it might be added) episcopally or papally in this Church; it might be said that even according to the New Testament the most diverse sociological organizations of such a community of faith are equally justified and have in fact existed; the claim of the Roman Catholic Church to be the sole legitimate organization of this community of faith of a juridically sociological character must be rejected.

Despite what has just been said about the provenance of the community of faith from Jesus, crucified and risen, we have here undoubtedly a very difficult problem that cannot be solved today as simply as it was formerly solved in traditional fundamental theology.

According to this theology, Jesus chose twelve apostles, thereby instituting the episcopate; when he took Peter from this group, he appointed the first pope. Consequently the problem arises as to how this Peter can be regarded as the first pope (even though he appears here and there in the New Testament to have a certain, even theological, importance) since he seems to have played practically no part in the Pauline communities. Why, it might be asked, did James not get a chance to be a kind of caliph of the community of disciples? Why is this episcopal constitution (which first appears as explicitly developed with Ignatius of Antioch and, in the third century, with Cyprian and others) something that not only can but must be? Why, as it might be formulated with traditional ecclesiology, are such constitutional structures belonging to the later period of Jesus' community of faith really *juris divini*, of divine law, instituted by Jesus Christ himself?

To all this, as I have already ventured to suggest, there appear to be a number of objections. But I would like now to suggest that there is certainly something like a divine law that comes to be, that can come to be. What then is the traditional teaching, stated also in Vatican II in *Lumen Gentium*, on the *ius divinum* of the papal primacy and the episcopal constitution, that is, of the monarchical episcopate?

In the first place this teaching states simply that such a structure is binding on the Church of the present time and also of the future and cannot be abolished by it. If we admit this, what is concretely practical about the teaching on *ius divinum* has already been grasped in its essentials. But then it can also be asked whether such a *ius divinum* must always have been clearly directly palpable, even in apostolic times. I ask: *Must* it always have been *so* clearly *palpable* as irreversibly binding? And I would answer that this is not necessary. To dispute such a necessity, such an explicit and formal palpability, such a *ius divinum*, is not to deny that these modern constitutional structures of the Church became perceptible more or less slowly (if we recall the First Letter of Clement or Ignatius of Antioch's theology of the Church at the turn of the first century) and then only in later history were increasingly clearly considered and in particular set up by the Church as permanently binding.

In order to make that intelligible I want to say that any history of one and the same reality follows a single track and that such a reality can be collective or individual. In both cases, in the light of a really humanly authentic anthropology, in principle it is quite possible to explain how in the course of a history such a collective or individual reality (a single individual or a collective society that is, however, essentially consolidated into a permanent unity) makes decisions on which it cannot go back and which bind it for later times; in other words, the idea of an historically free act of institution does not in any way imply that this free decision, because freely made, could also be revoked at will, that it remains permanently at the free disposal of the agency that made the decision. The history of freedom, as itself free, also follows a single track, creates what is permanently binding, what can be eliminated only by culpable rejection (if at all), since freedom in the last resort is the institution not of what is momentarily chosen but of what is irrevocable. This need not happen, of course, always and in every case, but in principle it is part of the true nature of a history of freedom.

Someone who has been married can perhaps get a divorce, but this cannot alter the fact that two people were married to one another as a permanent reality, binding for eternity. If I have followed a certain calling for forty years, I simply cannot revise my original, free decision in such a way as to be able to start again from the beginning at the exact point from which I started out forty years ago. Putting it very simply, history follows a single track, it is a kind of one-way street on which historically irreversible decisions are continually happening. On this one-way street, made up of historically free decisions, it is fundamentally impossible to turn back and start out again from this earlier point in a quite different direction, at least not if we assume that such decisions were admittedly not necessarily made to be binding in the light of the former situation, but are binding as corresponding to the *beginning*, which is the permanent law of the whole route.

In the light of these very simple reflections, I would say that I can imagine without more ado that the history of the Church at least during apostolic times saw decisions made about its sociological structures which, even though not coercive, were in accordance with its original and already theologically interpreted nature and cannot be reversed. And such historical decisions—which continue to be developed in a forward direction, but cannot really be simply abolished (with the Church returning as it were to an earlier stage of its history) as far as the Church's concrete sociological structure is concerned—in the sense of being irreversible, at least in their conformity with its beginning, can certainly be regarded as *ius divinum*. Whether such free decisions *juris divini* are still conceivable or not *after* apostolic times, is a question that can be left open here.

We might venture to say that the Church in apostolic times, from the fetal stage, so to speak, of its first origin, had certainly the right and duty to organize itself, to articulate itself, in a more concretely sociological way and at about the end of apostolic times did in fact acquire a constitution which, even though rudimentary, was nevertheless perceptible: a constitution which we describe today as Catholic, as of divine law, and with reference to which we deny the

Church any possibility of changing these ultimate constitutional structures of divine law. This need not imply that the decision in apostolic times in regard to a constitution must itself necessarily be based on an explicit will of Jesus to institute a Church, expressly stated in propositions. This, I think, cannot be proved and, even if we postulated theologically such explicit words of institution by Jesus, it would be useless from the standpoint of fundamental theology. On the other hand, I think we can and must regard such free decisions in apostolic times (a period which must not be unduly shortened, as is evident with the formation of the canon and the inclusion of later books) as wholly of divine law, without ascribing them to a verbally explicit will of Jesus to institute a Church. Such irreversible decisions, obviously in accordance with the essential nature and origin of the Church as Jesus' community of faith, cannot, it is true, be deduced juridically from certain historically palpable words of Jesus; but this is not necessary, they can still be regarded as constitutional structures of the Church which are of divine law in the sense explained.

They correspond to the institution or to the origin of the Church and as historical decisions they are authorized by the concrete historical situations into which the Church entered and had to enter. This, I think, is really all that is necessary.

Looking at the matter in this way, it also becomes clear that the Church's future is an open future. That is, if even divine law in the Church (the ultimate constitutional structures of the Church which rightly claim to be derived from Jesus) has a real *history* and, obviously, if this history, in which the Church lives and in the light of which it must assert itself and make its decisions in any particular situation, always continues, it must naturally be assumed that the Church as such in its concrete appearance (without abandoning the divine law which has accrued to it in history and without denying or obscuring its provenance from Jesus Christ, crucified and risen) still has before it an open and quite unpredictable history.

What the Church will look like in the year 2000 or 2500; whether the pope will then be in Rome, or somewhere else; whether there will still be all the bureaucratic machinery that we see and accept today in Rome and under which we perhaps groan; whether perhaps many other things of which we have no idea today will then be taken for granted; whether the Church will perhaps learn suddenly or slowly that women, too, can be holders of the priestly office; whether it will learn slowly that an academic training for the priest (despite all the respect I have for it as a former teacher) is not perhaps so absolutely necessary as we imagine today; whether it will perhaps become much clearer that leaders of a basic community, themselves emerging charismatically from the base, will also have sacramental approbation from above, and so on and so on: to all these, and to many other perhaps more important questions which we can regard as open, we cannot expect to find an answer purely deductively from theological principles or solely from ancient tradition.

From the very nature of the Church, which is an historical factor and whose *ius divinum* even has a historicity, the possibilities to be expected in all these things are endless. If in such transitional phases of Church history progress is too slow for some and too rapid for others, if in these transitional phases various things seem to be becoming obscure and uncertain, if then some people moan about the insecurity of the faithful, these feelings certainly need not be wholly wrong or stupid; it is a question of the phenomena of transition and of growth, which simply cannot be avoided in a real and genuine history.

From the time of Jesus, crucified and risen, to that of the Church today vast historical developments and transformations have taken place. These should be admitted without prejudice and without assuming, for instance, that Peter, when he heard the words subsequently recorded in Matthew 16, thought of himself as the first pope with a few hundred other popes coming after him and ruling in Rome with the aid of a complicated Curia. Such an idea could never have crossed Peter's mind. Nor did Paul rack his brain about leaving behind a collective or single person to rule a community; the pastoral Letters reflect the conditions of a later period.

The Church is always in history, always in a one-way history in which it never loses its legitimate past; and in this unpredictable, dark history of suffering the Church always comes from Jesus Christ, crucified and risen. Because, however, it is precisely sociologically organized, it testifies that God so loved the world that his love does not fail even as a result of our sin, but that, at least as far as humanity as a whole is concerned, he, the God of the grace that is victorious, not from us, but from God, prevails in the world.

This simple, straightforward message is simultaneously the most obvious, most mysterious, and most tremendous. That God himself is the ultimate content, the ultimate dynamism, the ultimate goal, definitively of this miserable finite creature, really not only in the plan but in the end result: this is something known only by looking to the risen Christ. That this salvation also actually prevails through him is the message of Christianity, a message that really exists nowhere else. And so that this message will always remain present in the world the Church is there; without it this message would not be definitive and final. Consequently, despite all its historicity and also despite all the historicity of what is called its divine constitutional law, the Church really has its origin in Jesus Christ, crucified and risen.

4

BRIEF THEOLOGICAL OBSERVATIONS ON THE 'STATE OF FALLEN NATURE'

I propose to offer here a few somewhat arbitrarily selected observations on the term 'state of fallen nature' (*status naturae lapsae*). The reason for the arbitrariness of the selection lies in the fact that a theologically adequate interpretation of the term would be possible only within the framework of a complete theology of the 'states' of man. In these brief observations, of course, it is not possible to give references to the sources of this theology and to the history of this term. Even so some discussion of the problems involved in these venerable elements of theological tradition may perhaps be useful.

We shall assume a certain acquaintance with the scholastic terminology used in this connection: pure nature, elevated nature, fallen nature, nature elevated and restored (*natura pura, natura elevata, natura lapsa, natura elevata et reformata*). The basis for this distinction is the Catholic teaching that justifying, deifying 'grace' as pledge of the intuitive vision of God (the state of complete union with God and of orientation to eternal life) is not due to man, not only if and because he is a sinner (through original or personal sin), but even prior to this insofar as the state of salvation is not unmerited in the same way as being created by God's free choice is unmerited. For a Catholic theology the created human being faces God and receives his definitive salvation and the orientation it implies of his existence toward this eternal salvation in the vision of God as free unmerited love of God, which in itself God could refuse man even though the latter already exists as a created being. If it is also assumed that man by this free decision can reject God's offer of himself and thus become a sinner; if furthermore it is assumed that God's offer of himself in forgiveness to the sinner as such implies a far more radical unmeritedness of grace than its unmeritedness on the part of the created human being as such; and if again it is assumed that this second and more radical character of unmeritedness is already involved in the grace of every human being by the very fact that the first human being sinned in a solidarity of weal and woe of the community of mankind, then all the above-mentioned distinctions in man's nature are really quite obvious. 'Nature' means man's reality as unity of mind and matter in self-transcendence toward God, insofar as this nature is the recipient of God's self-offering that, on the one hand, perfects man in deification and yet, on the other hand, is in no way due to this nature. 'Fallen nature' means the reality of man insofar as he is unworthy of God's gracious self-offering (as a result of 'original sin' alone or also of his personal sin) and in a certain sense has added a new and more radical unmeritedness to the unmeritedness of deifying grace as such. 'Nature elevated and restored' is man insofar as by God's forgiving grace (despite his previous sinfulness in the form of personal sin) and as a result of his free acceptance of grace he possesses a positive orientation to his own eternal goal, the vision of God.

At first sight then the idea of fallen nature seems to be clear. In Adam mankind fell. As a result of this sin on the part of the first human being, mankind does not possess the grace of deification through God's self-communication which is indeed unmerited but which it nevertheless requires; it is sinful. Humanity is fallen. The traditional view in Catholic theology is that each individual human being (with the exception of Jesus and the 'immaculately conceived' mother of Jesus) possesses this sinfulness before he enters by baptism (and/or by the free acceptance of grace in faith, hope, and love) into possession (the 'state') of sanctifying grace. 'Fallen nature' is a description of man insofar as he culpably lacks possession of sanctifying grace. Certainly it must be added that this state of man as culpably lacking grace (which is, properly speaking, the essence of being fallen) includes other peculiarities which determine the reality of man even when he has again obtained divine grace by justification: that is, he is in the state of nature fallen and healed. For the original justice of 'paradise' was associated with a freedom from the necessity of dying, from concupiscence, from suffering and pain, from ignorance and error. But these paradisiacal gifts are not returned to man when he enters, as a result of justification, the state of nature fallen and healed. In that sense then, the justified human being remains in the state of fallen nature, even though this necessity of dying, concupiscence, and involvement in suffering does not have the character of *'punishment* for sin' properly so-called but provides the dimension (in itself 'natural' and 'innocent') within which man is now expected to work out his salvation.

It cannot be denied however that there are many obscurities attached to this term 'fallen nature' which make it very difficult for us to appreciate its meaning today. In what follows we shall deal with these problems, without raising doubts about the fundamental justification of the term.

In our discussion of the problems, for the time being we shall pass over the question of whether and how the idea must or must not be maintained today of a paradisiacal state of freedom from death, concupiscence, and suffering preceding *chronologically* the state of fallen nature. The author has dealt with this question elsewhere[1] and has no wish to take it up again, at least for the time being.

Classical Lutheran theology regarded the essence of original sin and consequently also of fallen nature as consisting in concupiscence, the stirrings of which are opposed to the law of God and sinful, so that persistent concupiscence always makes man a sinner and he therefore remains a sinner even when he is justified by faith in God's forgiving grace: *simul justus et peccator*. The opposing declaration of the Council of Trent starts out from the assumption that the stirrings of concupiscence, unless ratified by man's free will, are not sin (since the justified person—who, as Paul says, is in Christ Jesus—is not condemned). For this reason concupiscence as such cannot constitute the real nature of original sin. The essence of original sin is therefore to be sought in the lack of justifying, sanctifying grace, while concupiscence is merely a consequence (not in itself sinful) of the loss of paradisiacal righteousness, which can remain in us without our being for that reason alone sinners in the proper sense of the term.

In this way, according to Catholic theology, original sin and consequently the state of fallen nature are transferred to a dimension

[1] On this cf. Karl Rahner, 'Erbsünde und Monogenismus' in K.-H. Weger, *Theologie der Erbsünde* (Freiburg, 1970), pp. 176–223.

which at least is not as immediately accessible to existential and religious experience as the dimension of concupiscence, which is in fact directly experienced. Original sinfulness here seems to become a mere theological postulate. All that man directly experiences of himself seems to be good: his intellectuality and freedom in which (since this is how he can know God) he has a positive relationship to God; his corporality, involving a 'natural' and as such innocent concupiscence which, after all, is nothing but the ambivalence of the material of freedom that must continually be processed by the history of this freedom. From this standpoint we can understand the axiom of at least one school in Catholic theology that has always remained undisturbed: namely, that fallen nature is distinct from pure nature only in the way that a person who has been robbed of his clothes differs from one who is naked from the start. If we leave aside the question whether and how the obligation and necessity (never, of course, denied in Catholic theology) of possessing justifying supernatural grace must work out empirically in someone who is not actually justified but in the state of fallen nature, what is really involved in such a view of fallen nature (if not commanded, then at least commended by Trent) is modern optimism as a whole from the time of humanism: man is free and good and the fallenness bound up with his natural being is understood in such a way that it does not infringe the goodness of this natural being. Man's nature as experienced is good and only good, even though it has the obligation of being open to deification by God's gracious self-communication. In this conception of fallen nature originating at Trent the fallenness of this nature properly consists only in the fact that this nature originally ('in paradise') possessed a grace-given perfection that it can now regain only in justification by baptism or by subjective conversion to the God of grace in faith, hope, and love.

Before we continue our investigation of these problems, a very different aspect of the meaning of fallen nature must be made clear. In all these questions Catholic theology in practice works with the model of infant baptism. The unbaptized child is regarded purely and simply as an originally sinful, unjustified human being; at the moment of baptism this human being is changed by the 'infusion' of sanctifying grace from a sinner into a justified, sanctified human being. Thus, from the very outset, an element of time enters into the notion of fallen nature. This does not mean simply that there would be no such thing as fallen nature if the sin of the first human being, understood as a particular historical event, had not occurred. An element of time is involved in the notion of fallen nature also insofar as this nature is regarded as ceasing to be fallen at the moment of baptism or of a subjective justification seen as happening at a point in time and at that point transformed into a nature fallen and restored, in which the original fallenness becomes perceptible only through the persistence of concupiscence and the absence of other preternatural gifts. In any case, within the life of the individual person, fallen nature as such belongs only to a certain period of time in that person's history and ceases with his justification. It is true that this theology is aware of the fact that God's universal salvific will embraces every human being always and everywhere; but in a sense it penetrates into the life of a human being only at a certain point in time, while his fallenness 'in Adam' determined him inwardly from the very beginning, making him a fallen nature; nature restored and elevated comes chronologically *after* fallen nature.

In the traditional textbook notion of fallen nature in Catholic theology then, we find an odd tension. This fallen nature in virtue of its temporality is a highly empirical factor: in the conception suggested by Trent, man *before* baptism is a sinner, deprived of sanctifying grace, under the power of the devil; *after* baptism he is justified and sanctified, divine grace has taken possession of him, is imparted to him after he had previously been without grace. At the same time in post-Tridentine theology this fallen nature is a very abstract transexistential factor, which as such cannot be experienced existentially at all and can become known only by theological indoctrination from outside, since man can experience himself directly only as good, personal-intellectual nature with concupiscence that in itself is inculpable, even though it carries with it also danger and struggle.

With all respect then for the Council of Trent and also recognizing that not everything implied in the textbook notion of fallen nature is *ipso facto* part of the Council's binding teaching, it may be said that the traditional notion does not possess all the clarity and internal homogeneity that might be desired. It suggests a temporality of salvation history prior to the temporality involved in freedom and its history. The unbaptized baby and the baptized baby (or the same child before and after its baptism) are distinct from each other as one human being under the power of the devil and another in the loving embrace of the power of God's sanctifying grace. This enormous difference, producing in the one an objective damnation (even if described as limbo) and in the other eternal bliss, is at the same time a difference which, as a theological postulate and as object of indoctrination from outside, lies beyond human experience in freedom and action. If the internal tensions in the notion of fallen are thus elucidated, this is not to deny the existence of theorems within traditional theology as a whole and in certain schools which make these internal tensions less tangible or (if they are fully developed) remove them all together. But they persist in the average textbook notion of fallen nature, even though (particularly as a result of a certain lack of theological interest) they do not disturb the normal theological consumer very much. Such a calm in the field of theology is still far from being a sign that the contentedly accepted answers to theological questions are correct or adequate. The calm is often merely a sign of theological wariness and lack of interest, since people do not understand and cannot show that these old problems have a fundamental significance and importance even today for modern man's self-understanding.

We are attempting, under modern perspectives and assumptions and with the aid of the conceptual equipment at our disposal, to say what is meant by the state of fallen nature and also what importance it has for a modern anthropology. With such a description, of course, problems arise as to how one statement or another is at the same time compatible with the dogmas of the Church's magisterium, which of course we have no wish to dispute or obscure. Here, in a brief essay, it is impossible expressly to examine all these problems. But the author may perhaps not be too presumptuous in thinking that he sees the problems and knows an answer to them, even if it cannot be presented here.

There really is something that can be called *status* or 'state' in anthropology of a philosophical or theological character. 'State' means realities connected with man that, on the one hand, are not simply part of man's metaphysical, transcendentally necessary nature and, on the other hand, are not odd, partial realities of man, but determine him as a whole in all his particular realities. They determine man always and everywhere. If there is about man a definiteness of this kind which, on the one hand, does not belong to his metaphysical, transcendentally necessary and enduring nature and, on the other hand, always and everywhere determines and binds this very nature, then this determination must be grounded either in God's free disposal of this nature or (and purely conceptually this seems at first an obscure and difficult hypothesis) in a free decision of man or of men, a decision which occurred 'at the beginning' of the history of all mankind in its entirety in such a way as to be and remain the factor determining the situation for *all* subsequent history. That this second conceivable possibility has in fact been realized (that is, is really also actually possible) can, of course, be known only from mankind's experience of salvation history. 'State' as concrete and inescapable situation for freedom in salvation history is therefore founded on God's and man's situation-creative freedom at the beginning. This means, of course, that we have developed theologically in terms of salvation history a concept of state that ought to be distinguished more precisely from other concepts expressed by the term 'state'. But we cannot enter further into this question here.

This state of man is originally grounded in God's free will in which the latter offers *himself* with his very own uncreated reality to the freedom of his intellectual creatures as meaning, dynamisms, and goal of man. Insofar as this free self-offering of God to his intellectual creature means always and everywhere the most radical opportunity and thus the most radical obligation for man, insofar as it not only hovers over man as an ideal possibility but is man's most real and innermost possibility (constituting also the possibility of the free acceptance of this self-communication of God), this freedom of love in which God gives himself to man really establishes fundamentally *the* state of man. It is really 'state', since it is not simply involved in the very nature of man who as already really conceived and existing must welcome the love of God imparting God himself as *free* grace that is not owing to him. It is really 'state' in the most fundamental sense, since man with his freedom can never get away from the situation that really determines him in which God with his infinite reality offers himself to man freely and lovingly and at the same time gives man the opportunity freely to accept this offer.

The state of elevated nature is man's most fundamental determination. It is not part of his nature, not because it is not internal to him, but because God's personal love in the light of God's own nature is always unmerited, must in fact be freedom and love. It is also deeply implanted in man, since (as distinct from the usual perspective in textbook theology from the Middle Ages onwards) the will of God for his own self-externalizing self-communication can certainly be regarded as the actual ground of creation and not as the will for a kind of subsequent elevation of the reality created by God. This state is not lost by man's sin and God's will for this state (assuming the existence of sin in the world) is the cause and not the result of God's salvific action in the world to overcome sin. This state is unconditional and cannot be abolished by sin. Man's freedom can sinfully say no to this state but cannot abolish it any more than man's freedom can abolish his nature and existence by saying no to them. To put it more clearly: this state does not hover above the reality of the world and man as an ideal postulate, which could be known only by a verbal communication from outside, from God, but is established by God's self-communication, which as a real offer to freedom is always and everywhere a real existential (that is, a state) of man, even though, through this self-communication of God, grace exists in the infant merely as an offer, in the mature person either as accepted (as in justification) or, in the sinner, as rejected. The state of elevated nature is really the unavoidable situation of man's freedom from which he can never escape.

He learns of this state as a result of a complex of experiences (in the last resort of a transcendental character) which must now be analyzed a little more closely. In this analysis it is not assumed that it could be made sufficiently clear always and everywhere by a single individual in the privacy of his life. The original and primary analysis takes place in the experience of the salvation history of mankind as a whole, culminating in the experience of Jesus Christ (the genitive is subjective *and* objective). Secondarily this experience is then reflected and interpreted in theology. This interpretation again appeals to the experience of the individual human being and confronts him with the question as to whether and how far in the history of his individual experience he can discover what this analysis in terms of salvation history and theology says about man.

All this is assumed here when we attempt to describe the experience of man's nature as elevated by God's self-communication offered always and everywhere. Man is the being with a radically unlimited transcendentality. But this is experienced *de facto*, not only as the condition of the possibility of a cognitive and active engagement with the categorial realities of the world, but also as endowed with the promise of an infinite fulfillment by God himself. If our transcendentality reaches out, not only to one object or another but also in a kind of paroxysm of absolute hope to the original unlimited unity of all that is, then (whether it can reflect on this or not) it is already sustained by God's self-communication, which we usually describe as sanctifying grace and which, at least in the form of an offer, exists always and everywhere. Insofar as this radical transcendentality of the human mind in knowledge and freedom is in fact the radicalness of a personal spirit, the sustaining ground of this radicalness—God himself—is experienced (reflectively or not) as freedom and love. Grace is experienced always and everywhere in man's existence. This proposition has no postulatory or mythological overtones if this experience is seen in the radicalness of man's transcendentality, a transcendentality that is not merely realized and understood as the condition of man's being-in-the-world, but (as given by God) implies the assurance in faith and hope (at least as an offer to free self-understanding) of finally reaching God himself, of being filled with the reality of God in himself. Man's ineluctable status-assuring self-understanding (which exists even if his ultimate self-destructiveness makes him refuse to admit it) consists in the fact that (also as intelligible subject) he recognizes that he is not God *and* that he respects himself as the recipient of God in himself. This (already existing or accepted or freely and culpably rejected) basic experience of man is originally not an isolated 'thought' occurring only spasmodically with the aid of a difficult reflection, but is veritably man's basic experience involved prior to any reflection in all thought and action.

In practice, however, this basic experience of divine origin and consummation is oddly fragmented in man. It is made by and in a human being who experiences himself simultaneously as one who is doomed to death and as one who is unable to gather the whole of his human existence with his knowledge and impulses integrally into this experience he has of a divine consummation. He experiences a contradiction between his concupiscence and mortality on the one hand and his absolute destiny to the immediacy of God on the other. The existence of such a contradiction cannot perhaps be deduced from abstract ideas of the realities involved here, nor will there be any attempt here to maintain that the individual human being in each case for himself alone experiences the contradiction so clearly as to be able theoretically to reflect on it. Of course, the contradiction also means that the two contradictory elements co-exist in one and the same person and for that very reason the contradiction really exists and can be experienced. What is involved in this contradiction is that man's state of grace, his divine origin and consummation ought 'properly' to exclude man's concupiscent situation, that is, it ought to place man's whole reality integrated and united completely at the disposal of man's freedom, in which, as empowered by God's gracious self-communication, man commits himself entirely to God. (The fact cannot be overlooked that actual death, which is not simply man's perfected self-determination as final and definitive but is also the culmination of man's incapacity to dispose of himself, is nothing but the most radical event of concupiscence in the sense in which it is understood here.)

If we really want to understand existentially and ontologically man's condition and situation, we cannot tacitly start out from the assumption that a particular state of man must either be sinful in the proper sense of the term (as habitual sin) or it must fit in consistently with the wholeness of man. Such an assumption would not only render impossible any understanding of man's 'physical evil' or lead to the conclusion that any evil of this kind can be understood always only as the consequence of moral fault in man. The contradictoriness of which we are speaking is experienced as actually existing and must therefore be conceivable. Man experiences his concupiscent distractedness and unintegratedness as something other than what must be regarded and experienced simply as obvious and innocuous, resulting from his corporality and biological origin. He feels this concupiscent condition as something that really ought not to be, when he measures this state against the claim involved in his transcendentality as radicalized by grace. In the light of this claim he cannot simply accept as justified and as a matter of course categorial realities which prevent him from realizing this infinite claim (and do not merely, as is obvious, fail to fulfill it). In the light of this claim he must protest against his concupiscent situation, and must feel (as Paul already expressed it in his Letter to the Romans) 'unhappy' about it. If this is denied or overlooked in a theory of fallen nature (because man's destiny with his transcendentality to God's immediacy is transferred to a dimension wholly beyond consciousness, where concupiscence can no longer be experienced as something that ought not to be), then the doctrine of fallen nature can be regarded only as a mythological interpretation of man, as an assertion that has no place in religious experience and is only indoctrinated from outside. At the same time, of course, the question of the source of this mythological interpretation of man itself remains unanswered. In brief, man experiences at every turn a contradiction present now and always between the radicalness of the claim of his deified transcendentality and the concupiscent situation in which he must realize it. The claim aims at integrating man as a whole into his assignment to the immediacy of God; but the concupiscent situation prevents this.

In biblical terms, we have the ability and obligation to love God with our *whole* heart, and yet we do not succeed in this. In Catholic theological terminology this contradiction (which ought not to be) is not described in itself as 'sin', since in another (Lutheran) usage the difference has been blurred between this contradiction and the act of freedom in which in a personal sinful decision man not only does not love God with his whole heart but actually rejects him. But this legitimate usage should not be allowed to minimize the contradiction between the duty of radical love of God imposed on man and what he actually achieves in his concupiscent situation. This sort of minimizing has often happened in post-Tridentine theology, since in that theology (which paid little attention to the religious experience of devout people) this concupiscence was abstractly related only to 'pure nature' and the fact was overlooked that this concupiscence always exists in the actual human being who by grace is always and everywhere permitted and required to fulfill divine claims, who in practice is never a 'pure nature' and can never experience himself merely as such.

If we maintain and regard as justifiable by the Church's official teaching the view that neither eschatological nor protological statements are part of reports of events from past or future but are legitimate conclusions from man's self-understanding (itself drawn from his present experience, sustained by grace, and thus implying revelation), then the question arises whether and how it is possible to draw from the experience of the contradiction of which we are speaking those protological statements which in traditional theology explain this contradiction by a primordial sin at the dawn of history, or whether these protological explanations are only more or less mythological elucidations of this disintegratedness of man experienced in oneself. Was there, it might be asked, *before* me a sinful 'Adam' whose action was the cause of my concupiscent situation or am I myself 'Adam', without any light really being thrown on my existence by an interpretation based on a cause sought in the most distant past? It must be said that, on the one hand, a Catholic interpretation of one's own existence and the experience of that existence cannot dispense with a recourse to history and that, on the other, all that can be said about this past as the cause of one's own concupiscent situation is no more than what is yielded by the present. If it can be assumed that the contradiction experienced between man's infinite destiny and his concupiscent situation must be understood as universal and that this contradiction moreover cannot be experienced as 'normal', then at the very beginning of mankind's history there must be a culpable event of freedom that explains this universal abnormal fissure in man. This aetiology presupposes the experience existing everywhere that a decision of freedom on the part of one person affects the other person's situation of freedom. But it is then conceivable that a decision of freedom occurring at the beginning on the part of all together provoked this abnormal condition, which as such obviously does not imply any personal guilt on the part of human beings who came after that beginning, but nevertheless creates a situation which as such ought not to be and is experienced as a contradiction.

It is difficult to say exactly how the beginning of mankind's history as set up by God as Creator is related to the 'beginning' of mankind's history established by human freedom of a culpable character. These two beginnings are certainly not identical, since the divine ordering of things as such cannot be understood simply (as Barth at first maintained) as the setting up of the creature precisely *as* contradiction to God, nor, however, can the second 'beginning' be understood as placed at a distance of an empirically *temporal* character in which everything possible within a history of freedom could have happened to prevent a later sin from being understood as a universal determinant of mankind's history. Consequently, the idea of a paradise of mankind at its origin lasting for a period of time is not only scarcely compatible with modern ideas of the evolution of the biosphere and of mankind, not only rouses suspicions of a mythology no longer acceptable, but also contradicts a serious theology of the beginning. The two beginnings must be brought so close to one another that a history in the usual sense of the term coming *between* them is inconceivable. The very first self-realization of creaturely human freedom must therefore have been a culpable act and the starting point of history. The idea of a paradise 'previously' implies the real necessity of a distinction between the two 'beginnings': origin of history from God, origin of history from sinful man (even though the establishment of this second origin can and must be conceived as an historical event in a metaphysically more abstract sense).

The idea of paradise has its legitimacy also insofar as it provides an explanation of the abnormality of the concupiscent situation in the light of a divinely given absolute claim. But in the last resort all these protological statements do no more than make man aware of the fact that he may not regard as normal the situation of his freedom between an absolute claim and the actually existing distracting possibilities, that he may not clear up this situation by settling for one side or the other of the contradiction, may not regard himself either as the subject of an absolute freedom for himself alone or as a being that can accept its concupiscent situation contentedly as a matter of course.

If concupiscence thus becomes an element of essential importance in the notion of fallen nature (before and after justification), this does not mean that concupiscence as such constitutes the real nature of original sin. But the essence of original sin will have to be understood now and in the future as the initially culpably caused absence of God's grace, sanctifying man prior to his decision of freedom: a grace that has an absolutely sanctifying quality prior to man's free decision, precisely because it is not a creaturely reality always ambivalent prior to the decision of freedom, but the self-communication of the holy God himself.

If we speak of a 'lack' of this grace, the term does not, or does not necessarily, imply that this 'lack' is chronologically prior to a (later) possession of this at first absent gift. All it means is that man, precisely as a member of this initially sinful humanity, although he ought to possess this gift, does not possess this sanctifying self-communication of God (as offer, as freely accepted, or as freely rejected). Whether he possesses this gift simply and as a matter of fact (at least in the form of a real offer) because of God's gratuitous salvific will in regard to mankind and despite the latter's initial culpability, is quite a different question. If and insofar as this 'infralapsarian' salvific will of God (which cannot be denied) can certainly be regarded as equally comprehensively and concretely effective always and everywhere and is not something at first existing only in God's intentions (in other words, as equally real as the impact of the beginning on all humanity) there exists in man prior to his free decision for or against God a dialectical simultaneity of 'original sin' (as lack of a claim to sanctifying grace from the very origin of mankind) and the grace existing always and everywhere as an offer because of God's infralapsarian salvific will. Prior to his personal decision in freedom man is *simul justus et peccator*.

He experiences the justification offered to him in the question put to his freedom by the absolute, never-to-be-silenced claim in his existence, in the radicalness of his transcendence, the demand for God himself as such. He experiences his sinfulness by experiencing the contradiction between his concupiscent situation and his absolute claim, a claim that can never be satisfied in this situation, since the definitive acceptance of God's absolute self-offering is not possible in a situation where a person cannot use his freedom totally to commit himself to a definitive finality. This does not mean that the experience of concupiscence in face of the absolute claim of proffered grace *is* in identity the experience of original sin, but only that it leads ultimately to this other conclusion about original sin. For if the contradiction between concupiscence and the claim of grace is traced back protologically to a sin at the beginning and man with his concupiscence originating *at that point* thus learns that of himself he has no claim on God's loving self-communication, then he knows his state to be that of original sin. If this original sinfulness as an inability to claim divine grace originating in a history of sin at its beginning is clearly to be understood as merely 'analogous' to personal sin, this is no argument against these reflections. For today it is certainly a generally accepted theological conviction that original sin and personal sin are two concepts that agree only analogously.

If this is how man's condition is regarded, the classical conception of original sin (lack of sanctifying grace) can be maintained and yet (as against a post-Tridentine theory) concupiscence can be more closely and more clearly intrinsically linked with original sin. The assumption behind all this is, of course, the proposition that man's concupiscent disintegratedness (that is, the impossibility of totally integrating his whole reality into the basic decision for or against

God) as such contradicts a self-communication of God (sanctifying grace) offered to man's freedom, a self-offering of God to man's freedom (at least in the form of an offer) which exists always and everywhere as an existential of man. But when man experiences and accepts his supreme vocation, sustained by God's self-communication, to love God with his whole heart, to love him divinely, then he can no longer experience and accept as a matter of course his concupiscent disintegration, his inability here and now to love God with his whole heart, but must experience it as something that really ought not to be, even though this something that ought not to be is not really sin prior to any personal decision but lies at a point difficult to determine between purely prepersonal evils (physical evil) and personal fault.

If concupiscence and, consequently, fallen nature are understood in this way, it should not be overlooked that this impossibility of a pure integration of human realities into the decision of freedom for God is not to be understood as the reality and experience of a mere privatistic inwardness, but also implies a situation of human corporality and especially of sociability. Sociological disintegratedness, the impossibility of complete harmony in society, unreconciled pluralism in society in all its dimensions, are primarily wholly part of that concupiscent situation of which a theological anthropology is accustomed to speak. This theology however does not merely note the banal fact of the concupiscent situation as now (still) existing, but also explains that this fact will be removed only with the end of history, since it was so firmly planted (even though by creaturely freedom) into the very beginning of this history that it cannot be removed by this history itself, since the latter, striving dutifully for its removal (the removal of alienation, etc.), again works from and with this concupiscent situation.

In the light of such a theology of fallen nature, of its concupiscent situation, the question ought to be raised about the peculiarity of a Christian ethic: that, on the one hand, it involves the precept of an approximative and asymptotic struggling and coping with concupiscence (with alienation, etc.) and, on the other hand, it cannot proceed as if this concupiscent situation could be purely and simply removed within the course of history. But it is impossible to deal further with this question here.

PART TWO

Priesthood

5

CONSECRATION IN THE LIFE AND REFLECTION OF THE CHURCH

In order to anticipate at once the following reflections as a whole, I would like to say that they are meant to make clear in theological terms the fact that in the concrete order of salvation (from which no human being can escape and which extends to man's innermost *a priori* definitive state) there is a sanctifiedness, or what may be called a consecratedness, a sacrality, of man, present in advance as the condition of the possibility of any ecclesial-cultic consecration, even though these latter consecrations elucidate in the most diverse forms and expressions the innermost and inescapable consecratedness of man here envisaged, while manifesting and locating it in the public-sociological area of the Church. Consecrations in the ordinary sense of the term (that is, baptism, confirmation, ordination, forms of consecration generally described as sacramentals for special functions, minor orders as preparation for properly sacramental ordination, and also consecration of virgins, consecration of abbots, etc.) do not establish for the first time a person's consecratedness, as if he had previously existed in a purely profane state; they are the ecclesial-cultic manifestations of a consecratedness conferred by grace, but always existing, embracing, and sustaining man's whole existence, always and everywhere present in the light of God's salvific will as offer of God's self-communication to man's freedom. That is really all that I want to explain and substantiate in the course of this essay. In this respect I think that what must be said has also its practical consequences in the spirituality of the priest and others consecrated by a sacrament or sacramentally and for the life of the Church, even though these more or less practical consequences can at most be mentioned only marginally.

In order to reach the heart of these reflections as quickly and as safely as possible, we may recall in the first place a theological datum that is certainly disputed by no one working in the field of Catholic theology: all consecrations, if they are to be meaningful and effective, are based on baptism. This (we may say, quite without prejudice) is the first basic consecration, the fundamental dedication, the fundamental initiation, which is the indispensable and necessary precondition for all other actual or conceivable consecrations in the Church. It is true that consecrations subsequent to baptism (for example, priestly ordination) in the area of the Church's sociological, public manifestation can assign to someone so consecrated tasks and powers that he would not (at least, not normally) possess without such a subsequent consecration. But this by no means alters the fact that a consecration of this kind, based on baptism, is an ecclesial-sociological expression of a particular kind, with a particular orientation, of *sacramental* consecratedness, of the incorporatedness and membership of a person in the Church, which in the dimension of the Church's sociological visibility is conferred only by baptism. Otherwise, in the very nature of things, it would be quite impossible to understand why all ecclesiastical tasks and functions, transmitted by other consecrations, should not be valid without being preceded by baptism.

Assuming all this, we now ask what is the position of baptism itself? Is it purely and simply the first and fundamental establishment of a person's 'consecratedness', of his admission into the dimension of the holy God and his love, in which God by 'consecrating' man imparts to the latter his own holy life? Or is baptism, albeit normally and as such necessarily, the manifestation (but an effective manifestation) of an internal consecratedness of man by grace, ontologically, existentially, and chronologically prior to baptism: a consecratedness which always and from the outset fundamentally determines man's existence, so that he simply cannot escape from this ultimate sacral sphere of his existence, even though he has either not yet reacted at all in freedom to this definitive state or exists freely in opposition to this existential established by grace?

It is the second view of baptism which we are supporting here. We maintain, then, that consecration in the diverse forms in which it appears in the Church is derived from a consecratedness more fundamental than ecclesial-cultic consecration and is not purely and simply a consequence and effect of the latter. This thesis is not obvious, it seems to contradict the view (more or less taken for granted) that any possible consecratedness is simply and solely the consequence of a consecration that takes place at a definite point of time as part of the public worship of the Church. Neither can it be denied that the formularies of the Church's official teaching on the nature and effects of baptism tacitly assume that there occurs for the first time and purely and simply in baptism what is usually described as the effect of baptism: infusion of justifying and sanctifying grace and of the supernatural habits known as the theological virtues of faith, hope, and charity; remission of original sin; the transposition of man from the kingdom of darkness and evil into the kingdom of God; of love, of friendship with God; the granting of the status of a child of God, etc. (Before pursuing our problems further, in order to avoid misunderstandings it should be stressed that it is not our opinion that simply *every* effect ascribed to baptism exists in man even prior to baptism; it is obvious that those effects which by their very nature belong as historical and sociological factors to the visibly sociological dimension of the Church are produced only by baptism itself, although there is no need to consider here more exactly which effects of baptism are of this character: whether, for example, what we called the sacramental character conferred by baptism must be numbered among these effects.)

We claim, then, that the fundamental effects of baptism (that is, the most fundamental consecratedness of man, man's existential always and everywhere) are present even *before* sacramental consecration, that baptismal consecration therefore comes after and is based on the consecratedness of man which is derived from grace, that this consecratedness as ontological and existential is the ground and not originally the consequence of baptismal consecration. We hasten to observe that this does not mean that the *efficacy* of baptism as sacrament on this fundamental consecratedness of man need be denied, even though our thesis of course makes the elucidation of the efficacy of the sacrament of baptism on this fundamental consecratedness more difficult than it was generally considered to be in normal sacramental theology on the efficacy of the sacraments.

This thesis, whose practical consequences will be indicated only at a later stage, implies, of course, a basic conception of the relationship between God and the world, of the nature of the supernatural endowment of grace and the vocation of the world and humanity to God's immediacy, of the nature of salvation history: a basic conception which, on the one hand, cannot be taken for granted in Catholic theology and whose interpretation, on the other hand, would of course go far beyond the scope of a brief essay. Hence only one or two modest observations in regard to the substantiation of this basic thesis are possible here.

How, we may ask, do we usually imagine the gracious, unmerited, and supernatural sanctification of man in the course of the history of humanity? We imagine the world, mankind and its history, first of all as a spatially and temporally extended reality of a profane character, even though created by God, into which God as distinct from the world and confronting it from outside enters at certain individual points and then acts by the revelation of the word and the communication of grace (the latter mainly through the sacraments). This is brought about by individual events coming on top of the otherwise profane course of world history, at different points, as additional to the ordinary course of things and which in principle can be individually located. These individual events produced by grace, occurring at definite points in space and time, may certainly belong together in God's intention and thus form the *history* of revelation and salvation as conceptually a single factor; they can also be linked together in the sociological-institutional dimension by the transmission of this successive revelation and by the religio-sociological institutions willed by God (for example, by the sociological factor of the Old Covenant and by the institution of the Church); but in the last resort this makes no difference to the traditional pattern of ideas, according to which the really constitutive events of revelation and inward sanctification by grace originally made their impact successively and from outside on a profane world and history. We think, however, that such an ideal scheme is inadequate and does not match up to the reality. God, in himself infinitely perfect and existing in glory, does indeed create in freedom a world and history absolutely distinct from himself, but he creates it from the outset as the recipient of his own *self*-communication by grace, in which from the very outset and always and everywhere he gives himself as the innermost dynamism of world and history and as their proper and very own goal.

What we call revelation history and salvation history is not the sum total of particular interventions of God at different points from outside into an at first merely naturally created world and history, but the history (the interpretation in space and time) of a self-communication of God in free grace in which God from the very beginning established himself in the innermost centre of the world as its salvation. As seen from God's standpoint then, his gracious self-communication to the world is not to be conceived as a kind of second initiative of God in regard to a natural world created in a first initiative, but as God's free will toward a world distinct from himself as the condition of the possibility of a more fundamental free will of God to bestow himself in love to the non-divine. Salvation history and revelation history take place from the innermost centre of the world and history where God as imparting his own sacred glory has always already established himself, is already always in immediacy the dynamism, sanctification, and goal of the world. Of course, this self-communication of God, through which he is the innermost centre of world and history, is always and from the very outset understood and willed as free offer to the freedom of the creature. Consequently, through the freedom of the creature in accepting or rejecting this self-offering of God, the latter has a history: that history which we call the revelation history and salvation history of humanity. But this precisely is the history of this self-offering of God conveyed by man's freedom to man himself, even though the history of man's freedom is itself the act of the free God and of the sovereignty of his own grace. What we otherwise usually call the sanctification of the world and of the individual human being is the free acceptance by creaturely freedom of the sanctification of the world and man, which has always been present in the form of God's real self-offering as the centre of creaturely reality as a whole. World and man become holy in an existential sense through man's freedom in accepting God, since they are always also sanctified prior to this by God as origin, dynamism, and goal precisely of this history.

Once again, may we understand what we call revelation history and salvation history in this way? Once again, I think we can. I would go further and insist that we cannot think of it otherwise if we see the relationship of God and the world to one another as we must see it today: that is, so that God does not appear as a particular element in reality as a whole, as incorporated into what we regard as the whole system of reality.

Why may we think in this way today, even in the light of the familiar data of traditional theology? On this, of course, only a few suggestions are possible here.

First of all, we may be permitted an allusion to Islamic theology, even though this goes beyond the scope of Christian dogmatics. Fischer-Barnicol writes,

> Islam has kept its understanding of revelation free from the internal contradictions which are unavoidable when the self-communication of the eternal to the temporal is nailed firmly to the historical crossbeam, to the time sequence. Then divine mercy is subjected to temporal ideas, as if it could be imparted only in slices, in installments, more clearly from one chapter to another, and completely only at the close and not in all essentials all the time. Islam's economy of salvation does not allow for a steadily improving performance over the course of history with a final examination at the present time when an official certificate is awarded which states that the truth is now known, understood, and expressed better than it was by the generations of believers who went before us. According to the Islamic view, God has revealed himself always and in all respects completely and unrestrictedly. Never provisionally, always finally. It is taken for granted that we shall appreciate this at the end of time when the religions of the book will be discovered in their unity.[1]

We need not and cannot simply share this Islamic view. Nevertheless, it contains a profound truth which we overlook or suppress in current theology. If we understand God's self-communication to the world in the form of an offer to freedom and history as one and whole and always present and allow it as such to have a history in the history of its own free acceptance by mankind's reflection (known as history of revelation in the word, which reflection must itself, of course, be controlled by this self-communication of God) and by freedom (known as salvation history), then we have a reconciliation between God's self-communication (which by its nature cannot be understood as happening 'in slices') and a true salvation history and revelation history as reflected in the Old and the New Testament.

[1] H. A. Fischer-Barnicol. 'Wortwechsel oder Gespräch—Zur Begegnung der Kirche mit dem Islam' in *Una Sancta: Zeitschrift für Ökumenische Begegnung* 31, no. 2 (1976): 150.

In fact, if man's whole history of freedom is governed by a supernatural, salvific providence of God and is thus as a whole oriented to God's immediacy, if all creation from the outset is established 'in Christ' and oriented to him, then this fundamental determination of all reality cannot be understood as at first existing in the mind and intentions of God. This determination of the world and of mankind's history must be objectively established in the world itself. It is a determination that does not exist only when it is objectified by explicitly verbal revelation; the latter simply makes evident objectively and as open to reflection what has always existed in the world as a result of God's self-communication to it. It is because of the presence in the world of this determination that we know that it exists also in the mind and intentions of God and not vice versa.

This becomes still more clear when we consider with Vatican II the fact that always and everywhere in the history of humanity there has been and is a real possibility of attaining supernatural salvation, that this salvation is possible only by faith in the strict theological sense and that this very faith is itself possible only if and when it is sustained by the grace that imparts God himself as its intrinsic principle. But this means essentially that the grace of faith (which in the last resort is God himself as uncreated grace) must be present always and everywhere in the world in the form of an offer and (as Vatican II expressly states) is rejected only when a person acts against the final decision of his conscience and even in this rejection remains confronted by God's offer of himself. But if this is the situation, then there is no point in regarding what we call the sanctifying grace of faith, hope, and love, as consisting in separate and intermittent offers by God, occurring only occasionally on the time-axis of an otherwise secular history. This grace (free and unmerited, of course) must be understood as an intrinsic existential of the history of humanity, but *in no way due* as a result of being present always as an offer to man's freedom and of having a history in this freedom itself. If the nature of creaturely freedom does not in the last resort consist in the ability to do something with this or that particular object but is the freedom of the subject to itself, then freedom and salvation history amount in fact to a freedom toward the subject endowed with grace and sanctified in the form of an offer prior to its self-determination. Incidentally, however, it may be noted that no lesser existential-ontological apriority can be ascribed to this *a priori* endowment of grace and sanctification, such as that which traditional theology assigns to what we call original sin.

We cannot go more closely here into the question of how this conception can be reconciled with the certainly correct and traditional view of the sacraments, understood as events of grace occurring at definite points in space and time. To deal with this question we must not start out from the model of infant baptism but must think of individual sacramental events in space and time as they occur in and with adults. But it is obvious here with reference to baptism and penance that these sacraments, even for traditional theology, without detriment to their efficacy, come upon a person who has already accepted in freedom the grace always offered to him and is justified. It is the person who *believes* and is *justified* in faith and love who is baptized, and only in such a person is the sacrament of baptism effective. In the sacrament of penance the penitent receives the word of forgiveness and must approach this word of forgiveness as already converted to God, his conversion being itself salvific and sustained by grace. Traditional theology also therefore presupposes a person already endowed with grace and justified. But this condition, which is presupposed, is itself sustained by the grace always preceding it and reaching the person in the form of an offer. Yet again this offer itself certainly need not be understood as an isolated event occurring for the first time and solely at the particular moment when it is accepted or rejected. Why and how exactly a real efficacy of grace is to be and can be attributed to the sacraments is a question that cannot be further discussed at the moment. In this respect it need only be said that traditional sacramental theology is also faced with the same problem as that which is linked with our own basic conception and that the latter consequently presents no difficulty that does not always exist whenever God's original turning to us in grace, sustaining all salvation history, is understood as an event occurring at a definite point in time.

Before turning finally to the implications for our theme of the basic conception of grace that sanctifies man, presented here by way of suggestion, an interim consideration must be interposed. We are occupied with those sacraments which might be described as sacraments of consecration: that is, with baptism and confirmation, also up to a point with the sacrament of matrimony and especially with the sacrament of order in its different grades. These sacraments have in common the fact that they establish, each in its own specific fashion, a permanent consecratedness on the part of the person who receives them. This consecratedness established by the 'status-conferring' sacraments (and this fact will in no way be denied) is, on the one hand, a reality which certainly cannot be conceived as existing *before* the sacraments but, on the other hand, lies within the historical, sociological dimension of the Church: reception into the visible Church through baptism, explicit authorization to participate in the visible Church's witness to the faith, the permanent bond of marriage, official authorization to participate in the function of leadership on the part of the Church's ministry through the various grades of order. These realities of course do not exist before reception of the sacrament and for this reason they are distinct from the real grace-given consecratedness and holiness which exists always and everywhere in the form of an offer to man's freedom; as such, these realities affect the dimension of the Church as a 'visible' society, leaving aside here the question whether as such they can be identified with the 'sacramental character' which the Church's teaching assigns as an effect to these sacraments *or* (which seems to me less probable) must be distinguished from the sacramental character.

Whether these realities in the sociological dimension of the Church must be understood (as appears to be usual) as a consecratedness and holiness already conferred by this Church as such, is in the last resort a question of terminology which in turn depends on the question of whether, in what sense, and with what justification we want to assign the predicate of consecratedness and holiness also to the Church as a sociological factor as distinct from secular societies or think that such a qualification for these realities should as such be strictly avoided, since holiness in the strict sense of the term can be understood only as participation in the glory of the holy God by his self-communication in grace, 'in sanctifying grace', in the grace which alone places the creature in the sphere of the blessed untouchability of the holy God. In whatever way we answer these ultimately terminological questions, while not overlooking the fact that the 'status' given with these 'sacraments of consecration' within the sociological dimension of the Church can exist also in sinners and therefore as such can be described only in a secondary and analogous sense as consecratedness, it is in any case a fact that these realities of the sacraments of consecration, constituting a status in the Church, refer back to the proper consecratedness of man by grace, that they should in principle be sustained by grace and *are* in fact so sustained even in the sinner, insofar as the sinner, too, is always determined by the existential of sanctifying grace in the form of an offer and a demand for its acceptance.

This connection between the real holiness of man through the grace which exists always and everywhere and the 'consecratedness' established by the sacraments of consecration has in principle always been seen in the teaching of the Church and of theology: these sacraments of consecration are supposed to be received 'in the state of grace' and they may never be understood as mere conferments of status in the sociological order of the Church, to which man's innermost relationship to God by the free acceptance of his consecratedness by grace is a matter of indifference; the sacraments of consecration are always also signs of this proper and innermost consecratedness of man and are always also the offer (effective by its very nature) of the 'increase' of sanctifying grace, that is, the offer of God's help toward an existentially increasingly radical acceptance by his freedom of the already always proffered holiness of man. The ultimate ground of this connection between the sacraments of status, the sacraments of consecration, and the proper holiness and consecratedness of man by grace lies in the fact that the Church is supposed to be and is the eschatological sign, the basic sacrament, not only of God's self-offering to man's freedom, but is also the basic sacrament which secures that this self-offering of God of itself is actually victoriously established in man's freedom; the Church as a whole is the holy, not only in the dimension of word and sacraments, but also in the existential acceptance of grace by man's freedom.

Presupposing this interim consideration on the relationship between the sacraments of consecration and the 'consecratedness' established by these on the one hand and the holiness and consecratedness of man existing always and everywhere because of God's self-communication on the other (the latter being always and everywhere the innermost centre and dynamism of revelation history and salvation history and not merely something that comes from outside occasionally at certain points upon an otherwise secular history), we can now attempt to consider a number of consequences which will lead us back more closely to the basic theme.

If someone has himself 'consecrated' (we are thinking now mainly of ordination, although what is to be said is true also *mutatis mutandis* of the other sacraments of consecration), he is nevertheless, prior to this consecration, not a secular, unholy person receiving through the sacraments, as something coming from outside in what seems almost a miraculous and magical fashion, a holiness which raises him in an elitist sense above the mass of secular, unsanctified human beings. What really happens in such a sacrament of consecration is the historical manifestation and the sociologically concretizing specification in the dimension of the visible Church of a holiness and consecratedness which has always existed inescapably in that person in the form of an offer in virtue of God's salvific will. The external and visible sign of a sacrament of consecration always refers the recipient to the ultimate and most fundamental depth of his own existence in which he has always been consecrated (whether he is explicitly aware of this or merely lives implicitly in accordance with it) by the self-offering of the holy God. The sacrament invokes this innermost consecratedness of the person and charges him to enter increasingly clearly and, existentially, increasingly radically into the experience of this innermost consecratedness of man; it charges and enables him to understand and realize his ecclesial-sociological consecrated status increasingly clearly and radically as the sociological concreteness and specification of his ultimate consecratedness which he possesses in common with all human beings, even outside the circle of those established by baptism as members of the Church in the narrower sense.

It is only from this standpoint that it is possible in the last resort to understand what is being said everywhere in the Church today: that those who are consecrated by ordination are each and all both servants of the Church and its members. The hierarchical separatedness of the person consecrated by ordination exists solely in the dimension of the sacramental sociological reality of the Church as such, not however in the 'hierarchy' of grace, of holiness, that is constituted by the diversity of radicalness in which human beings believe, hope, and love. The ordained person is called continually to discover afresh in himself this ultimate experience of the Holy Spirit, whom he shares with everyone, and to make it fruitful for the special task to which he is appointed by the sacrament of order. His official task in the Church is the concrete form in which he must also concretely accept his grace-given holiness and give it expression. However great the variety of ways of life and callings in which Christianity can be realized, the priestly ministry is not an additional task undertaken by the priest as supplementary to his being a Christian, but for him—for one who is called—it is *the* way of being a Christian. It is from this standpoint that the lifelong character of the priestly office can be made intelligible as the concreteness of inescapably being a Christian, even though this means that the concrete questions of the possibility or impossibility of priesthood for a time are not yet answered. 'Consecratedness' by the transmission of office in the sacrament of order acquires its ultimate truth and urgency in any case from that consecration which exists through grace.

A further problem must now be faced and I hope that the previous reflections may contribute, at least up to a point, to its answer. The problem consists in the fact that in recent decades, apart from the permanent diaconate, pastoral ministries have emerged in the Church, not based on any form of consecration and having behind them no more than a commission from the Church. In the light of this there is a special urgency about the question of the permanent significance and never ceasing importance of consecration in the life and in the reflection of the Church.

Before attempting in the light of our previous reflections to make a contribution directly to answering this question, there are still a number of preliminary observations to be considered.

We assume as a dogma that the papal primacy and the episcopal constitution of the Church are part of the Church's perennially valid essential structures, are of divine law, even though this divine law has had a history in the Church itself. We also assume that there is an office in the Church below the episcopate which is conferred in a sacramental happening called ordination. It is possible also to say without prejudice that imposition of hands is the sacramental sign of conferment of office in the Church today, as it was in the early Church, but that in principle it is within the Church's discretion to determine and to change the precise mode of the sacramental rite of ordination. But, in the light of these assumptions, it must also be said that the extent to which orders are sacramentally conferred and the grades of order are matters which lie within the Church's discretion. Today, for instance, the diaconate is undoubtedly a participation in sacramental ordination, but this is not a reason for claiming that Jesus himself expressly instituted the diaconate as a sacrament and as a specific participation in an office that must exist in the Church. In the Church's understanding at the present time the minor orders below the diaconate are not sacraments, but this does not mean that the medieval persuasion of their sacramentality must be rejected in principle; this opinion is still justified in the sense that the Church can institute such grades of order and also confer them sacramentally *if* it wants to do so and considers it opportune at a particular time. Nor is it impossible historically to assign a sacramental character to the consecration of deaconesses in the early Church. In general, then, without coming into conflict with a dogma of the Church, it can be said that there must exist in the Church an office that corresponds to the nature of the Church; that this one office implies a variety of powers corresponding to the Church's nature, such as the power to teach authoritatively, power to govern in the individual churches and in the universal Church or in the larger particular Church, sacramental powers; that the Church has the right and duty to confer in a variable and graded form a share in this one office and also to a limited extent to impart powers that are implicit in this one office; if and insofar as the Church confers, even to a limited extent, a considerable share in this one office (in the light of the importance of this participation and perhaps also in the light of its ultimate lifelong irrevocability), such a participation is or can be regarded as sacramental. Without this understanding, I do not think it is really possible to cope with the actual history of office, of ordination, in the Church. It seems to me that, in regard to the development, articulation, and division of what was originally one office, the Church has greater opportunities of variation than textbook theology ever recognized. This greater breadth of variation extends both to the possibilities of dividing and concentrating the power of office in a variety of ways and also to the determination of the holder of this power (man or woman, individual person or collective holder) and again to the question of the sacramentality or non-sacramentality of such a conferment of office.

In the light of these assumptions, we may now return to the problem. It was said that in the Church today there are pastoral ministries which do not presuppose any consecration, but are based 'solely' on a commissioning by the Church. In order to stress the urgency of the problem, it might immediately be added that, if the present development continues, the greater part of the administration of the one ecclesiastical office will be in the hands of those who undertake it 'solely' in virtue of a commission from the Church, without 'consecration'. I think that the problem should not be stated in the first instance as if its most urgent and most important aspect was the possibility in theological reflection and speculation of preserving enough significance and importance in the consecration of those who are today or will be tomorrow priests or deacons with a consecration whose sacramentality is (rightly) certain from the very outset. What we should and can say in the first place is that those Christians who undertake essential functions of the one office in the Church in virtue of a commission from the Church do not act 'solely' in virtue of this commission. They are in fact members of the Church, they are baptized and through this baptism their ultimate and never-ceasing consecratedness by grace (of which we spoke at the beginning) is symbolically and perennially present in the public, sociological reality of the Church; they regard their office as a participation in the one office of the Church in virtue of this ultimate grace-given consecratedness of their existence and its sacramental actuality in the Church; they, too, concretize and objectify this ultimate and most fundamental consecratedness of theirs in the office which they exercise. If and insofar as this office of theirs, based on a consecration, nevertheless differs (which is certainly not *a priori* to be denied) from the office of the priest or deacon, the real and fundamental difference between these offices lies not in the fact that a special 'consecration' as distinct from a mere commission belongs to the office of the priest or deacon but in the fact that these offices are different and have a different importance in the manner and degree of their participation in the one office of the Church. For the conferment of the office of presbyterate or diaconate does not imply a sacramental consecration as an addition to the transmission of the powers involved; it is sacramental because and insofar as it confers these powers and promises the grace necessary for their exercise.

Only in this way, I think, can we reach the real and still unsolved problem, which is twofold and which I can only describe as one that remains open. Whatever the rite by which office is conferred, ought not the Church in future to assign a pastoral ministry of some importance (as I certainly think it could do) in a sacramental rite? Ought it not to do so when this particular pastoral ministry, in practice and seen as a whole, is of the same importance as the pastoral ministry of the priest or deacon? Otherwise, is there not a danger that the ministerial priest properly so-called will be degraded to the rank of a mere cultic functionary when it looks as if all the functions he formerly possessed (that is, leadership of the community and official proclamation of the Gospel) had really nothing essentially to do with his office, since these can also be conferred by a mere non-sacramental commission? If we recall the fact that in the Church in the course of its history there were certainly conferments of office in themselves sacramental but not understood as such in theological reflection (as, for example, episcopal ordination in medieval theology), it is possible to raise even the (second) question: Is it not possible in practice in the Church of today or tomorrow that there will be conferments of important and enduring official powers which are so important that they cannot be conveyed otherwise than by a sacramental authorization, regardless of the manner in which this authorization takes place and even if its sacramentality is not explicitly taken into account?

There is no point in upholding the theoretical principle that the ordained priest is and must remain the proper leader of the congregation if the increasing shortage of priests means that without laymen as leaders the congregations will cease to exist. If this schizophrenia is allowed to proliferate, the Church will be involved in a tacit Protestantization which it has hitherto so abhorred, merely because of the desire (without convincing reasons) to continue to link the priesthood with an academic training and celibacy. Why, in fact? From the time of Pius X onward the requirements for receiving Holy Communion have been reduced to a minimum, while requirements for presiding at the eucharistic celebration have been extended to what might be called a European maximum, which seems unreal at least to the majority of people in the present-day world. If leadership of the community is an intrinsic and essential element of the priesthood, in which this function and that of the presidency of the eucharistic celebration are mutually dependent, then the very people who in fact in the future will be leaders of a priestless community should themselves be ordained priests and thus sacramentally recognized for what they are and what they accomplish as actual leaders.

It cannot be denied that the right of the community to have a sacramentally ordained leader takes precedence over the efforts of the Church (which certainly deserve respect) to have community leaders who accept the obligation of celibacy. No one can claim with certainty that for all times and for all cultural groups the association of priesthood in the unity of its governing and cultic functions on the one hand with academic training and celibacy on the other will be and will remain feasible to a sufficiently large extent. If this were not so, the Church ought incidentally to have pressed long ago for celibacy also in the Eastern churches and to have said that here, too, a sufficiently large number of celibate clergy would be possible. But if this dual trend of which we spoke causes us to have reservations, then certainly we must boldly face the question as to whether differently defined and delimited official powers may be conferred by a special 'consecration' in the Church in the new forms of the one sacramental ordination, if the above-mentioned laicization of the Church is to be avoided. Of course, it is clear *also* from our earlier reflections that this again is not simply a question of life and death, since there can be no office of importance in the Church which is not based on the holder's ultimate consecratedness and the visibility of the latter through baptism.

Here, I think, are open questions in theology which are not purely academic but have a considerable importance for the self-understanding and the spirituality of the holders of these pastoral ministries. Within the one Church in which all are sanctified at the centre of their existence so that this holiness is the ultimate sustaining ground also of all offices in the Church, there is certainly a real if secondary distinction between lay people and a clergy with a special consecratedness in the dimension of the sacramental sign and of a definite commission for an office which does not belong to everyone in the Church. But where the real dividing line lies between clergy and laity, where it *ought* to lie in the light of a theologically clarified understanding of office, these are questions to which the answer is still far from clear in every respect.

6

PASTORAL MINISTRIES AND COMMUNITY LEADERSHIP

After working out his ideas on the theme, the author felt that a preliminary observation would be appropriate. These reflections deal only with pastoral assistants who act as permanent and normal pastors in parishes without priests. Other pastoral assistants who are working interparochially and with reference to a particular field of pastoral care do not come within the scope of the present essay. There are pastoral assistants as understood here, and in the future there will inevitably be such in greater numbers (even though today their number varies greatly in different dioceses, and here and there—as a result of the problems with which this essay will deal—can be observed to be declining). This is so and will be so, even though a more general idea of the pastoral assistant can be developed, but to which what is said here does not apply directly and unambiguously.

Of course, it is possible to go to some trouble to avoid the use of pastoral assistants as understood here, to organize the structures of pastoral care in such a way that these pastoral assistants will become to a large extent unnecessary or cease to be so clearly visible. But (and this is what is assumed here) if in the future we are not to leave whole regions without local congregations bordering on other fully constructed communities, then there will be pastoral assistants in the sense understood here or it will be really be possible to find priests in sufficient numbers of the kind required for such communities. But both, as we hope to show, amount to the same thing.

PRIESTHOOD AND DIACONATE

A problem of considerable importance in pastoral theology and pastoral care in Central Europe today is that of the essential definition of the diaconate and of the function of what are known as pastoral or parish assistants and the relationship of these two 'offices' in the Church to the nature and function of the ministerial priesthood.[1]

In the Western Church for many centuries up to the present time, all that was known in practice and concretely of an articulation and gradation of office as one and whole in the Church, involved in the very nature of the Church as a grace-given and yet sociologically organized factor, was the episcopal office and the priestly office. The diaconate as known in the early Church had practically disappeared and remained only as a liturgically defined transitional stage on the way to the priesthood. Vatican II revived in principle the diaconate in the Latin Church as an independent office of a hierarchical and sacramental character. This raises afresh the question of the definition of the exact nature of the diaconate and of the relationship of the diaconate to the priesthood. This question is all the more difficult because the question of the nature of the ministerial priesthood again came to the fore at the same time and for a variety of reasons, with the result that the question of the relationship between diaconate and priesthood had to be worked out from the outset with two factors, neither of which as such was very clearly or comprehensively defined.

As far as the priesthood is concerned, the most important groups of problems are well-known. Should the office and task of priesthood be made intelligible in the light of the fact that it is conferred by a sacramental ordination, or is it the other way round? If the latter is the case, how is the nature of this office to be defined? Is its nature to be defined solely in the light of the powers which, according to traditionally Catholic teaching, are reserved exclusively to the sacramentally ordained priest: that is, in the light of the eucharist and

[1] It is impossible in a brief essay to give a full account of the relevant literature. Here we can refer only to the declaration of the German Bishops' Conference of 2 March 1977, 'Zur Ordnung der pastoralen Dienste', and the commentaries provided by Bishop K. Hemmerle and Professor K. Forster; the articles by W. Kasper ('Die schädlichen Nebenwirkungen des Priestermangels', *Stimmen der Zeit* 195 [1977]: 129–35) and Bishop P. J. Cordes ('Pastoralassistenten und Diakone', *Stimmen der Zeit* 195 [1977]: 389–401).

the sacrament of penance (together with the anointing of the sick)? Or, if such a definition seems too narrow and to contradict what seems in practice to be the task of the priest and what is suggested by the history of the priesthood, is it possible to produce a more comprehensive definition implicitly accepting these sacramental powers as part of his function but also covering comprehensively more meaningfully and concretely the priest's office as it exists in practice?

This, more or less, is the trend of all reflections on the subject today. By analogy with the bishop, the priest is seen as leader of a Church, as leader of a community which really is the Church in that locality. He must, then, have all the powers which necessarily belong to such a leader of a Church in a particular locality in the light of the theological nature of the Church as such. He is the leader of a local Church insofar as the latter is truly (in the theological sense) the Church at that point. Speaking in the name of the Church as a whole, he is the official proclaimer of the Christian message and at one and the same time the president at the eucharistic celebration; he has the function of guiding and maintaining in unity all other functions and their holders, constituting and sustaining a Christian community as Church, functions which, of course, cannot really belong exclusively to any single individual. It can confidently be said (even if this seems to involve us in theological and practical difficulties) that the task (and consequently the nature) of the priest is *to be a pastor*. Here at least is the basis for any understanding of the nature of priesthood. (This is also clear when the priesthood is seen in the light of the episcopal office, as in fact it must be seen according to the theology of the episcopate expounded at Vatican II.)

This is not to deny the fact that there can be (and, in certain circumstances, ought to be) priests who are concretely not pastors, either in the simple everyday sense of the term or as defined in canon law. That there can also be other priests is obvious from the very nature of a sociological function which, although ultimately one, can be variously differentiated; a particular individual power within the function as a whole can be given prominence in a single holder, the whole power can belong in principle to one person without being realized for that reason in every respect; someone can be the assistant of another person, even while possessing as such the same power, etc. In the light of such considerations the number of priests in the Church who are not pastors properly speaking also becomes understandable (and by and large legitimate). But all this in no way alters the fact that the nature and task of the priest is most simply and clearly understood in the light of the position of community leader, of pastor.

If the essence of the diaconate is to be defined, this definition must of course be framed in such a way that the nature of the diaconate is clearly distinguished from that of the priest. This is not so easy. If, that is, it is desired to define the diaconate as possessing (although under the overall control of the priest), apart from the two above-mentioned powers (eucharist and sacrament of penance), everything that essentially belongs to the priesthood, this must lead to embarrassing consequences. The deacon would then seem like a kind of minor priest and the question arises why he is denied power over the eucharist which, in a more profound and comprehensive view of the priesthood, is part of the function of leadership in regard to the community: a task of leadership also undertaken by the deacon, at least in practice in the present-day situation (especially in parishes without priests).

It seems appropriate, then, to see the task of the diaconate not as a curtailed, partial function of the priest and exercised under the priest, but as a distinct and separate function existing as such independently alongside that of the priest; this however does not imply any doubt about the fact that the deacon, with his independent task *alongside* the priest, is also in a congregation *under* the leadership of the priest who guides and unites it. This is no more than a formal outline of a definition of the diaconate; how its material content can be ascertained is something that will not be discussed further here. In this connection there are various theories, but not yet any real agreement.

In any case, it must remain clear that the deacon is not merely an auxiliary worker for the priest in the parish, but has a function which is *a priori* distinct from that of the priest, even though it must not be denied that in practice and concretely the deacon can and should undertake *in a subsidiary fashion* tasks in a parish that come within the scope of the priest's overall task. In the midst of all these difficult and troublesome definitions, which always seem somewhat arbitrary, it should not be forgotten that all these offices are ultimately extensions and concretizations in varying degrees of office as one and whole in the Church and that these extensions are largely a matter for the Church itself to decide and do not by any means need to be undertaken in the same way at all times and in all historical and pastoral situations.

PASTORAL ASSISTANTS

This complex array of questions becomes all the more formidable as a result of the emergence in Central Europe today of the office of what is called the parish or pastoral assistant, in addition to the two hierarchical offices and difficult to harmonize with these, either systematically or in practice. This new function is not a project formed in the light of a systematic and fundamental reflection and afterward put into practice. The opposite is the case. It was practice, without much theological reflection, that led to these pastoral assistants. And only when they had appeared on the scene to perform a task which was far from being theologically clarified did it become apparent that the questions must be asked about the theological significance of their function and its relationship to the two traditional offices in the Church.

There are too few priests willing to accept the obligation of celibacy; there are parishes without priests, where a regular eucharistic celebration and administration of the sacraments is no longer assured. An attempt is made to provide for pastoral care, first by concentrating the activity of the few remaining priests increasingly on functions which are clearly and exclusively reserved to them; then by assigning to persons who are not priests other functions which certainly belong to the nature of the priesthood (such as the official proclamation of the word in a particular community) but which traditional sentiment does not regard as so clearly possible only in virtue of sacramental ordination. For these tasks there are not enough deacons, but there are lay persons who have had a complete theological training and in that sense are on the same level as the priest. These are prepared to undertake in regard to an ecclesial community all functions assigned and transmitted to them by the diocesan authorities; in view of the pastoral needs, the diocesan Church officially assigns to these theologically trained lay people as many as possible of the tasks and powers as, on the one hand, a priestless community needs and as, on the other hand, are not certainly tied to sacramental ordination. That is why we have pastoral assistants. They are there in fact. But theologically they are a problem.

It is a problem that is keenly felt today. The declaration of the German bishops 'On the Organization of Pastoral Ministries' attempts to solve it. If we look more closely at the way in which pastoral assistants emerged, without previous theological reflection, it easy to understand where the problem lies and also how the German bishops reached their conclusions. Pastoral assistants are not to be confused with priests. If we attempt (as we ought to do) to understand priesthood not *solely* in the light of the two sacramental powers (since otherwise the priest could claim exclusively for himself merely the singularly unattractive and humanly frustrating function of the producer of an *opus operatum*), if, then, we rightly understand the priest in principle as the proper and unique community leader sacramentally prepared for this, then we must deny to the pastoral assistant (as the bishops do) the function of a community leader properly so-called. But if his existence is assumed as a fact and as unavoidable today, the attempt must be made painfully and discriminatingly to describe his function in a way that corresponds up to a point to the reality and yet distinguishes him from a community leader properly so-called, who is supposed to be the priest alone.

The same is true of the difference between pastoral assistants and deacons. We start out from the assumption that the diaconate is conferred sacramentally and incorporates the person into the official hierarchy; we observe that pastoral assistants do not receive their office through a sacramental ordination. We conclude that these two offices must be essentially different. We seek to define the diaconate on the one hand and the office of pastoral assistant on the other in such a way that the difference becomes clear, since the two functions must be distinguished in themselves and not merely in the way the office is conferred. A distinction of this kind may be possible in principle, particularly since (as we said earlier) the extension and gradation of what is ultimately and originally the one office of the one Church can be understood in a variety of ways and may vary also with the variations of times and of pastoral requirements. But in practice this distinction between the pastoral assistant and the deacon is also something that can be established only painfully and discriminatingly and the way to do this is by no means obvious.

We shall not however go further here into the difference between pastoral assistants and deacons, since the deacon's own particular function, which exists independently of any need of help for priestless communities, has clearly *a priori* nothing to do with the function of the pastoral assistant. Any attempt to ordain pastoral assistants as deacons in order to link them more clearly with the hierarchy would only obscure the problem: they would then be deacons, whose function as such is different from that of priests or pastoral assistants, and nevertheless exercise the function of both community leader and pastoral assistant. The question would remain as to how their function is distinguished from that of the priestly community leader.

Where does the difficulty lie in distinguishing between the pastoral assistant and the priest? If we consider the matter concretely, realistically, and sincerely, despite all sublime and well-meant distinctions the difficulty lies in the fact that the pastoral assistant in a priestless community has and exercises the function of the priest, with the exception of the two sacramental powers. From the standpoint of the community, such a pastoral assistant is the person linking them with the Church as a whole, just as the pastor is in a priestly community. In practice, concretely, and as distinct from subordinate parish assistants, both men and women, priests are distinguished from pastoral assistants in a priestless community only by the presence in the former and the absence in the latter of the two sacramental powers mentioned. Any assertion to the contrary is pure ideology or means that the pastoral assistant in a community without priests simply does not exercise the function that he ought to exercise in this pastoral situation and that in practice he is merely a subordinate parish assistant. This sort of thing is certainly possible, but it does nothing to alleviate the pastoral need that has led to the institution of pastoral assistants.

But if in practice, despite all sublime theological distinctions, the pastoral assistant in a priestless community exercises all the functions of a priestly community leader (apart from the two sacramental powers), we are faced with a dilemma. *Either* the functions actually undertaken by the pastoral assistant are regarded as by no means specifically priestly. Then what is truly priestly about the ministerial priest is reduced to the two sacramental powers reserved to him alone; the priest becomes a purely cultic functionary. It has been said often enough that this interpretation of priesthood is no longer acceptable today and we need not discuss it at length here. This narrowly ritualistic interpretation of the specifically priestly task is not only humanly intolerable, but also theologically wrong, since it is contrary to a modern ecclesiology and to the history of the priesthood. *Or* it is admitted that the functions actually undertaken by the pastoral assistant are at bottom specifically priestly or can be distinguished from priestly functions only by subtle, academic distinctions. But then difficult theological questions arise. If the commission to exercise permanently the functions of a pastoral assistant as a real community leader assigns an office that, judged soberly and sincerely, is more important and more comprehensive than the diaconate (and the lesser offices of the minor orders, which were regarded as sacramental in the Middle Ages), why should not or in principle (at least if the Church wants it) *could* not the conferment of an office of a permanent character be regarded as sacramental?

COMMISSION AND SACRAMENT

It is not a conclusive argument against the sacramentality of this commissioning to say that it does not take the form of an imposition of hands, since it is within the power and the discretion of the Church to decide the concrete form of the rite of conferring office. It also seems far from being theologically settled that a certain rite important for the Church can be sacramental only if its sacramentality is explicitly and reflectively perceived. (If this was necessary what would be the position of marriages of Christians outside the Catholic Church? Could they be sacramental? Were episcopal ordinations not sacramental in the Middle Ages, when their sacramentality was disputed?) If the Church (which is the basic sacrament) confers a permanent office of considerable importance for its own reality, can it simultaneously not want such an office to participate in the promise given by God to the Church? Can the Church prevent such a conferment of office from being an *opus operatum*, if this term is rightly understood and seen in the light of its derivation from the nature of the Church?

A further question: If in practice the leadership of the community is entrusted to pastoral assistants and this commissioning can be distinguished from a priest's community leadership only by subtle theories, if in a modern theology of priesthood the two sacramental powers reserved to ordained priests are basically articulations and extrapolations of the priest's fundamental task as leader of a local Church and official representative of the episcopal major Church and of the Church as a whole, by what right are these two powers denied to the pastoral assistant as community leader in a priestless community?

If someone as pastoral assistant is in fact appointed community leader, he is granted in this capacity the basic nature of the priest and at the same time refused the sacramental powers that flow from this basic nature. Is this theologically consistent? Ought we not almost to say that such a pastoral assistant possesses these sacramental powers in virtue of his basic function, but that they are 'suspended' in the same way as the newly ordained priest's power of absolution (which he possesses as such) is 'suspended' until he is granted the 'jurisdiction' which enables him to exercise it? It is possible, of course, to say that these sacramental powers are conferred only by imposition of hands in priestly ordination, which is the very thing that is lacking in the pastoral assistant. But this kind of argument does not dispose of the real theological problem. For it is not only a question of whether the appointment of a pastoral assistant as community leader without these sacramental powers (or perhaps only as 'suspended') is legal and must be respected. It can rightly be asked whether this procedure ideally corresponds to the properly theological nature of the powers and conferring of powers that are involved here. This can certainly be doubted or disputed.

Again, it is possible with the aid of acute perception to describe and with the aid of legal regulations to delimit the nature and task of the pastoral assistant in such a way that the latter is not distinguished from the priest merely because of the absence of the two sacramental powers. There can, of course, be people who have tasks in the Church, especially outside the strictly parochial sphere, whose function is unambiguously and clearly distinguished from that of the priest and who can, if it is so desired, be called pastoral assistants. In the present context however we have in mind only those with tasks in the Church who in practice in a priestless community take over the task (apart from the two sacramental powers) otherwise fulfilled by the pastor. In this case, too, the attempt can be made to distinguish between priests and pastoral assistants with the aid of subtle theological arguments. It is difficult to make an effective response to someone who takes the trouble to do this and is satisfied with the abstract conclusion. But it could at least be asked why these pastoral assistants did not exist in the past. If their office as different from the priestly office and as clearly distinguishable from the latter is supposed to flow from the very nature of the Church's pastoral care, it might be expected to have existed always or at any rate for a long time.

RESPONSIBILITY AND OFFICE

The question is how to resist seriously a tendency for the 'profile of the pastoral assistant to merge into the profile of the priest',[2] if the former is responsible for religious instruction, catechesis, training, counseling, and care for particular groups. If he can be assigned a 'commission to participate in certain tasks of the Church's ministry' and if such a commission leads in a priestless community, whether it is desired or not, to a commission to undertake all the pastoral care of the community, even if the expression 'personally responsible' is avoided, what really remains of the 'irreplaceability of the priest as leader of the community'? If religious instruction, catechesis, training, counseling, and care for particular groups are tasks which are undertaken *together* by *one* pastoral assistant in a community, is this a 'responsibility for certain specific fields' which belong to the lay person as such and have no intrinsic orientation to priestly orders? Why should such a complex and comprehensive task as a whole still not be an 'office in the theological sense of the term'? Is it possible so to organize concretely and in practice the pastoral ministry of a pastoral assistant in a priestless community that no sort of 'office without ordination' emerges alongside ecclesiastical office in the ordinary sense of the term or must we admit that what is exercised here is to a large extent *the* pastoral ministry normally con-

[2] This and the following quotations refer to the declaration of the German bishops on the organization of pastoral ministries mentioned in note 1.

ferred by sacramental ordination? If in a priestless community a pastoral assistant is the person to whom that community as a whole actually relates, it is pure theory to talk about the profile of a pastoral assistant not being alienated by an accumulation of the priest's functions.

The only way to get out of the undergrowth of these theological and practical difficulties is to ask again more precisely what was the situation and what were the circumstances out of which the institution of pastoral assistants emerged and whether these circumstances must be assumed to be unalterable. The institution of pastoral assistants emerged without previous deeper reflection simply because it was no longer possible to provide priests for all local communities. On the other hand, there are persons who have had a complete theological training and are prepared to undertake permanently even in a pastoral sense the leadership of a parish, but for their own part reject priestly celibacy. But it is taken for granted that the law of priestly celibacy remains unalterable. On this assumption (but only on this assumption) the institution of pastoral assistants emerges. Community leaders are sought, they are given everything that seems possible by way of powers, they are denied only the functions which are known from tradition to be reserved to the priest, without asking more closely in theological terms whether the powers and functions actually assigned to pastoral assistants are not (according to more exact and objective criteria) quite as important as those which are denied to them. People cannot and will not see this because otherwise pastoral assistants from the nature of the case would have to be regarded as priests; and in the Latin Church only a celibate can be seen as a priest.

It is therefore quite safe to say that the actual reason or the decisive precondition for the emergence of the institution of pastoral assistants is the law of celibacy. (We need only ask whether pastoral assistants would be possible in the Eastern Uniate churches with their married clergy or whether it would not be taken for granted there for a married 'pastoral assistant' to be ordained as a priest, since that would merely be a sacramental corroboration of the task which he performs or is expected to perform anyway.) When we say that the actual and necessary precondition of the emergence of this institution is celibacy, we are of course not denying that there are other reasons why someone who would be glad to undertake the office of a pastoral assistant nevertheless does not want to be ordained. But the other reasons involved in the sociological image of the modern secular priest, which create anticlerical prejudice against the priesthood, are so closely linked with celibacy that it is still absolutely correct to maintain that the law of celibacy is the precondition for the institution of pastoral assistants.

Let us assume that there were no law of celibacy for the secular priest. On this assumption there would not be any pastoral assistants in the modern sense, at least none who had undertaken this function as their permanent task in life and been appointed to a specific individual community. They would in fact be the real community leaders. In the light of their task they would regard the power of presiding at the eucharist and pronouncing the words of reconciliation as the natural consequences of their basic office. In a rite appropriate to the conferring of these powers they would receive from the Church the whole power of the community leader which develops out of the Church's very nature. They would then be sacramentally ordained priests, even though the ecclesial-sociological image of such community leaders (as married and perhaps exercising their office together with an ordinary secular calling) would differ considerably from the image of the priest today or even from that of a priest of the future exercising supra-local functions in the Church. In brief, without the law of celibacy, pastoral assistants in fact and in practice would become priests.

We can approach the question also from the opposite standpoint. We can start out from the axiom that a permanent task of fundamental importance in the Church should also be assigned by the rite envisaged for appointing someone to this taks. (For example, if someone exercises as his permanent task the functions of a deacon, he is expected to receive these functions by the sacramental rite known as ordination to the diaconate, even though the individual functions, regarded in the abstract, can be undertaken by a 'lay person'.) This axiom ought to be obvious, just as the obligation of baptism is obvious for someone who has already been justified by his subjective acts. The pastoral assistant ought therefore to be commissioned in a way appropriate to his actual function. If this function corresponds to the tasks of a deacon, he should be sacramentally ordained deacon. If the function of a pastoral assistant is in fact that of a community leader, he should receive priestly orders, since a partition between the function of the community leader and the function of presiding at the eucharist is contrary to their very nature.

CELIBACY

The whole question then centres on the problem of celibacy. In principle it is not denied by anyone but repeatedly stressed that the Church must give up the requirement of celibacy for the pastoral clergy if it becomes clear that this requirement means a considerable loss of badly needed pastoral resources. Provision for sufficiently large numbers of pastoral clergy is an obligation imposed on the Church as a matter of divine law, an obligation that takes precedence in a case of conflict over the Church's legitimate desire for a celibate pastoral clergy. Ten years ago, in an article defending celibacy, I wrote: 'If the Church cannot in fact find everywhere or in certain areas a sufficient number of clergy unless it gives up celibacy, then it *must* give this up, for the duty of providing a sufficient number of pastoral clergy is prior to the possibility and the desire (legitimate in itself) to have a celibate clergy'.[3] The numbers are increasing of those who maintain that this case of conflict exists now in Europe. (The co-existence of the Uniate Eastern churches with a married clergy and the Latin Church with its celibate clergy proves that the very nature of the Church does not require the question of celibacy always and necessarily to be settled uniformly in the Church as a whole.)

This is a problem that cannot be made dependent on the question of how many would want to be ordained priests if the Church abandoned celibacy, or whether giving up celibacy would alleviate the present shortage of priests. A Christian parish which by its situation, its structure, the number of members has the right to exist and live as a local Church, has also the right to a priest as leader of the community and of the eucharistic celebration. This is not a right that exists only when it can be fulfilled, not merely in this particular community, but also in all the others. And it seems to be prior to the right of the Church to a celibate clergy. In this essay, however, we

[3] *Geist und Leben* 40 (1967): 128.

shall not pursue further the question of priestly celibacy and the possible necessity of its abandonment.

What is important in our reflections is only the fact that celibacy is the actual reason for the creation of the institution of pastoral assistants, the actual reason why this institution leads to theological difficulties and pressures which really ought not to exist. If the circumstances which led to the institution of pastoral assistants are allowed simply to persist (that is, especially celibacy and the 'clerical' image of the pastoral priest resulting from it), there will inevitably emerge two classes of clergy: sacramentally ordained priests mainly undertaking supra-local functions in a diocese, on the one hand, and, on the other hand, pastoral assistants who are in fact the leaders in very many local communities and who do not really understand in theological terms why they are denied certain sacramental functions which are properly involved by the very nature of their basic function as community leaders, or why the attempt is made to explain with the aid of theological subtleties that a community leader who is a priest and a community leader who is a pastoral assistant are exercising two different functions.

Certainly we can agree with the claim in the bishops' declaration that 'there could be no justification for starting out to organize the pastoral ministry with a change in the conditions for admission to the priesthood by the Church as a whole.' It is true that we cannot 'start out' from such a change. But we might be faced with a pastoral situation in the Church calling urgently for this change. Neither is it necessary for these changes to occur simultaneously everywhere in the 'whole Church', particularly since the 'whole Church', if it is not to be identified with the Western Church, does not by any means have a celibate clergy everywhere. When the bishops' declaration says that such a change offers no assurance 'that sufficient priests will be at the Church's disposal in the long run', then, as we said, the counter-question can be raised as to whether a priestless community has the right to a (celibate or married) priest only if this right, which exists in principle, can be fulfilled simultaneously in all communities.

7

THEOLOGY AND SPIRITUALITY OF PASTORAL WORK IN THE PARISH

The theme of 'theology and spirituality of pastoral work in the parish' was chosen for me. The concrete and practical aspects of the theme must be left largely to others to explain. These *general* reflections are put forward by a priest who is not actively engaged in pastoral work in a parish, but he is sure that the true nature of the Church is more clearly and decisively involved in parochial pastoral work and, of course, in similar self-realizations than it is in theological reflection on the Church's faith as it is to be proclaimed: a reflection that is the business of the theologian, who has merely a secondary, albeit indispensable, function by comparison with this proclamation and the proclaimers. If we recall that, despite the importance of theory, practice is not only the execution of theory, but that the final, decisive, and complete theory emerges only from a practice on which reflection can never be complete, it becomes quite clear that the theorist can approach the practitioner only very modestly and unobtrusively, that he can offer the latter only very humbly whatever can be made of his theory and ask whether any conclusions can be drawn from it to put into practice.

The title, in fact, requires us to consider two themes: theology of parochial pastoral work and spirituality of parochial pastoral work. The first theme, theology of parochial pastoral work, is again, as such, very ambiguous. On the one hand, theology of parochial pastoral work can mean that we are asking about the theological nature of parochial pastoral work, of pastoral ministry precisely in the parish, and about the description in terms of Christian theology of the pastor's activity, since the latter is simply not a secular, social functionary and manager. But on the other hand, theology of parochial pastoral work can also involve the question of whether and how the pastor must be and remain a theologian if he is really to be able to fulfill his task, and why and how a study of theology continually renewed and carried further, a permanent contact with theological scholarship, must retain a place in the life of a pastor. As we said, theology of parochial pastoral work will be the theme of these necessarily brief preliminary considerations. What is to be said under the heading of spirituality of parochial pastoral work will, of course, become clear at a later stage.

THEOLOGY OF PASTORAL WORK IN THE PARISH

There really is something like a theology of parochial pastoral work in the first sense mentioned of the term. The parish and with it, of course, its leader, the pastor, are not merely secular, sociological concepts, but have a religious, dogmatic, spiritual content, which can exist and be understood only in the faith of Christianity.

The Parish as a Reality of Faith

If and insofar as the Church as one and whole is itself a reality of faith and not merely a secular sociological organization (even though the latter would serve a supernatural purpose, comprehensible only in faith) and if, however, this Church as itself a reality of faith has inevitably a spatial character, then it must also be said that a territorial parish within this Church likewise participates in the peculiarity of the one Church as a reality of faith. In the Catholic understanding of faith the Church as a whole is indeed one Church, but an episcopically (that is, spatially, territorially) constituted Church. This territorial structure of the Church is obviously in the first place an empirical and secular reality, but this very reality is nevertheless taken up into the mystery of the Church as the unity of human beings in the Holy Spirit and in the profession of faith in Jesus Christ as Son of God, crucified and risen, the historically palpable, irreversible self-promise of God as salvation of the world. This mystery of the Church as sacrament of the world's salvation becomes effective territorially, it becomes effective in space and time. The nature of the Church does not consist merely in the ubiquity of the Spirit of God, who is poured out equally on all flesh as innermost dynamism of humanity and its history. The nature of the Church consists even more in the fact that this undeniable although hidden ubiquity of the Spirit is manifested historically, sacramentally, sociologically, and incarnationally and that this incarnational and sacramental manifestation makes the ubiquity of the Spirit of God (unconfused and undivided) irreversibly and historically palpable in the world.

The Territorial Character of the Church

Thus the Church as sacrament of the world's salvation (as seen from above) has an unquestionably territorial character and this territorial character of the Church as sociological factor (as seen from below) shares in its quality as mystery (as, for instance, the water of baptism is earthly water and yet in baptism becomes the actual and effective manifestation of man's sanctification by grace). The parish, too, as a territorial factor participates in this quality which is part of the territorial organization of the Church. This becomes even clearer when we remember that the most effective and radical sacramental self-realization of the Church as the redeeming unity of human beings together in God occurs in the eucharist. Here the Church is present in its completeness and here it is unquestionably in place, in the local community, which is not absolutely necessarily but preferably and normally the parish community. It is understandable, therefore, that the New Testament, especially Paul, sees the Church first of all as the local Church, as (we may say without prejudice) the parish Church, at a time when there was still no difference between an episcopal and a parochial community Church. There can indeed be communities for the eucharistic celebration which are not parishes in the modern legal sense: personal parishes which do not have a directly perceptible territorial character, eucharistic communities which are not directly supported and authorized by the parish, monastic communities, etc. But when the eucharist is celebrated, people must always meet together in some place; if the eucharist is to be celebrated legitimately in this way at a chosen place, there must always be a relatedness to a local bishop or at least the explicit or tacit reference to the pope, who is not everywhere but resides in Rome. Hence it is clear that the Church's territorial character, particularly in its supreme realization, can nowhere be eliminated. And it is precisely this territorial character which is most simply and normally present in the parish community, *the* community, which is based on a primordial human reality that can never be wholly eliminated, on a group of people living together in a particular area. Precisely because this primordial human phenomenon, despite all opportunities for people to form a community or society for other reasons, can never be excluded from human existence and because it enters into the eucharistic celebration (as the matter of the sacramental sign enters into the sacrament in its unity with sacramental grace), the parish community participates in the territorial structure of the Church, which belongs to the latter's substance, since it is part of the Church's sociological, historical, and incarnational nature.

The Parish—A Tangible Spiritual Reality

A parish is not merely a secular concern belonging to a religious society as a police district belongs to the state, but a spiritual reality in which a person learns or can and should learn that not only his temporal existence but also his cosmic-spatial existence is sanctified and encompassed by the grace of the holy God of which it is the incarnation. Of course, this theological thesis of the spiritual potentiality of human beings living together is not merely an indicative, but also an imperative. As the person who baptizes is required to provide water, the Church must provide a local group of neighbours in order to be able to celebrate the eucharist and thus fully realize itself historically and sociologically as sacrament of the world's salvation. This sort of local gathering of neighbours, of course, is not to be understood merely as a physical and geographical reality, but as a truly human factor of a genuinely neighbourly fellowship in righteousness and love, such that this human reality can enter into the eucharistic celebration. And it is to this human reality that the imperative resulting from our theological thesis on the spiritual quality of the territorial parish refers. This imperative, of course, must be fulfilled in the first place through all the other functions which belong directly to the parish as such, even though this does not mean that these other tasks of a parish as such are merely means to the end of forming this territorial community which is to be the human substratum of the eucharistic community. But all the rest of the functions of the parish as such (religious education, religious courses for adults, welfare work, etc.) also contribute to the formation of such local neighbourliness in the full human sense of the term, even to the formation of a spiritual community as such, and may and must therefore be appreciated and promoted also from this standpoint.

Advancement of Human Fellowship in the Secular Sphere

This imperative for the formation of local neighbourliness can and should relate, as far as it is possible and necessary, to more than is directly envisaged or implied by the specific tasks and functions of the parish. As far as it is possible and necessary, the work of the parish and the pastor may and should relate to the secular reality of local neighbourliness as such. Let us assume that parish and pastor, when necessary, make the greatest possible effort to see that a spatial agglomeration of human beings becomes even in the secular sphere a genuinely human fellowship, a truly human fraternity living together in mutual knowledge of one another, in sticking together, in trust, and providing mutual help. By this very fact they are contributing to the conditions in which a real spiritual community in common praise of God, in a common acknowledgment of expectation of the coming Lord, in unity in the Holy Spirit, can be realized in the eucharistic celebration; in this way the eucharistic celebration is not merely a casual external assemblage of individuals looking for the satisfaction of their personal needs as they might look for this in a department store. If a country-parish priest, in a place where it is possible and humanly appropriate, meets the farmers and farmhands after mass for a meal in the local inn, this, too, can be a consequence of this spiritual imperative established by the above-mentioned theological thesis. If, as hitherto, we tried to envisage the theological quality of the Christian local community, of the territorial parish, in the light of the eucharistic celebration, this does not mean that the theological character of the parish is solely based on the act of worship; all that was intended was to make clear as simply as possible the fact that the territorial parish has a theological quality.

Insofar as the rest of the functions of a parish have, on the one hand, an independent theological significance and are not merely means to the end of the eucharistic community, but have, on the other hand, more or less necessarily a local basis, even in the light of these other functions of the parish there emerges a peculiar theological, spiritual quality; it is not merely an unavoidable secular reality, but is assumed in its human spatiality into the mystery of the Church.

THE SIGNIFICANCE OF THEOLOGY IN PAROCHIAL PASTORAL WORK

As indicated at the beginning, the term 'theology of parochial pastoral work' has a second and different meaning. In the latter sense the term means purely and simply that theology has and must retain its place and its importance in parochial pastoral work. Parochial pastoral work directly aids the realization by word and sacrament of Christian existence in the community as such and provides also for the Christian life of the individual, who as an individual Christian can never exist in a Christian way entirely outside the Church or, therefore, outside a community, and yet in his individual existence is not simply absorbed collectivistically either in secular or in ecclesial social life.

Priority of Pastoral Activity to Theological Reflection

This task of making the Christian reality effective in word and sacrament, in community and individual existence, is therefore something different from and prior to theology, which, even if it grows out of and is directed to Christian practice, is in fact theoretical and scholarly reflection on this more fundamental Christian reality. To that extent, the pastor is not really a professional theologian and need not be one in the sense of being engaged in scholarly reflection. If we define exactly and straightforwardly the really correct relationship of theory and practice (if, for example, we keep in mind the correct relationship from the Catholic standpoint of bishop and theologian), then we cannot regard the relationship between pastor and theologian as if the pastor were more or less only the retailer distributing to individual consumers the commodities produced by a large-scale theological industry. Proclamation comes *before* professional academic theology and is not simply a way of expressing and transmitting the latter. For theology reflects on the reality presented to it in the proclamation and ritual self-realization of the Church.

Reflection as a Constitutive Element of Practice

True and important as all this is, important as are the consequences of all this also for pastoral work (which cannot be considered here in detail), it remains true nevertheless that even theology properly speaking—academic theology—has its place and its importance in pastoral work. For a certain element of reflection is contained from the beginning as a constituent part in any practice, in any fundamental self-realization of the individual, of society, and of the Church, and cannot be excluded from it without practice itself being destroyed. Practice and theory are not identical, but are not placed side by side as separate areas, purely and simply independent of each other. If only because of these ultimate peculiarities of the relationship of theory and practice, close reflection on the element of reflection known as theology, which is itself a constituent part of practice as such, can never be irrelevant to practice.

Positive Approach to Theology—for the Sake of Human Beings

The pastor must have a positive attitude to theology properly so-called, since the latter, seen more closely, is itself involved in his proclamation and since this reflex theology helps him to grasp and express more clearly and purely what he proclaims, even though the experience of his own proclamation always contains more than what academic theology as such, working reflectively and systematically and historically, can understand and objectify of it, Today, there are in addition all the necessities of an academic theology that are involved in the present state of proclamation. The pastor is not a ritualist, a magician, or a spellbinder who can simply rely on the *opus operatum* of traditional verbal formularies and sacramental rites. He is required, to the best of his ability and by the word of proclamation and sacrament, to produce in the recipient of his pastoral efforts the existential preconditions for a genuinely human, believing reception of those realities which he offers in word and sacrament to man for the latter's salvation. The recipients of his efforts are not merely simple and straightforward human beings sustained by a homogeneously Christian milieu who rely purely on his formal authority as an ordained expert on religion and accept what he says. They are educated people living in the midst of the contradictions and pluralisms of a secularized world who do not get their view of life only from their pastor; they are also people who are Christians by choice and who live in crises of faith. How is a pastor to proclaim the Gospel and the message of the Church to these people with any hope of success if he has no contact with modern theology, a theology which is attempting to consider and cope with all these critical inquiries addressed to Christianity by the world of today? How can a pastor perform adequately the task imposed on him of interpreting Scripture if he is not to some extent applying the methods of modern exegesis and noting the conclusions of modern biblical studies? Unless he has a basic knowledge of these studies, how can the pastor's homily amount to any more than a lecture on his own pious opinions which he presents as best he can in the light of a biblical text? How can a pastor, addressing educated and uneducated Christians, distinguish between the really binding substance of faith and other perhaps traditional but nevertheless time-conditioned interpretations of this faith? How can he avoid imposing on people today as a matter of faith burdens which they are not bound to bear and perhaps cannot bear, if he is not also aware to some extent of the efforts of modern theology to bring out these distinctions? If he is not constantly in touch with present-day theological work, is it possible for a pastor to go beyond the traditional catechism formulas, to retain, enlarge, and change that vocabulary and those horizons of understanding and ways of access of an up-to-date proclamation which are necessary today and are in fact being established in the first place by academic theology?

Contact with Theologians, Reading New Books, Keeping Up with Periodicals

It is obvious that the ordinary pastor with so much work to do on the one hand and with his limited intellectual and spiritual possibilities on the other can gain and maintain only a limited contact with modern academic theology. It is also unfortunate that academic theology often makes too little effort to convey its questions and its conclusions to the ordinary priest in such a way that he can utilize them in his pastoral work. But this in no way alters the fact that the pastor in his own way must be engaged in theology and must remain in contact with modern theology. He ought also always to be reading discriminatingly and after consultation selected new publications and unhesitatingly to set aside a certain time for this if he is not to continue forever performing his task with an outmoded theology which he learned many years ago or if he is not to sink back to the theological and spiritual plane of an innocuous childish faith, the faith he brought with him to his first studies in theology, only to lay aside the latter also as useless after he had been ordained. If he is to carry out his mission responsibly, the pastor must really exploit the opportunities of further education offered to him in training courses and similar arrangements. Deanery conferences and similar institutions ought not to be merely friendly gatherings of clerical colleagues or conferences of pastoral managers, but should also provide a little theological work and further education. Where it is possible the clergy should also have the courage to do some biblical theology, working together on a text in preparation for a sermon. The existence of theological reviews should not be constantly threatened because of the small number of subscribers; they should be bought and read by the pastoral clergy. In a word, theology of pastoral work in the title of these reflections means also that theology is and must remain an indispensable element of pastoral work itself.

We now come to the second part of our theme.

SPIRITUALITY OF PASTORAL WORK IN THE PARISH

In view of the range and the difficulty of this second theme, it is obvious that only a few, somewhat arbitrarily selected observations are possible here, particularly since spirituality of parochial pastoral work as such of course integrates into itself everything that pertains to Christian spirituality as a whole and consequently cannot be described here in its whole range and in all its depth.

A Preliminary Reflection

In order to get some idea of the particular themes implied in the overall theme of the spirituality of parochial pastoral work, we may first mention a more general consideration. This preliminary consideration might be summarized in the thesis that the spirituality of parochical pastoral work as such must be the spirituality of a basic community today and of the team directing it.

First of all, there are basic communities of the most varied kinds (which cannot be described here and distinguished from one another) which are justified and meaningful, which are different pastorally and in terms of the present canon law from a parish community. We cannot explain here the meaning, justification, and limits of such basic communities. Without going into that question, we are starting out from the persuasion that, even as compared with these basic communities of the most varied kinds, the parish communities will maintain their irreplaceable importance today and in the foreseeable future, that they are not merely fossils from earlier pastoral epochs, nor are they simply administrative districts of episcopal major Churches, but are, remain or must become real Christian communities on the spot (as we tried to suggest in theological terms in the first section of the first part of this chapter). Allowing for all this, however, it must be said that by their very nature and seen from both sides these basic communities and these parishes do not simply exist separately, side by side, but to some extent interpenetrate and depend on one another. In other words, if and insofar as a parish community is more and should be more than an administrative area of an episcopal major Church, if and insofar as it is or is to become a truly Christian community in all dimensions of Christian existence, with the eucharistic celebration at its heart, actually based on local but authentically human neighbourliness, then the parish, too, has in itself as its centre, as its most compact realization, what might be called a basic community.

Core Community as Basic Community of the Parish

It is not without reason that we speak today of a 'core community' also with reference to the parish community. A present-day parish must certainly offer a welcome to everyone: it cannot neglect Christians by choice (for example, people who have a merely casual and qualified attitude to Christianity and the Church) and it must not become a ghetto for a few pious Christians from a very particular and restricted social milieu, sheltered from civilisation, society, and politics, and having a sectarian and bourgeois character. Nevertheless, an authentic and living parish today cannot be sustained merely by the power of the major, episcopal Church and its administration; it must likewise be sustained from below, from the base, by the faith and by the spiritual and not merely folkloristic attachment to the Church of convinced Christians and their fellowship; consequently it must itself form and carry within itself something like a basic community. But if all this is assumed, the thesis stated above is understandable: the spirituality of a parish, of its pastoral work and pastor, is today (in a positive, but not, of course, in an exclusive sense) the spirituality of a basic community.

Parochial Pastors—All Priests and Lay People Officially Active in the Parish

All that, of course, amounts only to a very broad and incomplete framework for articulating the question of the spirituality of a parish, of parochial pastoral work and of parochial pastors, particularly since parochial pastoral work and parochial pastors are not in principle to be understood as referring merely to the function of the pastor in charge of the parish, but as related to all those who are engaged together officially and as full-time workers in this pastoral activity. Nevertheless, and even though we are making a somewhat random selection, we may now ask: What must be the special characteristics of the spirituality of parochial pastoral work and parochial pastors, if it is to be the spirituality of a basic community, of a core community and its representatives?

In order to answer this question, even though obviously only very partially, it is possible to suggest two headings which are linked with each other in a kind of dialectical unity: loneliness of faith and fraternal fellowship of faith. With all due reservations, these are the headings under which the spirituality of parochial pastoral work today is to be characterized. What does this mean?

The Loneliness of the Faith of 'Parochial Pastors'

I shall speak first of all of the loneliness of the faith of those who have to carry out this pastoral work in the parish. In itself *fides qua* was always a matter of personal responsibility, it involved the decision and freedom of the individual: a decision of faith that he could pass on to others less than anything else in his existence, that he could not leave to other authorities and could not base on grounds already present. But formerly this faith found expression in a homogeneously Christian milieu even though the outlook of the public at large was secular and indifferent; it was possible to believe what more or less everyone seemed to believe, at least in public and in ordinary conversation, so that it almost looked as if, within the dimension of faith, the individual could be relieved of what had seemed the irremoveable burden of responsibility, of the decision for faith against unbelief, of hope against all hope, of unrequited love. It is different today. Christian faith must now be continually realized afresh, in the atmosphere of a secularized world, against a background of atheism, in face of a technical rationality whose advocates declare *a priori* that all statements which cannot be justified in terms of this rationality are meaningless or (to use Wittgenstein's term) belong to the realm of 'mysticism' about which we can only be silent.

Decision of Faith More Radical Than Formerly

In such a situation the solitary responsibility of the individual in his decision of faith is necessary and required in a much more radical way than was formerly the case. Consequently, part of the present-day spirituality of the Christian in general, and in particular of those who have to represent this Christianity publicly by carrying out pastoral work, is the courage for a lonely decision contrary to public opinion, the lonely courage analogous to that of the martyrs of the first centuries of Christianity, the courage for the decision of faith that draws its strength from itself and does not need public support.

Personal Experience of God and His Spirit

This loneliness of the individual's conscience in regard to faith must have, however, an absolutely positive side in order to be able to endure. If it is to persist, it will live out of a wholly personal experience of God and his Spirit. It has been said that the Christian of the future will be a mystic or he will not be a Christian at all. This statement is very true if we mean by mysticism not singular parapsychological phenomena, but a genuine experience of God emerging from the depths of existence. According to Scripture and the Church's teaching, properly understood, the final conviction and decision of faith does not come in the last resort merely from a didactic indoctrination coming from outside, supported by public opinion in secular society or in the Church, nor from the purely rational arguments of fundamental theology, but from the experience of God, of his Spirit, his freedom, bursting out of the innermost centre of human existence where it is wholly real, even though it is an experience that cannot adequately be reflected upon or verbally objectified. Possession of the Spirit is not merely something known to exist as a result of didactic indoctrination from outside, but experienced from within. The solitary Christian in silent prayer in the final decision of conscience, not rewarded by anyone, in unlimited hope that must no longer cling to any calculable assurance, in the radical disappointment of life and the powerlessness of death willingly permitted and accepted, in the night of the senses and the Spirit (as the mystics say), etc.: this solitary Christian experiences God and his liberating grace, as long as he accepts these experiences (just indicated) and does not run away from them in an ultimately culpable fear, even if he cannot interpret and attach a theological label to the experiences of God and his grace transcending all individual realities. The Christian today must live from this loneliness of fundamental religious experience, he must clarify this experience and increasingly appropriate it in radical freedom. Only then does the theological indoctrination of Scripture and the Church's teaching acquire its ultimate credibility and existential practicability.

Independence of Public Opinion

This loneliness, with the scope it gives for freedom, with its negative side of being independent of ordinary public opinion and its positive side of admitting the experience of God in his Holy Spirit, is above all characteristic of the spirituality of those who represent Christianity in their pastoral work in the parish.

The pastor and his assistants in the parish today cannot be functionaries and managers representing a sociological factor called 'Church' and promoting its ideology in competition with others. They must be people who have had in solitude a living experience of the Spirit. They do not really need for that reason to talk about their experience (although Paul eventually did so). But the proclamation of the objective message of the Gospel and the Church must in any case be sustained and inwardly illuminated by their own solitary experience of the Spirit. To put it quite simply: those engaged in parochial pastoral work must themselves be spiritual persons. This is obvious, it is easily said, and yet it is the most difficult thing that is demanded from these people. If they can manage this most difficult thing, then everything else they have to do is easy. If the apparent lack of success in their work, their disappointments in pastoral activity, thrust them back, so to speak, into loneliness and forsakenness, this experience at its deepest level is the mystical phenomenon of that lonely and silent night in which a person silently encounters the mystery of God accepting him, sheltering him, and assuring him as a perhaps bitter but final consolation his ultimate freedom—assuming that the pastoral worker has come to learn better than to run away from the mysterious experience of God in ultimate loneliness and forsakenness. A primary characteristic of the spirituality of pastoral work today is loneliness in the sense in which we have at least tried to outline it.

Fraternal Fellowship and Its Experience of the Spirit

A second characteristic of the spirituality of pastoral work today, linked with the first in a singular dialectical unity, is fraternal fellowship in which the same all-sustaining experience of the Spirit is possible. This is a phenomenon which is perhaps only now becoming clearer, of which we older persons can speak only hesitatingly and cautiously while awaiting its future. It seems to me that this phenomenon is something that we older persons never experienced or experienced only in the traces it left behind. In the light of our background and education we older people were also spiritually individualists, even though we gladly carried out the liturgy together as our obvious, objective task and duty. We need only look back into the past of the Church and of its life. We can see then that experience of the Spirit, 'mysticism', was understood and lived as obviously a purely individual occurrence on the part of the individual person for himself alone. When did anyone think of a common experience of the Spirit, when did anyone long for it or know it as it came about evidently on the Church's first feast of Pentecost, which presumably was not the occasion of a casual local gathering of a number of individualistic mystics, but of an experience of the Spirit by a community as such? An experience of this kind, of course, cannot and is not meant to relieve the individual Christian and to spare him that loneliness of the most radical decision of faith, since human individuality and solidarity are not factors that can be set off against one another or substituted for one another.

From Spiritual Individualism to Common Experience of the Spirit

This does not imply that an experience of the Spirit in a small community as such is *a priori* impossible, even though we older members of the clergy have never or scarcely ever known anything of the sort and still less attempted to bring it about. Why should there not be something of this kind? Why should not younger Christians, including the clergy, find an easier way to such a joint experience of the Spirit? Why should not something of this kind be more easily possible and more necessary today and in the future than it was formerly? Why could not phenomena like joint counseling, genuine human communication in the form of properly human conversation and not merely of superficial technical explanations, group dynamics, etc., be accepted, exalted, and sanctified among Christians by a common experience of the Spirit of God, so that a truly fraternal fellowship in the Holy Spirit emerges? In the last resort this sort of thing need not take place in extraordinary, apparently almost parapsychological circumstances like those seen sometimes in enthusiastic groups of American Pentecostal movements. There is no need to speak in tongues, nor need there be any attempt to produce phenomena of healing by imposition of hands. But if people perhaps have little or no time for such things, that is far from saying that there simply cannot be any sort of communitarian experience of the Spirit at all. Why should there not be a really spiritual discernment of spirits undertaken jointly?

Why is the prayer to the Holy Spirit at the beginning of a meeting of a parish council or a pastoral team concretely and practically merely a pious opening ceremony, after which everything goes on as it would at a secular gathering, making use of purely rational arguments in the style of any sort of management? All this can be put forward by older people like us only very humbly and self-critically in the form of a question. But in this connection the younger clergy should at least suspect and try both cautiously and courageously to realize and test opportunities in the Church and consequently in pastoral work which are not yet by any means exhausted.

Growth of a Spiritual Team

A team engaged in pastoral work in the parish might perhaps slowly become a properly spiritual team, a fraternally spiritual fellowship, might have or slowly but courageously try to acquire a spirituality lived together in the proper sense of the term. I will not venture to offer any prescriptions as to how exactly this could happen. But it does not mean that there are not starting points or ways of access for this kind of spirituality in fellowship as such, even though they must first be sought and tested with patience, even though a critical transposition of occurrences in group dynamics into a properly spiritual event has still to be made, even though prayer together and Scripture reading together (purely as such as outward rite and as the study of exegesis by several people together) do not yet amount to a spiritual event. Here only the modest surmise may be expressed that in the future which has already begun a pastoral team must become a spiritual fellowship with a communitarian spirituality if it is really to do justice in adequate measure to its task in pastoral work.

8

THE SPIRITUALITY OF THE SECULAR PRIEST

I must declare from the outset that I am not exactly going to attempt to answer the question raised by this theme in the form of a plain, straightforward thesis, affirming the existence of a spirituality peculiar to the secular priest as distinct from lay persons and members of religious orders and at the same time indicating to some extent in what precisely this peculiarity consists. It is impossible for me to defend a thesis stated so unequivocally, but that is not the same as saying that this spirituality certainly does not have a specific quality of its own. What I can say, then, amounts only to some preliminary observations on the subject, which fall short of an answer but may explain why I am not venturing to make a clear decision on the essential question.

(1) It might be said that there are as many diverse spiritualities as there are different human beings; or, if we want to reduce the number of these spiritualities (which is identical with the number of human beings) to a manageable size, we could say that there are as many spiritualities as there are more or less stable, diverse types of human life and occupation. Every human being has his unique and never recurring individuality. If spirituality is simply a question of coping with our life's work in a Christian way, there are as many spiritualities as there are human beings. But if these human beings, each of them unique, both differ from one another under the most diverse aspects of sex, age, calling, social position, specific historical situation, etc., and come together under these aspects as groups, and if then the peculiarities of such groupings necessarily determine the spirituality of the people in these groups, the most diverse spiri-

tualities can be distinguished in the light of these considerations and we can rightly speak of a specific spirituality related to age, sex, historical period, nationality, calling, function in the Church, etc. This is as obvious as it is important, if we want to elucidate more exactly a spirituality appropriate to a concrete human being and assigned to him by God.

In this sense it is obvious that concrete spirituality (for example, as the concrete Christian way of coping with his life on the part of a secular priest) is inevitably different from that of a lay person or a religious, if and insofar as this calling and task of a secular priest differs from that of a religious or a lay person. But this statement of the obvious, whether the result of reflection or not, is not an answer to our question. A concrete secular priest is also a man, a human being in a particular historical and sociological situation, at a certain age, in a particular situation in the society of the Church and in secular society, with a particular physiological constitution, and so on. The concrete definitive form of his spirituality is therefore dependent on all these factors, a number of which he shares with some human beings, and others with other human beings who are not secular priests. If then we do not want to distinguish too many types of spirituality for the requirements of shaping a life in practice, the question arises as to whether the specific character of the spirituality appropriate to the secular priest as a result of what is certainly the peculiar nature of his vocation is of such consequence that it cannot in practice be neglected in favour of forms of spirituality in which people today are distinguished from one another under other aspects and for other reasons much more essentially than, say, a modern secular priest from a modern religious or from a lay person living a truly and radically Christian life. Seen in this way, the question of a specific quality of the spirituality of the secular priest that is of considerable practical importance as compared with other factors determining a person's concrete spirituality has not yet been answered.

(2) For the time being, however, we may disregard this problem of the question of what truly existential import the specific character of his vocation (which must certainly not be denied) brings to the spirituality of the secular priest, if this import is compared to what is brought into his life by other factors which he shares at all times (or at least today) with people who are not secular priests. But if we

disregard this question and simply ask about what is specific to the spirituality of the secular priest (which undoubtedly exists) if and insofar as this state of life is distinguished from others, from those of lay persons and religious, we are faced in turn with the question of how to define the nature of the secular priesthood and to deduce from this the peculiar character of the spirituality of that priesthood. But then we are faced with a new question which is not easy to answer, as is evident from the great and confused discussion of recent years about the nature of the ministerial priesthood.

Is this nature to be defined in the light of the sacramental powers which belong to the ordained priest as distinct from the lay person? Is the priest to be understood in the light of his mandate to proclaim the Gospel, even though the ministry of the word has its culmination in the exhibitive word of the sacrament? Is the priest to be regarded fundamentally as a (at least potential) leader of a local Christian Church (regional or personal in character)? Is his nature to be defined in the light of the episcopal office? Is he simply the concrete bearer and representative of all the peculiar qualities with which the Church confronts the individual Christian, from whom it is distinguished, even though he, too, is simultaneously a constituent member of this same Church? These and similar questions cannot, of course, be worked out and answered in detail here. But, even if we assume that they have been answered in a general way and feel certain that the different aspects of the priesthood as indicated are not mutually contradictory but form together an integrated nature, many questions still remain open with reference to this attempt to deduce from the nature of the priesthood a spirituality specific to the secular priest in which these essential elements really gain a considerable existential weight.

We ought first to ask what diverse elements in the nature of the priesthood really have a considerable importance for the priest's spirituality. For example, if we really take seriously the active participation of lay people in the eucharistic celebration, it may not be simply taken for granted, for example, particularly by a young priest today, that the sacramental powers as such have existentially a considerable importance in his life. As distinct from the outlook of an older generation which stressed the existential and consequently spiritual significance of belonging to the sacral sphere distinguishing the priest from the lay person, perhaps a young priest of today will grasp more easily and more clearly the existential importance of his life and consequently the considerable influence on his spirituality of his task of proclaiming the word of God. But, even if we leave aside the delicate question as to which of the different elements of the nature of the priest are of decisive importance for his spirituality, there still remain further questions. For a start, the specific quality of a spirituality derived from the nature of the priesthood belongs, of course, also to priests who are members of a religious order. In this sense, then, there is no difference between the secular priest and the priest belonging to a religious order.

There can be no doubt that spirituality in the orders of priests over the past centuries has been deduced more from the priesthood as such than from what is specific to the religious state as distinct from the secular priesthood and that, consequently, until recently no one saw any problem in the fact that spiritual directors in priests' seminaries were mostly regulars. Although things are now gradually changing, until very recently it was scarcely possible to suggest that such a spiritual director, not being a secular priest, could not understand at all or at best only from outside the spirituality he was supposed to instill in his students. If the spirituality of the secular priest, then, is determined by his priesthood, the question remains open as to how it is distinguished from that of a priest in a religious order. At the same time it is scarcely possible to be satisfied with the explanation that the spirituality of the priest in a religious order involves an addition to the priestly character that is determined by the specific qualities of the religious state. This would mean that the spirituality of the secular priest is defined merely negatively and it would still not be clear what distinguishes this spirituality from that of the priest belonging to a religious order.

A further question arises if we want to define the spirituality of a secular priest in the light of the all-around, complete nature of his priesthood. We may ask whether the essential elements of the priesthood are of very considerable weight for the existential Christian attitude, for the spirituality of the secular priest, if we take into account the motivations which assume these essential peculiarities in the different historical, cultural, and sociological situations in the world and in the Church. Of course, if we want to do so, we can deduce from the nature of the priesthood the character of a spirituality corresponding to it. But is not this spirituality utterly pale, or easy to confuse with the spirituality of a Christian as such, or merely the sum total of precepts for fulfilling properly the tasks and the duties of his state on the part of the priest, if it is compared in its abstract nature with that priestly spirituality which differs with different times and situations? If we consider priestly spirituality in the Church under these aspects, differentiations begin to appear that make it impossible to reduce this spirituality to a common denominator, unless we take refuge in what is wholly abstract and therefore cannot be binding.

What did a priest or bishop (in practice, the same thing) look like at the time of the Pastoral Epistles? What did a missionary as mentioned in the *Didache* look like (if we want to regard him as a priest)? What was a cleric like under the strict control of a Cyprian in the third century? What image of the priest did Chrysostom see reflected in his first 'mirror' of the priesthood? What is the type of the secular priesthood presented in the community life of Augustine with his clergy? How did a medieval parish priest behave in his parish? Assuming that they were not merely caricatures of the priesthood, what were prince-bishops and warring popes really like? What is the spirituality of a specialist theologian, of a Curial official, of a worker-priest? What is the image of the priest in the *Ecole française* or as suggested by Pius X? We have only singled out quite arbitrarily a few of the variations in the course of history of the image of the spirituality of the secular priesthood. But these alone make it clear that the secular priest's spirituality is so greatly differentiated by the different cultural and ecclesial situations in which it has to be lived that what is common threatens to disappear as a theoretical, abstract idea behind these differences or in practice is scarcely different from the general Christian attitude of all times and all states of life.

In addition to all this, there is a further question to which we can draw attention only in passing. Is the secular priest's celibacy in the Latin Church to be included among the essential elements of the spirituality of the secular priesthood? If it is, then we have here a spirituality different from that of the priesthood in the Orthodox and Catholic Eastern churches. If not, then this spirituality of the secular priest, deduced from the nature of the priesthood, but in which celibacy has no part, is so general and abstract that it cannot be very helpful, since it leaves out a very typical element in the life of a priest in this Latin Church of ours. But if we decide on an affirmative answer to the question just raised, a great deal still remains obscure. For it is not at all clear from what standpoint the secular priest observes the celibacy that is supposed to determine his spirituality. Is the meaning and motivation of this way of life identical with the meaning and way of life observed in accordance with the evangelical counsel of chastity by members of religious orders? Or is this celibacy of the secular priest in the last resort to be assimilated to the unmarried state contrasted by Jesus in Matthew 19:12 precisely with that accepted 'for the sake of the kingdom of heaven', without however suggesting that the former, enforced by circumstances, must necessarily be considered immoral or un-Christian?

If the celibacy of the secular priest has to be regarded as identical with the single state of the religious (at least on the assumption that it cannot otherwise be lived truly and in a way commensurate with human dignity), then between the spirituality of the secular priest and that of the member of a religious order there would be a convergence which would render any further distinction between the two spiritualities a matter of idle speculation, since (in Germany, at least) the financial situation of the secular priest and that of the regular on the whole (apart from wealthy professors of theology among the secular clergy) can in practice scarcely be distinguished; it is the same with obedience, which as applied in the religious orders today amounts to little more than the secular priest's acceptance of his bishop's directives. If it is said that secular priests may live as individuals while priests in religious orders have a community life with its own social structures, it can also be pointed out that in practice the life of a religious is often very isolated and, on the other hand, in practice and in theory the secular priest is not debarred from leading a community life, as we see it lived in various forms and to varying degrees of intensity, for example, by Oratorians and other communities of secular priests.

(3) A further difficulty in defining a spirituality peculiar to the secular priest arises from the fact that, for very far-rcaching and profound reasons, no human and no Christian life can be lived in the light solely of a single basic attitude or precept. Every human life must necessarily grow out of a plurality of attitudes which can never be wholly united under the control of deliberate human planning, but must be left in obedience to God, to his providence and his decrees.

Even the most radical Christian way of life not only cannot but may not be determined and shaped in the light of any single precept. Neither flight from the world nor love of the world, neither action nor contemplation, neither passive identication with the down-graded nor struggle to change social conditions, neither theology of the cross nor theology of glory, neither renunciation nor human enjoyment of the world, neither life nor death, nor any of these things *alone* and as such can be the sole precept or the sole formative principle of a Christian life. We are not going to explain at length here why this is so, why really Christian life-styles in all their variety and differences of emphasis (which are necessary and justified) can essentially have only a single and absolutely final radicalness: that is, to entrust the plurality of life (which can never be completely rationalized) calmly and silently to God; to project life plans and life-styles, aware that none of these can be realized and certainly may not be realized in 'chemical purity', if they are to remain Christian. Even Francis of Assisi's life of poverty, radical as it was, did not display any monomaniacal exclusiveness; a radical 'corpselike obedience' in a religious order is necessarily combined with a person's own free self-determination which cannot be subject to anyone else's approval. Humility is human only if the humble person is not merely humble, etc.

What is at once so obvious and at the same time supremely wise is what makes the distinction of life-styles and spiritualities so difficult. If we want to set apart the meaning and spirituality of the religious life from the life-style of the Christian in the world, we run into the danger of proclaiming and canonizing a monomaniacal radicalness of certain attitudes—escapism, renunciation, otherworldliness, etc.—which cannot actually be made effective and which are simply not human and still less Christian. If it is claimed that these distinctions between the religious life and life in the world are not completely exclusive, but involve only differences of emphasis, of priorities among possible structural principles of a Christian life, this is certainly important, but it also obscures again the distinctions between the two life-styles as we first come across them, especially when these variable and fluctuating shifts of emphasis have to be translated once more into the life of the individual or the Christian in the world as such. Then it is possible for the religious, without being disloyal to his vocation, to enjoy life uninhibitedly and spontaneously to a considerable degree, injuring no one, but not experiencing the reality of the law of the cross; and conversely a Christian 'in the world', governed by the law of the cross, can live in the shadow of continually renewed self-denial. But if we take refuge (not entirely without justification) in the concrete differences in the outward mode of life in order in this way to clarify the difference between religious life and life in the world, we have certainly pointed out differences (for example, in clothing, in the external life-style, etc.), but we have not answered the question of how these differences have a considerable influence on a person's innermost feelings and on spirituality itself. We have to allow also for this basic difficulty when the nature of the spirituality of the secular priest is to be defined. It is clear from the outset that it is determined by a large number of contrasted peculiarities.

It is also understandable that the concrete situation in which a particular secular priest is living is of decisive importance for the place where the emphasis is to be laid among these dialectically mutually opposed peculiarities of his priestly existence. If a Roman Curial cardinal and an African priest in the bush or a worker priest in a French factory are all priests, the 'dosage', the emphasis among these individual dialectically opposed peculiarities, is vastly different for each of these priests and it is difficult to speak, except in a very abstract way, about a common spirituality. The conditions of life in which the nature of priestly spirituality must be realized are so diverse that the 'mixture' of contrasted essential peculiarities inevitably takes such varied forms that the one spirituality appears concretely to be determined almost by one peculiarity alone, the other spirituality almost solely by the other peculiarity, even though in every spirituality (if and insofar as it is Christian) *both* peculiarities must exist. Unfortunately, it is not possible here concretely to describe such historical examples of these diverse spiritualities in detail.

(4) With all these difficulties, another solution might be suggested. Let us see in what this consists and whether theoretically or at least practically it is effective. It consists in the thesis that the spirituality of the secular priest in itself is materially the same as that of other Christians in the world and is distinguished from the latter only formally insofar as (in addition to the obligation which rests on other Christians in the world) a second obligation to the same spirituality

arises for the priest when he comes to practise it: an obligation arising from his special office, which as such must also urgently impel the secular priest to practice this spirituality.

This thesis certainly has its attraction. In a sense it recognizes completely a spirituality of the secular priesthood, but it evades the painful effort to mark out the content of this spirituality as distinct from that of the Christian simply as such; instead of this it can remind us that *every* Christian is called and obliged to the *perfection* of Christian existence. From that standpoint what we call 'the evangelical counsels' (in certain circumstances, also the celibacy of the secular priest and other spiritual obligations laid down by canon law for him) do not imply a higher degree of Christian perfection as such and thus of the spirituality characterized by the counsels: all that they do is to provide for those aspiring to the one perfection of love of God and neighbour common to all Christians different conditions of life and special aids by which they are distinguished from other Christians. In favour of this thesis it can be said that it provides a simple explanation of the immense variety of spiritualities of the secular priesthood, since this variety is basically identical with the diversity of serious Christian living which is found among normal Christians as a result of differences of age, culture, sociological status, etc. The thesis could also be recommended because it prevents from the very outset any pretence on the part of the clergy to be a spiritual elite; the cleric, too, has nothing else to do but to become as good a Christian as possible, but he has an additional obligation in this respect arising from his special vocation. But, despite its apparently neat solution of the problem, the thesis also has its difficulties.

In the first place, would not this thesis have to be regarded as valid also for the religious, so that no further distinction between different spiritualities in the Church could be made at all? But have we not then thrown out the baby with the bath water? Are we not contradicting a unanimous tradition in the theology of spirituality which always sought to distinguish essentially between several spiritualities, at least between that of Christian lay people and that of religious, as Vatican II made clear, even though, as the Würzburg Synod stressed, one and the same goal of perfection of life is common to Christians in the world and to religious and their different ways may not be distinguished as higher and lower realizations of Christian existence? This seems to be a real difficulty, at least when we recall the fact that priestly celibacy in the West brings priestly spirituality very close to the spirituality of the evangelical counsels, despite the query we raised earlier in this respect.

A further difficulty about the thesis just formulated consists in the fact that, at least at first sight, the office of the priest obliges him to fulfill his life in certain ways that do not otherwise occur in a Christian life in the world and that consequently his office does not involve merely a new, additional obligation in a Christian life, but materially determines this life as distinct from that of the Christian lay person. This seems obvious and certainly finds expression in all descriptions of priestly spirituality. There should be really no dispute about this. But we ought to look a little more closely and introduce more exact distinctions if we want to make clear why and how the specific official obligations of the priest also introduce *material* peculiarities into his *spirituality,* assuming that such peculiarities have considerable existential importance in the life of the priest. For example, the question might be raised (however tiresome it might seem to some people) whether participation in the eucharist in the way proper on the one hand to the priest and on the other to the lay person is really considerably different in the existential spirituality as such: in other words, in the *opus operantis* necessarily sustaining the *opus operatum.*

If we raise doubts about the view that the sacramental power proper to the priest as such is what substantially distinguishes the priest's spirituality from that of the laity and then go on to ask what other official tasks and obligations impose a special character on the content of priestly spirituality, then presumably we shall be referred to the ministry of the word: the obligation of the priest in the name of the Church, in a missionary spirit, in season and out of season, with his whole existence, to stand up before an unbelieving or purely secular world for the Gospel of God, his forgiving grace, his crucified and risen Christ as the irreversible self-promise of God to the world. Such a ministry of the word must undoubtedly leave its mark on the innermost life of the priest. So, too, on his spirituality. But if with the Second Vatican Council's theology of the Christian laity we stress the laity's ecclesial mission in the world, if we are clear that a lay person really radically convinced and leading a radically Christian life in the modern atheistic or secularized world simply cannot avoid or may not avoid bearing witness to his Christianity by his life—of which bringing the word to his fellow men is a part—then this determination of the content of the secular priest's spirituality in the light of his ministry of the word is again not so absolutely clearly convincing and does not distingish priest and layman so obviously, as long as we assume that the layman, too, lives radically a real spirituality, as he ought to do. If we take these things into consideration, the difference between the two spiritualities is very greatly reduced and amounts more or less to the fact that the priest in virtue of his office has simply an additional obligation really to live one and the same Christian life, one and the same spirituality, which he has in common with all, and so also to bear witness to the Gospel which it is his official mission to preach.

The reader may deplore the apparently irregular course of these reflections and blame us for not having the courage to put forward a metaphysically and theologically clear and decisive theory of the spirituality of the secular priest as distinct from that of the laity or of the religious. I think, however, that this vacillation in the last resort springs from the very nature of the problem. The one Christian life from the one Holy Spirit in the one following of Christ takes concrete shape at different times, in different callings, under the influence of different charisms, in thousands and thousands of forms, always new, always different, continually surprising, and yet in all these countless variations remaining the same. Both because of the innumerable possibilities of the concrete development and because of the ultimate unity of this life and this spirituality, it is enormously difficult and even a little futile to work out a kind of Linnaean botanical system for all these countless forms of spirituality and set them out neatly within the scheme, only to discover once more that the concrete spirituality of a particular human being, because of the plurality of its elements and the different stress laid on these elements, could again be brought simultaneously under different types of spirituality; and it is by no means certain from the very outset that the specifically priestly element even in the life of a holy priest must be the particularly and all-around determining characteristic of his spirituality.

(5) Bearing in mind all that has been said up to now, including all the queries, we may attempt in conclusion very briefly to say something more about the content of the spirituality of the secular priest.

It does not really matter whether what we have to say applies only to the secular priest or whether a priest in a religious order, or even a lay person, can claim it as true also for himself. Neither would we want to claim that what is said here about the spirituality of the secular priest is valid for all times and for all historical and cultural conditions everywhere in the world. We are speaking of the secular priest in our own country and at the present time. But it must again be expressly stated that this spirituality cannot be defined (either theologically or humanly) in the light of the spiritual 'exercises' planned for the secular priest in the Code of Canon Law hitherto in use. The spirituality of the secular priest necessary today in our country will not become a reality as a result of retreats based on monastic spirituality.

It may sound old-fashioned, but it seems to me also that the spirituality of the secular priest needs to be deliberately cultivated, to be systematized and exercised. The importance of this insight, derived from the monastic life (which, it seems to me, still has its value) was formerly exaggerated and the unsuccessful attempt was made to bring the secular priest's spirituality into line with a system aimed at producing ascetical and spiritual profit. This, of course, did not work, and it is even less likely to work today. The spirituality of the secular priest will be a truly Christian endurance of the life that is particularly his own and really involves a spiritual task for him. This, however, does not exclude but, in fact, includes a certain system, exercises, an agenda for each day, planning in advance, the coherent organization of his time, etc.

It can certainly be said that the secular priest today must regard himself as the preacher of the Gospel, commissioned by the Church. He must be convinced that this calling of his can be fulfilled only with the involvement of his personality and his life, that it is consequently not a task only for part of his time, for office hours. From this it follows that the priest's professional task and consequently his spirituality cannot consist merely in the completion of a number of measurable individual achievements, that the rest of his life, too, is subject to the always overwhelming demands of the law of his priestly calling. Precisely in order to be able to fulfill this calling, the priest certainly needs leisure, a sphere of privacy in his life, recreation; but all these things must be determined by what is properly the law of his life and do not amount simply to a right that can be taken for granted and must not be disputed by anyone. If the priest's task, to be paid for by his life, is to spread the message of the Gospel, if that very message requires him with Jesus to take the side of the poor and deprived, then I do not know whether the prosperous life-style (adopted as a matter of course by a majority of the clergy in this country) really corresponds to the spirituality required of the priest. In other countries, even in Europe, it is different. There priests are mostly poor, simply because they can scarcely do anything about it. But does not Christian spirituality consist in realizing without affectation a life-style that brings the priest at least close to the poor, so that people can see that there is someone here who renounces, for the sake of the kingdom of heaven and without reward, something that no one could prevent him from keeping?

A revision of the average life-style cultivated by the German clergy would do them good, particularly before external circumstances compel them to do so. Such a revision today would certainly be a part of a modern spirituality of the secular priest. If we look to Jesus, it seems to me that it is not absolutely clearly a part of our spirituality to be counted in the German Federal Republic mainly, almost entirely and rightly, among the defenders of present social conditions. To be honest, we priests in this country are not particularly obviously and impressively the conscience of the nation where this conscience ought to prick us—and not only with reference to the struggle about the abortion laws. Such a socio-critical involvement is not merely part of the priest's professional task, but ought also to leave its mark on his spirituality, since it brings with it resistance, opposition, and similar experiences which must be understood as participation in the lot of Jesus. The priest of today can bring life to the preaching of the Gospel only if (as well as and as far as it is granted him) he is a mystagogue of that ultimate, internal, religious experience of God and his grace without which no one today can in the long run resist the pressure of his secularized environment and remain a Christian. But this assumes that the priest himself, as well as and as far as he is capable of it, has that personal internal experience of God without which he would be degraded to a cultic and ecclesiastical official celebrating magical and today no longer credible ceremonies.

We said elsewhere that the Christian of the future will be a mystic or he will not be a Christian at all. If this statement is true in any sense, it is true especially of the priest. We may be very sceptical in regard to religious imports from the East. But is the spirituality of the normal priest such that he can rise to the challenge of this Eastern spirituality and that he can have a justified feeling of superiority on the basis of his innermost experience and the treasures of the Christian mystical tradition? Have we not too many priests here who rely on traditional popular piety and help to cultivate it, almost like enthusiastic chairmen of local associations for Christian folklore, but do not see that for socio-political reasons the 'people' are increasingly melting away; who do not see that the 'people of the future' are settled somewhere quite different; who simply ignore their properly missionary task of making new Christians out of pagans? Undoubtedly, there ought to be invested in this priestly task of proclamation rightly understood a spirituality which already exists here and there but has not yet acquired the clarity and obviousness which is the condition of the priest's effectiveness today.

9

THE SPIRITUALITY OF THE PRIEST IN THE LIGHT OF HIS OFFICE

The theme here is 'starting points for a spirituality of the priest in the light of his office'—of his office, that is, both as it is seen in what is properly the binding teaching of the Church and theology and also as it confronts us today in its historically conditioned concreteness.

First of all, a few preliminary observations:

(1) When I was invited to take part in this conference,[1] I had to stipulate (more from necessity than from my own choice) that I should be allowed to talk *freely:* that is, I would not bring with me a carefully prepared, written address. There may be advantages in this procedure insofar as there will not be any attempt to cover too much ground and consequently there is less danger of talking over people's heads. But the condition put forward and accepted has the disadvantage that I am liable to go round and round the point, to say and to stress some things and leave others in the background or forget them and thus to speak vaguely about a matter which certainly deserves exact and well-considered treatment. I must ask you, then, from the very outset to allow for this disadvantage and forgive me. In view of my declining strength, the pressure of other work, and my age, it would have been simply impossible to adopt a different procedure.

(2) You are listening to an old man. I certainly don't feel young; I am in my seventy-third year and at that age a person knows very exactly his limitations and particularly his limited opportunities of

[1] This lecture was addressed to priests in 1976. See List of Sources.

practical experience. *You* are really pastors who have borne the burden and effort of pastoral work for years and decades; I have always been a teacher and, although very occasionally engaged in pastoral work, for the most part theologizing and philosophizing in my ivory tower. I am aware of this and must ask you also to allow for the fact and forgive me if this address turns out accordingly. Moreover, if we are talking about the priestly office and the spirituality it involves, each of us has inevitably a concrete image of this office and the spirituality resulting from it which is concretely determined also by *our* life, by our experience of life, our sociological, ecclesial situation—so much so that none of us can adequately portray this concreteness of our image of the priest and the image of priestly spirituality and consequently we impress on this image features that may well be legitimate, but which are not present in this way in the priestly image of another colleague. And if the same thing is noticeable also in the present lecture, that is, if you have the impression that I am going on and on about things which are of no interest to you, which really do not affect you, which strike you as odd, this, too, of course is an unavoidable situation which, we might say somewhat pretentiously and pompously, is part of the historicity and individual relativity of one man's perception of truth, particularly in his old age.

(3) I would like to say right from the beginning that I completely agree with what Father Zulehner has said about this theme as a whole and I think that what he has said about Type B as the type to be preferred today (since it brings out more clearly than Type A the special features of the present-day priestly situation and spirituality[2]) is in perfect harmony with my own opinion. And I even have the impression that there is is nothing particularly that I can add to his comments, except at most to observe that this conception is absolutely legitimate and can be maintained in the light of the dogma of the priesthood.

(4) Obviously there are plenty of concrete individual types of priestly spirituality. Each of us has the right to give concrete shape to the possibilities of priestly existence and priestly spirituality as they occur in our own life. It is clear that a priest who allows his

[2] P. Zulehner, 'Elemente einer pastoralen Spiritualität' in *Priesterliche Spiritualität heute*, ed. S. László (Vienna, 1977), pp. 13–40.

spirituality to be shaped and conditioned in the light of his particular office and task will have as his ideal (and as what, in fact, he realizes) a spirituality and a priestly image differing according to whether he is a teacher of religion in a city school or living as a country pastor. Each way has its concrete justification. The conservative and the 'progressive', the intellectual and the simple, devout person, the quiet spiritual adviser (or what we might call 'the spiritual man'), and the apostle creating a sensation in the world: all these types can be justified and we must simply get used to accepting one another, acknowledging their right to exist, and not insisting that as priests we must all be molded in the same pattern. Each of us must gradually crystallize out of our own situation, our own temperament, and our own life history the priestly image and the type of spirituality that are right for ourselves, naturally being humbly aware of the fact that what we present is *a* priest, not *the* priest. All this is obvious, but, if you look into the concrete circumstances of our lives as priests, you will see that it is by no means so simple in practice and that this apparently simple norm is very often infringed.

I would now like to put forward some very general ideas on office and spirituality.

I

We begin with a very simple thesis: priestly spirituality is first of all simply Christian spirituality, Christian life in faith, hope, and love. Priestly spirituality is not (at least, not primarily) a kind of extra to a normal Christian life, but (while, of course, determined by the concrete life task of the priest as distinct from other Christians) the spiritual, Christian life of a Christian purely and simply. Today this is really obvious in the light of the practice and nature of the priesthood. It is obvious in the light of *practice*, for, exactly like other people, we have to live in a secularized milieu, we are impugned and called in question by a world of secularized values with its rationalism, with its technocracy, with its crowds, etc. One way or another, like other Christians today, we are living in a diaspora; neither for them nor for us are faith and Christian life and the hope of eternity to be taken for granted as something that we could pass over, so to speak, as unimportant for us and then find greater scope to develop a sublime spirituality as our special job or as a kind of hobby. We are poor, tormented, frightened, threatened by the world as a whole, by politics and industry; just like the others, we are caught up into the whirlpool of secularization; faith in God, in an eternal life, the persuasion that our freedom is to be exercised responsibly before God, all these things create exactly as many difficulties for us as they do for other people. If this were not the case, it would not be an advantage, but a sign that we are living out of touch not only with our time, but also with our office and our own life, since we cannot really live this office and this life otherwise than in a genuine confrontation with our time and situation, society, culture, and lack of culture.

Priestly spirituality, then, is first of all Christian spirituality which, as such, is required of every Christian if he wants to be a true Christian and not merely a conventional or folkloristic Christian. But if we say this, the question will inevitably be raised as to what exactly this Christian spirituality is. We can, of course, say that it is life out of faith, hope, and love, it is life from the Holy Spirit; we can say that it is life from the Spirit of Christ, life from the Gospel; we can say that it is life from the following of Christ; we can say that it is life from the hope of eternal life, out of an ultimate responsibility in which we are aware that, whether we want it or not, we are living our life to the very end in freedom for or against God. We can say that Christian spirituality is life oriented to God's judgment, it means coping with sin that cannot be eliminated by referring to social or psychological constraints, etc. We can say all that, it is all true, and here and now there is really nothing more that I can say; to say anything more precise would require at least an eight-day retreat.

Simply to provide a spur, a question that is meant to be disturbing, I would like to add the following in regard to this Christian spirituality which is basically identical with priestly spirituality. When we speak of 'spirituality' (whether the term is a good one, very understandable, or pastorally useful is another question) we mean 'life from the Spirit'. But then the question arises as to just what this is supposed to mean. And the crucial point for us personally and in our pastoral work today is whether we not only succeed in getting this 'pneumatic', spiritual dimension of our existence into our own heads or the heads of other people by an abstract, conceptual indoctrination (which today will be more or less ineffective), but whether we can discover this Spirit as what we really experience in ourselves.

And this is extraordinarily difficult today in the age of sociological criticism of ideologies, in the age of natural science, in the age of Freud, in the age of depth psychology and of the psychological corruption of human beings. Is there in fact anything of this kind? Have you ever really experienced the Spirit of God? Suppose you say: 'Yes, I was once touched, or I was at one time devout, or I had the impression that there is some sort of God who is good, who quite likes me, although he allows children in Vietnam to be killed by napalm bombs'. In that case you ought to unleash on this claim of yours to have discovered the Spirit in yourself all the corrupting elements of psychology, of sociological criticism of ideologies, of rational psychology, technology, etc., and then ask if anything remains or if all that is left are merely words like 'God of love, grace, Holy Spirit, God's indwelling', etc., to which we cling because of some sort of feeling that in the long run we cannot do without this sort of thing. Are these words not all mere husks, long ago deprived of meaning in a long historical process from the time of the Enlightenment?

I said earlier that I cannot answer this question now. The reason why I raise it at all is in order to make clear what are the innermost structures that a Christian, and consequently a priestly, spirituality must have in order really to cope with these problems.

At most I can add only a few words which seem to be even more abstract and merely refer to the matter under discussion without getting to the root of it. In the last resort spirituality is man's absolute transcendence, beyond any categorial reality in him or outside him, into the absolute mystery that we call God; it is ultimately a transcendentality dying, crucified, becoming torn apart with Christ, not as a theory but as what happens in us in our concrete existence when we confront this life with its ultimate dependence on the incomprehensible mystery of God and achieve the acceptance, the endurance, of this life concretely with Christ through all categorial breakdowns, through all death, through all disappointment. Of course, such an experience of our own absolute transcendentality, crucified with Jesus into the absolute mystery, has a history in us. This is something that comes into existence slowly, we reach these things only gradually; perhaps there will be some people who never notice it or do not consider and cannot express in words what has taken place in them. At the present time, I think, at least the priest (we shall come to practical matters later) should slowly come to see that something of this kind exists.

For the moment that must suffice to mark out the problems involved in the first statement that I wanted to make, to the effect that priestly spirituality today more than ever is simply Christian spirituality and not an addition to the Christian life. In this sense spirituality is understood as truly Christian life emerging from the innermost centre of our own existence and not merely as a fulfillment of religious conventions prevailing in Christianity and in the Church. Spirituality, Christian spirituality, is the active participation in the death of Jesus and, since he is risen, in that death as successful and as assumed into that ineffable, incomprehensible, not controllable, not manoeuvrable ultimate mystery *quod omnes* (as Aquinas would say) *vocant Deum*.

II

Coming now from the first part of our reflections to the question of priestly office. It is obvious that our priestly office must also determine the character of our spirituality and even provide its essential foundation. Not, properly speaking, as an external addition to our Christian life, but as the radicalness of that life which is required from us as official representatives of Christianity and the Church. From that standpoint we must ask what we actually understand by this priestly office. For you know just as well as I do that in the last decades there has been a tremendous amount of writing and discussion about the nature of the ministerial priesthood and some very diverse opinions have been expressed. Clearly, I cannot explain and work out all these things again here. I would like to say from the outset that what I am putting forward here by way of commentary on these themes is not to be understood and interpreted as the sole possible, more or less official theory. In Catholic theology today there is a great deal that is obscure, that is being discussed and giving rise to very varied opinions. This is because very many questions in the history of dogma confront us today as a result of our attempt to gain a more exact and impartial understanding of these things: questions, for instance, of the relationship and connection between Jesus and the Church, of the existence of seven sacraments, of the relationship of the sacraments to the Church, of the possibility of a further development, and of the possibilities and limits of changes in the sacramental life of the Church.

If you read Hans Küng to the effect that Jesus did not institute a Church, or if theologians like him are saying that (whatever Trent may have defined) the sacraments are, of course, not instituted by Jesus Christ, however little I share these views and however much I have opposed them, I do not advise you to raise an outcry against them in the name of orthodoxy, but quite impartially to ask first of all how these views came to be expressed. We must note, for example, that it was about a thousand years before it was known that there are seven sacraments. Or if you really take seriously the most modern exegesis on what is known as Jesus' 'imminent expectation', if you take seriously the historical, concrete, theological relativity of the human consciousness of Jesus (a consciousness that could be developed, gain new experiences, produce new formulations), then, of course, questions like those on the understanding of the Church and the priestly office are not actually as simple to answer as Catholic theology assumed even as recently as thirty years ago. So much by way of preliminary remarks.

In regard to the priestly office I want firstly to issue a warning against a misunderstanding. To express it very cautiously, as this office is conceived today in concrete practice and in the Church's official teaching, normally (not allowing for emergency situations, but leaving these aside for the moment) only the legitimately ordained priest in virtue of his sacramental ordination can preside over and lead a legitimate eucharistic celebration. This we can certainly assume as a fixed point of theology on the nature of the priestly office, notwithstanding all the problems it implies. But we need not deduce from this that the priest must necessarily see his actual nature in the light of that fixed point or give expression to it in his spirituality. Not that anyone is forbidden to do so. But to say, because this power of consecration as part of his priestly existence is reserved (at least in the ordinary way and in the normal case) exclusively to him, that this is also necessarily the proper, most fundamental, and most decisive point from which he gains his own total understanding of his nature is something that is not (at any rate, not logically) demonstrated by this priestly reservation.

For we can also see an extraordinarily great historical variability in the official nature of the priesthood. No one denies, for example, that Ignatius of Loyola wanted to found an order of priests, and Pope Paul firmly restrained us Jesuits from imperiling or dissolving the priestly character of the order. If we look at the life of Ignatius of Loyola, it is clear that he certainly wanted to be ordained. I would say, however, that this was simply because, for him, it was concretely the most practical way and the condition of the possibility of getting on with what he really wanted to do. In his own spirituality he was not at all terribly insistent about saying mass; if I remember rightly, he waited for a whole year after his ordination before he got as far as that, but then he said mass very gladly and with immense devotion. But with his first companions he went into prisons and ministered to the sick. For him it was enormously important to be in the closest possible contact with the poor and the socially underprivileged of his time in the prisons and to go into the hideous hospitals of that period, to convert prostitutes in Rome, perhaps also to run a school to inspire pious princesses, etc. In a word, what he in fact did seems open to the inane verdict or objection that it could all have been achieved by people who were not priests. Against this, it must be pointed out that precisely in view of historical variability and of theology it is impossible to describe anything as properly and solely priestly, as what *only* the priest can do. That is to say: preaching the Gospel, ministering to the poor, defending the underprivileged, following Jesus in this sense, prayer, a mystical sphere of one's own existence, are just as much part of the priestly office as—and I do not mean it in a pejorative sense—'being able to say mass'.

How can this thesis be substantiated merely with an appeal to actual images of the priest in history, in which the function of presiding (in the strict sense) at the eucharist was by no means always and necessarily the central feature? How can such a thesis or such an image of the priest be demonstrated more precisely in terms of dogmatic theology? Here I am touching on opinions and theses which I really do not want to pass off as the Church's official teaching, views about which we can think what we like. In a question like this, where there is no really clear and binding official teaching of the Church, the theologian has no choice except to follow his own opinion.

Dogmatically and 'ontologically', from the nature of the case, the absolutely primary datum is not the pope, not the bishops, and not the priests, but Jesus Christ, crucified and risen, who simply would not be the Risen One, would not be, as Vatican II says, the indefectible, irreversible sign of the salvation of the whole world, who would not be the sacrament of salvation for all times, if he had not with him by the invincible power of his grace the Church of the believers, of those who love him, of those who follow him. Such a Church which, as one and whole, is primarily the permanent sign of salvation, the permanent sacrament, which is God's presence permanently established in the world, such a Church as a sociological reality has an office, a power of government, which must be seen in the first place as one and whole.

Such a power of government can and must be split up into definite individual functions. The Church has always a function of government—not just of any kind like that of the state or of some other society, but one which is part of this indefectible nature of the Church which maintains to the end of time the presence of Jesus Christ as the irreversible sign of salvation. This one office is first and foremost one and whole. We cannot go on for ten hours or so here about dogmatics or ecclesiology and consequently cannot worry about how this ultimately one office is split up, articulated, and shared, and where in all of this divine law ends and merely ecclesiastical law begins; this is true even if we say that the papacy and the episcopate (and perhaps also a presbyterate split off from the episcopate) are of divine law—all of which is by no means obvious.

I would venture to say that, abstractly and in principle, I could imagine the whole Church as consisting of pope and bishops (in the sense that every priest is also a bishop). I would not want this. But what articulations of the ultimately one office are present unchangeably in the Church itself by its very nature (or, we might say, by the will of Christ), and what further articulations of office are left to the Church's free decision, is an extraordinarily difficult and obscure question. All through the Middle Ages there were minor orders and St. Thomas was sure that all minor orders were also sacraments, that, consequently, the conferring of these orders was also sacramental; the subdiaconate, too, was obviously regarded as a sacrament. In addition, of course—and this again is a difficult and obscure question which I cannot examine closely here—even when people speak of a divine right of papacy, episcopate, and presbyterate, it must be remembered that these factors as expositions and articulations of the one office nevertheless have had a history in the Church. How am I to answer a Protestant exegete when he says that the primitive Church, as described in Paul's Letters (or elsewhere before Ignatius of Antioch), had a presbyteral constitution, since the apostles were still alive and were the true bishops, and so on? I can get out of the problem by admitting absolutely that even divine law has had a historical development in the Church and yet remains divine law, even though there was a long struggle before this development itself came to be recognized in the later Church in its own irreversibility and validity. Such a development toward irreversibility can certainly involve also an element of decision and of free institution by the Church, and yet the result of the development can be described as of divine law.

Why am I talking about all these odd things? It is from this standpoint that we can understand the great variability of the image of the presbyter in the Church, in other words, how functions expressly portrayed there can later fall into the background or even drop out completely, while other elements which were present at most in a rudimentary or potential way stand out more clearly than formerly. Consequently, even among such a large number of factors involved in a concrete priestly mandate, one or another may become more relevant to priestly spirituality and later cease to be so. Father Zulehner has drawn attention to some of these factors: representative of God, the person leading the community, etc. These are features which were wholly legitimate in a former priestly image, since they could also have a positive meaning even in their ambivalence; they could even have predominated in the image of the priest in former times, but that is no reason why they should have the same importance for all times. Nor can this plurality of features in the priestly image be regarded as a basis for the question of whether there are certain things that can be done by someone who is not a priest. Even if there are, it is wrong to conclude that these things are not fundamental for priestly existence and priestly spirituality. A priest might say: 'My priestly self-understanding and my priestly spirituality have their living roots in the fact that, welcome or unwelcome, I proclaim the unique message of the kingdom of God, of the crucified and risen Christ, to rich and poor, to privileged and underprivileged, that I commit my life to this task which I regard constantly as the centre of my life, that I do not regard it as any kind of casual occupation, but as something in which I am investing my whole life'. Such a person has a concept of the priesthood that excludes as irrelevant the question as to whether another person, a pastoral assistant, a layman, can do anything of this kind. This is not to deny that priestly existence can also be seen in the perspective of the altar.

It might be said that the actual core of a priestly existence and spirituality, in the light of which the latter can be understood, may also be grasped and lived by someone who is by no means a priest. I would answer that such a person obviously ought to be ordained a priest. I would also say that if there are or must be pastoral assistants today who are permanent official leaders of a parish which is without a priest, then in God's name let them be ordained. Why? Because it would mean no more than giving them the sacramental ratification and palpability of what they really are. The same is true of someone who in practice does what is essentially the task of the deacon. By ordination nothing is really added that he did not already possess, but what he had is sacramentally palpably secured in the dimension of office in the Church. If someone were to tell me that this is an outrageous idea, I would ask him how he would cope with another situation. Suppose a person comes to the priest and tells him: 'I am really living as a Christian in imitation of the crucified Christ, I believe, I hope, I love, I sacrifice my life for my neighbour, I live my life more or less after the fashion of Mother Teresa in Calcutta, but now, Father, I have discovered that I was never baptized'. Is the answer: 'For God's sake, whatever you did up to now was of no account; it was certainly not Christianity, it was not life coming from the Holy Spirit'? No, here was a Christian, here *is* a Christian. Baptize him. Why? So that the life he is already living can be seen expressly in the dimension of the sociological and historical palpability of the Church.

We find the same thing in Aquinas. In his theology it was taken for granted that anyone who came into the confessional had in reality (in virtue of his repentance) already been forgiven by God. The whole late scholastic and post-Tridentine controversy about attrition and contrition and the like would have had no real meaning for Aquinas. In other words, for St. Thomas, the penitent received the sacrament *because* he was the sinner once more justified, which does not mean, however, that the efficacy or the causality of the sacrament is denied. This is something I cannot explain here and now. In other words, the conception of a human and official task which in a sense precedes its sacramental ratification is certainly one that is involved in other comparable cases of the Church's sacramental life. What I wanted to say ought, of course, to be developed in a more exact theology of the relationship between word and sacrament, but this is not possible here. All I want to say now is that the priest can certainly regard himself today as the officially commissioned mystagogue of the faith of the parish and as its leader, as minister in all dimensions of its life, including the eucharist as the culmination of the sacramental word in the Church, and, therefore, I think, could by all means consider his priestly spirituality as the radicalness of his Christian existence and not as something added to it.

It would be possible, of course, to ask more closely what is 'official', to raise the question of whether it is necessarily identical (in the light of the Church's dogma, not that of its present legal practice) with 'lifelong'. But all that must be left aside here.

Before attempting to pass on to some more concrete images resulting from this way of understanding the priestly office (today both dogmatically justifiable and appropriate to our time), I would like to call attention only to one more assumption: that is, that with priestly spirituality, office absorbs a person's own life and life absorbs office. Here we find a difference from all other forms of work in society. Of course, a master shoemaker or a businessman, a diplomat or a politician, will develop out of his specific calling (if he pursues it in the right way) quite definite attitudes also for his personal life, his ethic, etc. But, from the nature of the case, since the officeholder here attests the whole of human and (by God's self-communication) deified life as such, and works for and must concern himself with the formation of the Church as the historico-sociological presence of this vast, gracious endowment of the world as a whole, this is something that cannot be understood as a particular calling *in addition to which* it is possible to have an independent private life in the strict sense. And, conversely, if the priest is someone who wants to be radically Christian and surrenders power over his whole life to this Spirit of God whom he can experience at the heart of his existence, then priestly existence is not a supplementary task, obligation, and burden of Christian life, as it might perhaps otherwise seem to be. Of course, just like members of religious orders in their own way, the priest is thus up to a point authorized and condemned to be (if I may use the ugly word) something of a religious 'pro'. All this involves problems: the danger of overexertion, the danger of a mere legalistic ritualism, the danger of attempting to reserve for oneself a private sphere which cannot absorb one's personality. I did not want to do more than allude to these things.

III

In the first part of my comments I could do no more than mark out the questions of office and understanding of office on the one hand and that of spirituality on the other. I am well aware of the aphoristic and very vaguely selective character of what I have said up to now. I want to attempt now to become a little more concrete and to point to aspects of the image of the priest today which belong to it possibly from the dogmatic nature of this office and necessarily in our present situation.

When I was considering these things, I did not pay much attention to the very cleverly and correctly designed chart of such aspects by Father Zulehner. I approve of it and find it very good, but I shall permit myself to allude to these aspects in a slightly different way.

The first thing to be said perhaps is that the priest of today must be someone who can pray in a personal way. This does not mean, of course, that someone else, a lay person, who is not a priest in the Catholic Church, could not manage, cultivate, and do the same thing just as well. And it certainly does not mean that this capacity for personal prayer for a priest (since he is the official representative and the commissioned mystagogue of the faith of the parish and its leader) is something that is merely *presupposed* to his priestly existence *as such*. No, the priest as such ought to be someone who is able to pray personally and not only as officially carrying out the liturgy or reading his breviary, but by his very nature and going far beyond these duties. This ability to pray ought not to be seen as a sectoral occupation in his life, but as a basic structure of his existence, since he is the very man who ought always to accept, as dependent on it, the presence of the absolute mystery facing every man and truly to live it in freedom.

I have, of course, a very bad conscience and almost an aversion, in face of my own inadequacy, to saying anything of this kind. But how can a priest today, confronted by man's rational scepticism, proclaim something of the faith if he has not a genuine, original, religious, and spiritual experience in a sense entirely absorbing him, from which he simply cannot escape? How can he do this unless in his concrete experience of life, in his disappointments and in his fundamental joys, in his love, in fidelity, in his dependence on other people, in his responsibility, in his grief, in his confrontation with death, he is always someone for whom all this means the approach, the closeness of God himself? At a time when there is not a homogeneous Christian public opinion to support our proclamation of the faith and to make it almost inescapable for the normal human being, at a time when none of this exists any longer, we cannot simply say in the light of Scripture: 'That's how it is, there is a loving God and there are grace and eternity, etc.' I must discover in myself and also in others and make increasingly clear such a religious, original experience of existence (which can be freely rejected but is inescapable) open to the mystery of God, and then speak from this centre. How precisely this is done and how it 'comes off', and how an actual failure in this respect can be given a religious interpretation, are additional questions which cannot be discussed here, since that would take us too far. But we ought to be able to start out from an original, religious experience in this sense, which is prior, not in time, but by its nature, to verbalized, objectified Christianity as officially taught and institutionalized; otherwise we shall get nowhere today. How many people we then reach or do not reach is another question and not one that is really of the greatest importance.

Anyone, I might say, who has taken up music seriously will not allow his attitude to music to be affected by the fact that there are musical philistines for whom it is no more than complicated noise. It is more or less similar in the sphere of religion. The priest under any circumstances ought to be a man of personal prayer, a mystic. I do not want to presuppose or to develop any theology of mysticism. In the classical understanding of mysticism it has been seen too much as a higher sphere of religious experience, accessible only to a very few chosen individuals. I do not deny that such a conception has a certain importance and contains some truth. But in the last resort, measured against the extraordinary psychological states of mystics like John of the Cross and others, faith, hope, and love are not something lying beneath these states, something merely ordinary, but that which permeates these extraordinary phenomena of submergence and the like and is wholly accessible as properly religious experience also to the normal Christian and particularly to the priest—in fact, to anyone who faces in freedom the radical incomprehensibility, depth, and absoluteness of his existence toward God.

A second thing that might be said is that the priest of today and tomorrow is the poor priest who willingly admits this poverty into his actual existence and gives it a positive emphasis there. There can be no doubt that the Church, measured against social conditions elsewhere, is increasingly becoming a poor Church; the only question is whether or not we accept this poverty as the occurrence, the jump-off base, for man's ultimate crucified transcendentality (radicalized by grace) into the incomprehensible mystery of God. In this sense poverty has of course, not only an economic, but also a cultural dimension. Certainly the priest today (like yesterday and tomorrow) should not be a philistine, an uncouth person, or anything of that kind. But the fact remains that if a professional ventures to carry his whole existence into a very special dimension of possible human existence, he must in some sense be the poorer, must be prepared for renunciation in regard to other dimensions. This holds quite generally. Could you imagine a musician practising at the piano for eight hours every day and then having an equal interest in other hobbies and occupations which are possible without any reservations for other people? He renounces one thing or another and we priests, who, in a sense, invest our whole life with all its resources, tasks, and possibilities in this religious existence, can nevertheless enjoy a glass of wine, do a little photography, or get away for a holiday, etc. The priest should certainly not use his piety as an excuse for cultural, intellectual, scientific philistinism, but he should see clearly that he must have the courage to be poor even from a cultural standpoint, not to have his finger in every pie everywhere, not to be keeping up with everything, not even to be tempted to do this sort of thing, and not to think he has to use a thousand secular privileges to win support for his task.

In this sense there is also a kind of cultural poverty of the priest that is part of his nature and his life. It is by no means our task or our duty to want to be in the top class in all the dimensions of the very differentiated cultural, intellectual, scientific, and artistic life of the present time. We should not renounce these things out of philistinism, uncouthness, laziness, or lack of interest, but in this respect we should *want* (occasionally to a very considerable extent) to be poor, if only because no one, with his time, with the finiteness of his resources, and even with the finiteness of his heart, can do everything at once and because this kind of renunciation, this crucifixion of the inward person, a renunciation of quite legitimate dimensions of human existence, is in fact the way in which we constantly break through into the mystery of God himself.

The fact that there is then also something like a spiritual poverty is really obvious to someone who provides himself with a few key words from the theology of mysticism. I get worried and uncomfortable sometimes when I hear my fellow Christians and preachers of the Gospel proclaiming that the meaning and fulfillment of life can be found only with and through and in God. Of course, in the last resort, this is true. But at the same time do we not often forget that God is the meaning of our life as the God of incomprehensible judgments, as the God whom we simply cannot take into account as a fixed and definite factor in our life, as the God of freedom, as the God of incomprehensibility? In mystical experience there is something that is described as 'night': in other words, as poverty, as an ultimate innermost threat to our existence, to which the only response is to summon up the last resources of faith, hope, and love for this incomprehensible God. Of course, we Christians should be cheerful, serene, uninhibited, showing people that it is possible and desirable even at the present time to find space in our lives for something like joy in the senses, for festivity, celebration, serenity, for laughter, lightheartedness, and frankness.

All this is true and enormously important, but we need not act as if we did not also break free from ourselves to fall into God's incomprehensibility where we know nothing more. In face of this world of horrors, of inevitabilities, of dead ends, of terrors, of 'Auschwitzes', how can I offer today a theodicy, a justification of God? How can I put forward credibly such a theodicy, if I am not sure that there is in the last resort nothing left but man's capitulation, also in spiritual poverty, before God. If someone today can go to his death serene and composed, confidently and happily, there can certainly be no objection to this. But neither can there be any objection if, in an ultimate tribulation, in an ultimate poverty, torn away from ourselves, we have to die into the darkness of what is called God. In brief, there is a kind of spiritual poverty that we by no means want to deny or suppose. The troubled Christian who feels that too much is asked of him, the Christian who prays with Jesus 'My God, my God, why have you deserted me?', who consequently does not by any means die with Socratic serenity, is not perhaps the only possible and conceivable Christian, but he is also a genuine Christian who attains the peak of his perfection precisely in the abyss of his spiritual emptiness and poverty.

This threefold poverty—economic, cultural, and spiritual—is part of Christianity, of Christian existence, and of Christian spirituality in general, but nevertheless for that very reason is something required particularly from the priest and particularly today.

In the third place it must be said that the priest today is primarily the servant of the faith of others. Father Zulehner has rightly made the extraordinarily important statement that we cannot assume today the existence of Christians as baptized, as already indoctrinated and structured by a universal, homogeneous, Christian public opinion, but must be mystagogues of faith for them. Consequently we have no reason for not accepting without prejudice this necessity of ours to be continually learning the faith afresh. We need not behave as if we were not threatened in our faith and could take it for granted. We should not trifle with temptations of faith on the ground that they are not doubts of faith in the strictly moral theological sense; we do not need to make blunders like this. There is certainly also a religious experience that embraces all these possibilities of a Christian existence in struggling with temptation, in poverty, in darkness, in a sense in joy and peace, and that can really give a person the feeling or, better, the existential experience, a final awareness, of actually not being able at all to escape or lose God, since God's apparent remoteness itself attests and makes present God precisely as God. But this again does not exclude the fact that we ourselves have also a history of faith, that we must be lifelong adventurers of God in ever new situations.

Formerly, Christian spirituality was conceived as an ascent to a height of what was called 'Christian perfection', with the ways and stages of this ascent in a sense outlined and marked out in advance by the theology of the spiritual life. Today the older priest is less likely to have the impression that he has become more perfect than he was at the beginning; he will see himself as someone who is led by God's providence in his life history through continually new and surprising situations, in which he can never say from the outset what will happen and how he must cope with it. When St. Teresa of Lisieux was apparently tempted most of all in the final stages of her life (as compared with earlier stages), for that very reason she had reached the summit of her perfection. The courage to recognize from the outset that we are involved in a lifelong adventure which cannot be calculated in advance is part of our priestly existence today if we want to be the servants of the faith of others.

There is a further point. And now I really am getting onto thin ice. I am absolutely convinced that, apart from a special vocation from God (which may certainly exist), a priest like myself should and must devote his life—all his time and all his strength—to normal priestly functions, and that the present shortage of priests makes it impossible for the Church to do without this kind of commitment. Nevertheless, as a result of a number of experiences, I think that a certain spirituality associated with true worker-priests (if not the concrete calling itself) might be a critical, generative factor for our priestly life. The courage to be and to remain sociologically inferior, to live a life in which one belongs in some way to the underprivileged, to the plebes; the courage to lead a life in which one is no longer the village pope, in which one does not simply belong to the educated classes and where academic status counts for nothing; the courage to live shoulder to shoulder with the poor where life is bitter, monotonous, dull: all these things are characteristic of the mentality of genuine worker-priests (and I know some of them) who do not want to be worker-priests in order to abandon (like certain types) their priestly self-understanding. This is a mentality which could have a critical sting, an evocative power for us.

I must say that for me these people represent something of a threat to a well-provided bourgeois existence and may frighten us out of assuming that this existence is normal and to be taken for granted. A number of conclusions may be drawn. Although what I said earlier remains important, I think that the priest today must be something of a nonconformist. That is not to say that he should be an inveterate grumbler, forever complaining, continually at odds with his bishop and with Rome: all these infantilisms are ruled out from the beginning. But if the Church is permanently a Church also of sinners and if this sinfulness has its effect on the exercise of office, if, in this way, office by its nature necessarily leads to the temptation to institutional harshness, crudeness, reactionary attitudes, it cannot be said that a certain critical dissociation from what is actually practised in the name of office in the Church is something that is incompatible with a present-day priestly image. This should be sufficient on this topic.

The priest of today will necessarily always be overtaxed: overtaxed between what he is and what (as he himself knows) he ought to be, overtaxed by people, overtaxed by the Gospel, overtaxed by his office, overtaxed by his time. It should be noticed that this is itself the concreteness of his existential transcendence, not his speculation about transcendence. Consequently it is possible to face this continually excessive pressure with a certain composure. It acquires a positive meaning. It can be admitted that it would be terrible if I no longer had to distinguish between what ought to be and what in fact I am and what I achieve. To be able and to have to entrust our own finiteness, wretchedness, even sinfulness, completely and utterly to God and his grace: all this is part of Christian and priestly existence. As priests, we are not and need not be the sort of people who can imagine that they have done everything well and as the great experts and men of achievement ought to make a triumphant entry with flying colours into God's eternity. With Teresa of Lisieux we shall have to admit that we come at the end of our life as wretched sinners to God and it would be a terrible self-deception to think that we had 'made it'; we have the right (if I may put it in that way) to feel in a blessed defiance that we are the people from whom too much is expected. The fewer priests there are, the more we shall be in this sense the ones who are overtaxed.

It is impossible to do much more here than to suggest the headings under which some other points might be considered. In his present-day priestly existence the priest must be familiar with theology. I am not saying this simply because I have been teaching this strange science all my life. Anyone who has to proclaim the Gospel responsibly today—not merely to a few schoolchildren eager to learn and young enough to accept everything without reserve, but to the present-day despisers of Christianity—is in a difficult situation. He cannot preach that kind of neo-Protestantism which is prepared to sell off cheaply the true, Christian, completely Catholic faith, he may not offer people no more than what their superficial humanism prepares them to accept from the outset; but neither may he use expressions or adopt attitudes in regard to the faith he offers which create unnecessary difficulties for others. I think it must also be said that Rome, feeling bound to address the whole world at once, is in a desperately difficult situation. And it seems to me that Rome has not yet come round to saying the things that have to be said in a way that avoids sufficiently the difficulties and abrasions which could and ought to be avoided. Rome, too, ought to do more theology. But this is true also for us. Despite all 'mystical existential experience' coming from this innermost centre, we are the ones who have to present a verbalized doctrine which itself comes from the Church and requires, not only personal religious experience, but also a continually fresh recourse to the Church's teaching and to the work that is and must be accomplished by theology for the understanding of the Church's teaching.

There is a further point that I can indicate also only as a problem, without answering it. In the Church's practice there was a period of sacramental enthusiasm when it was tacitly assumed, if not explicitly taught, that grace is conveyed primarily and actually more or less solely in the sacraments as such and exclusively there. This is wrong and contrary also to present-day mystical, religious experience. It remains an open question also for our spirituality whether we are really drawn in an ultimate existential radicalness into our destiny precisely in the sacramental celebration of the death and resurrection of Jesus, or at the point where we see our life as a failure, or where we die, or where we go on living in an ultimate incomprehensibility of an unselfish love or freely exercising a responsibility that is not radically accepted or recognized by anyone else. Obviously a priest should attempt to direct his religious life so patiently, so impartially, so lovingly that he has always a positive relationship (one that stimulates his religious existence) to sacramental events in the Church. But a religious life of grace, experience of the Spirit, and sacramental life are not simply identical, and the priest, although he is the functionary of the sacramental aspect of the Church, need not act as if they were. If for any reasons at all, connected with his individual lot in life, someone cannot honestly claim that carrying out the eucharistic cult or administering the sacraments is even existentially the high point of his life, he has no need to lie, no need to talk or act as if it were. He can always do this sort of thing with sufficient involvement, if he goes about it in a reasonable way; he can also, of course, celebrate the eucharist simply when he wants to do so, like Ignatius of Loyola or Philip Neri, the latter having his full, consecrated chalice in front of him for hours, sipping from it every quarter of an hour and for the rest living immersed in God. All I wanted to do was to point out that experience of grace and sacramental celebration are not simply the same thing and that the two are often separated even in priestly life and a person's individual organization of his life and lot can be readily and naturally accepted in this respect.

I had wanted finally in a nonpolitical sense to refer at least briefly to the political dimension of priestly spirituality. What I mean by this will be understood by anyone who reads without prejudice and with good will the paper produced by the joint synod of the dioceses of the German Federal Republic in 1978: 'Our Hope: A Profession of Faith in Our Time'.[3] I do not think that we must or should practise politics in a banal, commonplace sense. But I think that the unity of love of God and love of neighbour, the knowledge that where we stand by the poor, persecuted, underprivileged there is or can be an intimate experience of grace, and that an ultimate transcendentality of man radicalized by grace into the mystery of God and a self-renunciation in love of neighbour represent the two aspects of the one Christian life, the unity of love of God and love of neighbour—in the last resort, that is what I understand here as the political dimension of priestly spirituality; and that is something quite important.

Insofar as we experience this transcendentality of grace in the following of Christ, we cannot say as a result of an abstract reflection that we are equally indifferent to poverty and riches, higher status and lower status. Jesus fought (but not as a political revolutionary) unequivocally on the side of the poor, the persecuted, the plebs, and did not rise above them in glorious neutrality. The synodal paper says more or less that we can put up with the opposition of the educated and the clever, but that the Church cannot dissociate

[3] 'Unsere Hoffnung' in *Gemeinsame Synode der Bistümer in der Bundesrepublik Deutschland,* Official complete edition, vol. 1, ed. L. Bertsch, S. J., et al. (Freiburg, 1978), pp. 84–111.

itself from the disappointment of the poor, of the disappointed, of the persecuted; nevertheless, the Church has been and remains today too much a Church of the middle classes. This does not mean breaking out at once in wild revolution against it. But it does mean that we ought to feel a sting and an unease in regard to the image of our Church and that the priest ought to feel these things in his spirituality since he, too, experiences God's grace only where he becomes poor with the poor and counts them among his friends. In that sense there is something like a political dimension to our own spirituality.

PART THREE

Life in the Church

10

ON THE THEOLOGY OF WORSHIP

It is obvious that in an essay of a few pages only one or two somewhat arbitrarily chosen remarks can be made on the theology of worship. From the outset there is no intention of having recourse explicitly to the teaching of Scripture or the Church's magisterium. If the starting point of these reflections consists mainly in general questions of sacramental theology as a whole and of the Church's actual worship as such, as distinct from other sacramental happenings that thus remain somewhat in the background, this may be admitted from the outset. Anyone who understands and can accept what is said here can easily draw for himself further conclusions with references to worship in the strict sense.[1]

It seems to me that in the Church's consciousness there are two different conceptual models for God's grace as it operates in human history. I use the expression 'conceptual models' because the question of whether the ways envisaged here of considering grace are in reality mutually contradictory will not be raised at all, still less decided. Nor will it be claimed that they are regarded in the Church's actual sense of faith as strictly isolated and wholly disconnected from one another and mutually contradictory; it is not denied that the two models exist together in the Church's concrete awareness, even though the emphasis on one or the other is considerably different. Nevertheless, they are different. And this diversity itself arises from a still more universal and fundamental difference in the ways in

[1] The reflections in this essay touch closely on those put forward under the title 'Considerations on the Active Role of the Person in the Sacramental Event' in *Theological Investigations,* vol. 14 (London/New York, 1976), pp. 161–84.

which God's relationship to the world is seen. But this, too, is something that cannot be discussed here.

The *first* way of seeing the operation of divine grace in the world considers that operation first of all and primarily as an intervention of God in the world at a definite point in space and time. The world is regarded in the first place as secular, both because of what we call 'nature' and because of the inherited sinful state of this history of the world and humanity. If, then, forgiving and deifying salutary grace (as God's self-communication) is supposed nevertheless to be present in the world, this presence is conceived as an intervention of God at a certain point in space and time, as (we might say) 'actual grace'. This conceptual model of grace is based on the implicit assumption that grace can be an unmerited gift of God only if it becomes present and only where it becomes present in a secular and sinful world to which it is mostly denied. From this initial position it is easy to understand the sacraments. They are then seen as events at certain points in space and time (with a quite definite modality which need not be examined more closely here) where grace comes to be in a world otherwise deprived of it. It is easy then to understand the causality of the sacraments: they produce something not otherwise available. From this standpoint also it can be understood why in a theology of the sacraments dominated by this conceptual model the baptism of infants (who are assumed to be previously lacking grace) is regarded as the ideal type for sacraments as such, even though with particular sacraments (of the 'living', etc.) qualifications and reservations have to be made. But even in cases in which a sacramental event presupposes a 'state of grace', this state is regarded merely as an objective and moral *precondition* and not a something which itself acts as a cause and is manifested in this sacramental event (as such always coming freshly 'from outside'). Even with the sacraments of the 'living', which presuppose the presence of justifying grace, the model of infant baptism remains predominant: grace is effected in the sacraments, not as being brought there to historical and ecclesial manifestation, but as produced purely as the effect of the sacraments.

The *second* way of considering the operation of grace starts out from the assumption that the secular world from the outset is always encompassed and permeated with the grace of the divine self-communication. This grace is always and everywhere present in the world. It is, of course, present either in the form of a pure offer to freedom (not yet decisively possessed) with 'infants', or in the form of acceptance with the 'justified' person or of rejection with the sinner (a rejection which does not mean that it ceases to be the sinner's demanding and orienting existential); but it *is*, always and everywhere. Its unmeritedness does not prevent it from being the existential always and everywhere present at the very heart of human existence. In the last resort, world as 'nature' is not plain and obvious reality, totally involved with itself, to which grace is added (so to speak) subsequently as the result of a kind of secondary decision of God; from the outset God is lovingly seeking in freedom to bestow himself and, because he so wills in freedom, because he wills grace, he must create a 'nature' to which he can impart himself as free love. Nature is, because grace has to be. From the outset, as ground of nature, grace is the innermost centre of this nature. Consequently, nature is never actually purely and simply secular; it is always nature graciously endowed with God himself. When and where it finds expression in personal freedom, this freedom means the acceptance of this innermost centre of reality, acceptance of God and thus of salvation history.

This salvation history is not made up of successive spatio-temporal interventions of God in an otherwise secular world, but is the history of freedom (of God and man) which accepts this innermost and enduring deification of the world, gives it historical expression and thus itself constitutes the history of this deification of the world. In this way grace is understood, not primarily as 'actual', but as 'habitual' grace. There is a salvation history as history of divine and human freedom, but the latter is precisely the history of the ever present deification of the world by God's self-communication, through which alone salvation history can be conceived at all and hence the history of the world must be understood even in a true and radical sense as history of God. The sacraments accordingly are not really to be understood as successive individual incursions of God into a secular world, but as 'outbursts' (if we can express it in this way) of the innermost, ever present gracious endowment of the world with God himself into history.

This manifestation of the ever present deification of the world in historical events is, of course, involved not only in the sacraments, but wherever man accepts himself as such in freedom. Properly speaking, this is something taken for granted in Catholic theology. For this theology teaches that *every* 'salutary act' sustained by divine grace is a realization of this grace and consequently its 'augmentation' implies a more radical acceptance by man's freedom and the establishment of deeper roots in man's existence. Grace, then, occurs, not only and not even primarily in the sacraments, but wherever a person accepts and realizes in freedom his existence as it is, as radically and immediately dependent on God. If this Catholic teaching on the deification of our free acts by grace (by the 'theological virtues') is correct and taken seriously, then there is actually no merely secular sphere (in the dimension of truly existential freedom) lying *alongside* the sacral sphere, the latter being made up of sacramental and ecclesial occurrences. In ordinary language what is known as the sacral sphere (comprising sacraments, liturgy, worship) is better understood simply as a definite individual materialization (fundamentally necessary and binding on man) *within* that sacral sphere which is brought into existence by the grace that is everywhere present and effective and which coincides concretely with the sphere of existential freedom as a whole as a reflex self-awareness of the grace everywhere present and effective, finding expression in the sphere of the explicit word and the ecclesial community.

As we said earlier, we wanted first of all only to put forward these two conceptual models of grace, without opting absolutely for one or the other. The first conceptual model will certainly not be simply rejected here: it elucidates the unmeritedness of grace, the unpredictable historicity of grace in its realization, the sacraments as causes of grace (a doctrine which must be maintained in accordance with the Council of Trent), although this does not imply that these truths can be maintained and expressed only in the light of this conceptual model. This, it seems to me, is not the case. If grace is understood (as in the second model) as universal ground of salvation history, it does not for that reason cease to have an actual history, for it must be realized concretely in the history of man's freedom. As man's 'nature' is realized in history and nevertheless is the universal ground of this history, the same is true of grace. It is the ground of salvation history, which is itself realized in that history. Without simply rejecting the first conceptual model, then, it is possible to maintain that the second is at least more intelligible and easier to reconstruct for people today. In particular it gets away from the idea that salvific grace necessarily takes the form of an intervention by God from outside at a definite point in space and time: an idea which for people today somehow savours of the miraculous and mythological. In a more extensive substantiation of the legitimacy and sufficiency of the second conceptual model, it would, of course, have to be shown more precisely that here, too, there is a place for a rightly understood theory of sacramental causality, that there is a difference between a baptized and an unbaptized infant, that infant baptism, even if not absolutely necessary, is at least meaningful and something for which parents must accept responsibility in an ecclesial community. It is impossible to explain all this more closely here; but it can be done and has been done elsewhere. All we are looking for here is a further elucidation of the nature of Christian worship in the light of this second conceptual model.

Admittedly there are many aspects of the nature of Christian worship which are left out of consideration here. We are not considering really explicitly the communal and sociological character of Christian worship, which is derived from the nature of the Church and ultimately from the unity of humanity in its salvation history. We are not considering the differentiations of the Church's worship as they arise out of the diversity and the unity of word and sacrament. We are not asking here when we have liturgy in the proper sense of the term or how it is distinguished from private prayer and private gatherings for prayer. The idea of 'feast', or 'celebration', which finds expression preeminently in worship, is not under consideration here. We are not speaking about the political or eschatological character of worship. We are not asking whether or how the sociological and hierarchical character of the Church must be brought out in worship. The general anthropological presuppositions of worship are left aside. Many other things which ought to be considered in a theology of Christian worship remain unmentioned. As we said, all we are attempting here is to consider a little more concretely the conclusions in regard to worship that can be drawn from the second conceptual model of grace. If all aspects of grace itself could be explicitly described or assumed as clear and apparent, it would also be possible to deduce from this second conceptual model of grace an entire theology of worship in all its aspects. The possibility is all the more obvious since grace by its very nature has a communal, sociological character, orienting man in every respect, and consequently also as a social being, to God. But, since it is impossible here either to elucidate or simply to presuppose these aspects of grace, our reflections must remain fragmentary.

In the light of this second conceptual model the Church's worship is not the installation of a primarily sacramental sphere in a profane, secular world, it is not an event otherwise without roots in reality, but the explicit and reflex, symbolic presentation of the salvation event which is occurring always and everywhere in the world; the liturgy of the Church is the symbolic presentation of the liturgy of the world. This does not diminish its significance. For its significance consists in the very fact that it presents the liturgy of the world spatio-temporally and in sociological explicitness and thus conveys to man an explicit and reflex enactment of this liturgy of the world, of salvation history. The liturgy of the world, in which anyway we are always involved and which reaches its culmination in the cross of the Son, is seen by man in his dreary existence only through a haze, obscured by the banal ordinariness of life. It has to be reflected and elevated to the explicitness of the word and its sociological presence. It is true that something of the explicitness and reflection of this liturgy, which is identical with the whole history of humanity, is necessarily always part of man and his history, and consequently there are religions always and everywhere. But this reflex explicitness of the world liturgy as it comes to be has its own history and it is not left to our discretion what point we want to occupy in the history of this process of becoming explicit. As history of the world's freedom, this liturgy attains its irreversibility in Jesus Christ, his cross and resurrection; and if and insofar as we have come in the history of our individual freedom to know this culmination of the universal history of salvation, of the world liturgy, it is no longer left to our discretion whether or not we want to allow this historical achievement of the explicit irreversibility of salvation history in Jesus Christ to be reflected and made explicit also in our life, whether or not we take part in bringing out the reflex explicitness of the culmination of the liturgy of the world in the liturgy of the Church.

As existences incarnate in space and time, we Christians are subject not only to the 'must' of allowing man's transcendental essential realities and his existentials (of which grace, too, is always and everywhere a part) to find explicitness in some conceivable way in space and time, but also to the 'must' of giving to the actually attained culmination of this history of spatio-temporal explicitness of grace in Jesus Christ space and time in our own life: of celebrating (which is the same thing) the Church's worship. When we say that we celebrate the death of the Lord until he returns, we are saying that we are giving space and time explicitly in our own life to the culmination of the history of the world liturgy which is present in the cross of Jesus (the culmination of both this history itself and also its spatio-temporal reflex explicitness). Consequently what happens in worship of this kind is not something that does not occur or has not permanently occurred elsewhere in the world, but something that occurs always and everywhere or has occurred for all time and for everywhere in the world, and is explicitly celebrated, stated, and appropriated. This ecclesial worship is important and significant, not because something happens in it that does not happen elsewhere, but because there is present and explicit in it that which makes the world important, since it is everywhere blessed by grace, by faith, hope, and love, and in it there occurred the cross of Christ, which is the culmination of its engraced history and the culmination of the historical explicitness of this history of grace. To anyone who has (or might have had) absolutely no experience in his own life of this history of grace of the world, no experience of the cosmic liturgy, the Church's liturgy could only seem like a strange ritualism, as strange as the sacrificial action of a Vedic priest who feeds the gods and thinks that by his action he is keeping the world on its tracks.

As we said earlier, at this point the essential qualities of Christian grace, as they find expression in the Church's worship, ought to be explained more precisely. It ought to be shown how this grace is the ground of an ultimate unity of mankind in itself and with God; its eschatological character as pledge of the final consummation stressed, it ought to be made clear how in the history of freedom of the world this grace has already found its irreversible victory in the cross of Christ. It ought to be shown (and this is of decisive importance) how this grace has its history in man's day-to-day existence with its splendours and failures and is actually experienced there. Only then could it be really shown and made clear how these aspects and characteristics of this grace are given a new, reflex manifestation and presence in the celebration of the act of worship. It is impossible to explain all this in greater detail here. But perhaps enough has been said to indicate in what the real ground of the Church's worship and the right understanding of it consists.

The pastoral situation for gaining a genuine understanding of the Church's worship is very complex today and consequently obscure. Certainly there are many people even today who come to learn through worship itself, through its outward shape and through the natural way in which it is carried out, that God's grace becomes an event here in the midst of a world which they experience only as profane and godless. There are certainly people like this. It is certainly right to use every possible means to shape the act of worship in such a way that it operates on its own account as an event of grace in a secular world. Where there are (still) people like this (for a great variety of historical and sociological reasons) and where the attempt to leave the Church's worship to make its own impact and its own appeal is largely successful, it will be possible still to bring home the idea of worship from the standpoint of the first conceptual model of grace. But the fact cannot be concealed that to very many people today worship is at first seen as a kind of magical procedure and as an old-fashioned ritual now devoid of meaning, while they have the impression that a true encounter with God (if it is possible at all) must take place in the dull bitterness of ordinary life with its experiences of hope, responsibility, love, and death.

These are people who find themselves and God in 'life' (as they say) and not in ecclesial-liturgical ceremonial. If a way of access to the Church's liturgy is to be opened up for them (and they seem to be the great majority today), it can only be from the standpoint of the second conceptual model of grace. It must be admitted readily and without hesitation to such people that grace, encounter with God, can occur and does actually occur in the ordinary routine of secular life. Prior to any kind of defence of the Church's liturgy, for these people in the first place there must be produced a clear way of access to the depths of their own existence, where God has communicated himself from the very beginning and where he offers himself to man's freedom. In the first place a mystagogy (if we may use the term) of the mysticism of ordinary life is necessary; it must be shown that he whom we call God is always present from the very outset and even already accepted, as infinite offer, as silent love, as absolute future, wherever a person is faithful to his conscience and breaks out of the prison walls of his selfishness. With these people such a mystagogy is a necessary presupposition for an understanding of the Church's worship. If this understanding is to be awakened, they must be shown that worship is the explicit celebration of the divine depth of their ordinary life, that what clearly appears in it and consequently can be more decisively accepted in freedom is what occurs always and everywhere in the ordinary course of life. These people must be helped to understand that the very fact that God is worshiped in spirit everywhere (and not only in Jerusalem) is itself made explicit and celebrated in the worship of the Church.

It is perhaps an exaggeration to describe (as I once did) the transition from the first to the second conceptual model of grace as a 'Copernican turning point.' It is an exaggeration, since the first conceptual model never entirely alone and on its own account determined the sense of faith of people in the Church; an exaggeration also because care must certainly be taken in preaching not to overlook for the practice of the Christian life *those* aspects and characteristics of grace which are less explicit in the second conceptual model. The transition cannot be regarded as so sharp, since the second conceptual model does not exclude the fact that the acceptance of grace offered universally is always a free act of the human person and thus makes the salvation event into an *historical* happening and since this free acceptance of universal grace itself depends again on God's free decision, which can neither be theoretically explained nor worked out in advance. But these aspects of grace, which are more clearly and more immediately evident in the first conceptual model, may also not be overlooked or passed over in silence in a theology of worship. On the other hand, it also remains true that the second conceptual scheme offers people today a better way of access to the understanding of grace and thus also of worship. Consequently priests ought to make sure that this model is really present in their concrete preaching. Then worship will be seen, not as a strange, reserved, special region in secular life, not as divine liturgy *in* the world, but as the divine liturgy *of* the world, as manifestation of the divine liturgy which is identical with salvation history.

11

THE SUNDAY PRECEPT IN AN INDUSTRIAL SOCIETY

MEMORIAL OF SALVATION

In order to say something intelligent about Sunday and to cover somehow all the problems involved, we ought *first* to ask about the exact meaning in the Old Testament of the Sabbath precept, of sanctifying the Sabbath. Undoubtedly there were religious and social reasons for it. The precept was meant for all in Israel: slaves, as far as there were any, normal and ordinary people, the better off, and even the beasts. But I do not want to say more here about this Sabbath precept.

Second, something ought to be said about the historical and theological aspects of the adoption of this precept in the Church of Jesus Christ. Here of course (and this has primarily and directly nothing to do with Israel) should be mentioned the peculiarity that the Church continually celebrates afresh in the weekly liturgical sequence the resurrection of Jesus as a unique historical and fundamental salvation event. A theological content is thus available which was not present in the Old Testament celebration of the Sabbath, even though behind all these celebrations there is a basic human datum: the fact that man can celebrate and should celebrate in a temporal sequence the anamnesis (memory) of events that occurred once and for all in salvation history. Admittedly, this is a theological problem for its own sake and extends to these solemnities as a whole. I do not know exactly what the situation was in the Old Testament or in later Jewish times, if and in what sense the Sabbath observance had anything to do with the exodus from Egypt. It might be said anyway that the Sabbath precept in Israel, too, had an anamnestic (commemorative) dimension in terms of salvation history and was related at least to God's rest on the seventh day of creation. In a word and in any case, in the Christian celebration of Sunday there is a reference to a quite definite event of salvation history, so that the question arises as to how, why, and for what existential-ontological reasons man is the being that can celebrate historical events which are apparently simply past. And what is the meaning of such an anamnesis? Is it merely historicist reflection, inspired by a certain historical curiosity, on a past event which nevertheless cannot in this way really be brought up again out of the depths of the past? Is it possible with the aid of this kind of recollection to make something like this present in the proper sense of the term or, so to speak, continually to repeat it? But in regard to this second point also I should not discuss here the Christian acceptance of the Sabbath precept as a way of recalling the death and resurrection of Jesus.

PRECEPT OF THE CHURCH

Third, however, I want to say something quite different. Although somewhat disguised in the ordinary course of preaching, according to the Church's universal teaching, there is no Old Testament precept which, as such, is still binding on Christians. And among these abrogated precepts is that of the Sabbath observance. If a Christian preacher insists on the Church's Sunday precept by recalling the thunder and lightning of God's holy covenant on Sinai, he is telling lies, he is asserting something that simply does not make sense. We must say, then, that the Sunday precept properly speaking is not a divine precept, either in the light of man's permanent nature (as preternaturally or supernaturally elevated) or in the light of the Old Testament: it is and remains a precept of the Church. That the Church has a right to issue a precept of this kind and that this right and the fulfillment of the precept by the individual Christian have also deeper, more universal foundations and grounds, this again is a different question. That a human person is a worshiping being, that the Christian in his religious existence must necessarily relate again and again to the death and resurrection of Jesus, that, consequently, he must (to express it somewhat prosaically in terms of moral theology) from time to time take part in the eucharistic memorial celebration of this death and resurrection of Jesus, all these are deeper reasons justifying the Church's Sunday precept; but the requirement of attending mass on Sundays and, as we used to say, abstaining from servile work is a precept of the Church and basically no more than that. That the concrete form of this precept, its interpretation, the strictness or elasticity of the interpretation, are conditioned historically is something we have certainly experienced in recent decades.

BINDING UNDER PAIN OF GRAVE SIN?

Fourth, if we recognize soberly, honestly, and without dissimulation, that it is a question here of a positive precept of the Church, then (independently now of the question of a conceivable or not conceivable, a desirable or not desirable, further development of the concrete shape of this precept) it is in any case clear that the precept is open to all the restrictions and interpretations appropriate to a human precept, which simply does not directly involve man's eternal nature nor, consequently, his permanent supernatural determination by grace as such. Obviously, a positive precept of the Church is open to many more possible interpretations and can more easily cease to bind in the concrete individual case as a result of excusing causes or other reasons than a properly divine precept of natural law or a divine precept of the supernatural order as such. It can really be taken for granted also today that an individual can consider himself dispensed in the concrete from the Sunday precept of participation at mass, not only because of sickness, but for other sound reasons. There is no need here to go into the casuistry of how there can be reasons for dispensation from the obligation of Sunday mass, or what these are. That is a different question, with which other people can amuse themselves. In any case, on the one hand we should take this Sunday precept seriously (even though it is no more than a precept of the Church) and, on the other hand, we have the Christian's liberty to interpret and apply these human statutes and precepts with a certain magnanimity and inner freedom. I do not know if this could be a practical rule of thumb (that is somcthing for the moralists to consider), but I would say that whenever and in whatever cases the inner existential and supernatural justification of the Sunday precept is not conclusive for the individual case, the Church's precept as such is not to be regarded in that individual case as binding under pain of grave sin.

We might presumably attempt to justify this proposition from various aspects. It might even be said that the Church can by no means impose an obligation, as we say, under pain of grave sin, unless it is also required for deeper reasons by natural law or supernaturally by law or morality. But we may also perhaps leave aside a universal justification of this kind and face the situation at the present time. There now exists in fact in the Church a mentality (which is not opposed by the institutional Church) which regards the Church's precept (even though it amounts to more than this in its formal implications and authority) as not really binding under pain of grave sin, unless participation in the eucharistic sacrifice is seriously required as a result of an existential and mental-spiritual necessity. What exactly do I mean by this?

ANALOGY WITH OTHER PRECEPTS

From the very nature of the case and in the light of his faith, a normal Christian is obviously aware that he must frequently take part in the celebration of the eucharist, whether there is a precept of the Church to that effect or not. An obligation of this kind, which arises, so to speak, from the nature of things and which already or again exists as an institutional arrangement quite independently of the properly official precept of the Church, can certainly not be proved to be binding in the concrete every Sunday. But a Christian should have the good sense to admit that he would certainly be basically, if not perhaps also expressly, denying his inner, fundamental, essential relatedness (conferred by baptism) to the incarnational structure of the death of the Lord (that is, to his sacramental presence in the eucharist) if he simply did not bother about mass over a long period. This is an obligation that can, of course, become concrete, even if it is impossible to demonstrate mathematically exactly when and where. It is like living in the same house with my mother: Who is to say when I have to talk to her? And if she lives elsewhere, it is impossible to demonstrate on what day I must visit her or for how long. Nevertheless, as a human being and as her child, I have a serious moral obligation toward this woman to realize my personal relatedness to her in the concrete by visiting her. How often that should be cannot be calculated mathematically. Attendance at mass likewise may depend on all kinds of circumstances: on the state of my religious development, on my opportunities or difficulties of being present, on my entire subjective, particular character, etc. One person will perhaps commit a serious offence against love for his mother if he is living in the same town and does not visit her for months. For another, a quarterly visit may be quite sufficient.

EXISTENTIAL OBLIGATION

It is rather similar with the mass. I would say that a Christian ought to know (precept of the Church or not) that he has an obligatory relationship to the Church's eucharistic celebration as the memorial of Jesus' death and resurrection by which he is redeemed. And where an obligation of this kind seems in the light of a reasonable, serious, and scarcely disputable human judgment to find concrete expression, so to speak, and to be concentrated in an actual celebration of mass on a particular Sunday, the Church's precept becomes one that we normally describe as a morally grave obligation. It becomes binding under pain of grave sin.

Where this is not the case, the Christian ought to take part in the eucharistic celebration at least every Sunday, if only because he really should occasionally do something Christian, the omission of which does not bring him at once into serious conflict with God. But apart from that radical obligation, I would claim that the Church's precept is not concretely binding here and now under pain of grave sin. Like the speed limit on the motorway, it is a standard which we must observe in a spirit of both Christian freedom and seriousness. At the same time, the question remains completely open as to when and where in a normal human life there can be an absolute dilemma between the fulfillment of a precept and grave sin (which would lead to eternal perdition). This is not to be tried out in regard to the Sunday precept in particular, since this is not an appropriate test case.

Fifth, we must have regard for a number of consequences of the development of modern industrial society. These include the five-day work week, the varying work periods, the fact that it is very difficult to impose the Sunday precept and participation in the eucharist as binding on people in certain occupations (bus conductors, for example, and the service sector as a whole); the fact that in some places the obligation can be fulfilled by attendance at Saturday evening mass, which, despite biblical analogies, really amounts to a departure from the Sunday precept; the present-day opportunity of other evening masses which in a religious sense and existentially may be more appropriate and convenient for modern people on a weekday than a Sunday mass in particular; the fact that the weekend of Saturday to Sunday or even merely Sunday is rightly seized on by people in the large industrial centres as an opportunity to escape from the concrete cage of the metropolis, to enjoy a longer period of recreation, etc. These and similar facts raise for the Church the question of the situation in principle and generally today in regard to what is known as the Sunday precept.

Briefly, it might be said that this Sunday precept as such, being a positive precept of the Church and not directly a commandment of God, is subject to the Church's discretionary decision and consequently could be abolished. That is not to say that the Church could dispense itself from the task of continually reminding Christians of their relatedness, to be concretely realized, to the sacramental celebration of mass and not merely to the death of the Lord as such. Nevertheless, the Church could abolish the Sunday precept properly so-called and, for example, leave it to individual Christians to decide how to realize this essential relatedness to the eucharistic celebration in their concrete life, likewise how often they would do this and on what days, etc. This is a real possibility.

REASONS FOR MAINTAINING THE TRADITION

At the same time, however, it must be pointed out that it is difficult to say whether the Church *ought* to make its pastoral decision (which cannot be simply arbitrary) on these lines, or could even be *permitted* concretely from a pastoral and human standpoint to do so. In the first place, even at the present time in our modern industrial society, the individual days are not absolutely reduced to a secular level. Monday to Friday amounts in fact to something different from Saturday and Sunday. It might even be said that the two days of the weekend have acquired, as a result of secular cultural and civilisatory developments, more clearly and firmly a special position in regard to the other days. They are freer than they could be formerly. If the farmer's wife nowadays gets her milking machine working comparatively quickly on Sunday, she has in any case more leisure than she had even twenty or thirty years ago, when each cow had to be milked separately. And there is ample evidence that the weekend in secular terms possesses more clearly that civilisatory and cultural status which makes it suitable for a special and even religious demarcation of Saturday and Sunday, or simply of Sunday. Allowing for the greatest magnanimity in detail and in regard to particular groups of people, these and similar reasons could quite appropriately move the Church to keep to the *joint* celebration of the eucharist and the death of the Lord on a particular day.

Of course, many other reasons could be mentioned. Even in a modern society of people supposed to have come of age, the stability of a general practice is something wholly appropriate and useful. It might be said that, even in regard to religious matters, it is unreasonable to leave people too much to their own initiative as isolated individuals. We might point to the fact that even at the present time there are also secular celebrations of important historical events, commemorated in a joint service on a particular day. Whether these are national feast days or youth initiations is immaterial. In any case, while admitting the Church's freedom in principle, as emphasized above, to abolish the Sunday precept (if it seemed better to do so), it might nevertheless be asked if the Church today could and should uphold the precept if it is rightly understood. For whatever cannot be proved conclusively to be necessary in the light of man's nature must not be regarded on that account as superfluous.

It must be remembered that man lives and can live not only from those things whose metaphysical and transcendental necessity can be proved. It must be remembered that a person cannot expect whatever he does or ought to do or what is perhaps even required of him to be proved to be irrevocably necessary. It is impossible to prove transcendentally that we ought to shake hands when we meet or part from someone. Nevertheless, it is reasonable to do so and anyone who denies this in principle, maintaining that theoretically we might just as well rub noses, is an idiot who is determined from the very outset not to admit the undemonstrable and yet factual and meaningful realities of human life which must be respected if life is to go on. Of course, the Church can appropriately keep to the Sunday precept, as we said, justifying this by a reasonable explanation, interpretation and eventually the application of casuistry to the precept. In my opinion, if the Sunday precept is maintained and interpreted with Christian freedom, it will not involve any unsurmountable pastoral difficulties, not even in the present-day society.

INFLUENCE ON SECULAR SOCIETY

There is a further consideration. It is basically true that the cultural and civilisatory development of modern society, with its faceless masses, its flexible working hours, etc., has brought with it a situation which is not particularly favourable to the Church's Sunday precept. But we can at least raise the question of whether the Church must look on, so to speak, indifferently or passively at these secular developments and then introduce slight changes in present arrangements in order to give effect to the pastoral conclusions from secular reality as it is and otherwise to do nothing. We could certainly ask why the Church (for good reasons and without claiming a predominance over the secularized, profane society) should not intervene to influence directly the trend of development in that society. After the Russians, at the beginning of the Bolshevist regime, had introduced an absolutely flexible working week which inevitably made no distinction between Sunday and any other day, they apparently gradually came to see that their plan humanly and reasonably was not particularly wonderful or glorious and, if I am correctly informed, returned to a common rest day. The opportunity could arise for the Church to contribute, perhaps even with merely secular and human arguments, to the further development of secular society in a direction more favourable to the Sunday rest, the Sunday precept, the Sunday celebration, more than the trend seems to have been up to now. It would indeed be a good thing if on one day the noise in the streets were to cease more or less entirely, if there were one day no lorries were traveling, etc. All these and similar things are quite possible. It is not by chance that, in West Germany at least, league football matches are played on Saturdays.

All I wanted to do here was to suggest briefly that there are circumstances in which the Church has not only the abstract right but also the concrete opportunity, without offending non-Christians, positively to steer the development of secular society to a point at which the Sunday precept and the Sunday celebration would fit more conveniently into the total framework of civil life. Perhaps we could find more suitable times for the celebration on Sunday. Perhaps a number of things which at present appear merely as reluctantly granted concessions might one day become normal and obvious, while some other things, now maintained as part of the tradition from former times, may be dropped. If, as J. A. Jungmann always insisted, the Sunday celebration is to be seen in the first place as a responsibility of the parish as such and not, properly speaking, the individual's wholly personal responsibility, we might eventually come to the conclusion that masses at six or seven o'clock on Sunday mornings impose unnecessary torment on the clergy. We might perhaps arrange a splendid and beautiful common celebration only in the evening of Sunday, or even on Saturday. We could then say that any particular individual (a bus conductor, for instance, who has to work at this time) has no need at all to attend mass on that Sunday, since this is not primarily his own private and personal religious obligation, but, if he has any obligation at all, it is as a member of this parish, which can in fact choose to have a joint celebration and at a time which, from the nature of the case, cannot be convenient to every individual.

12

BASIC COMMUNITIES

Action 365[1] forms and gives life to something that can be described as, or aspires to be, a basic community. On such a sociological and theological theme it is possible, of course, only to put forward a few aphorisms, and even then only very vaguely and without substantiation. Only with these reservations can I venture to consider the theme. I want first to consider Christian basic communities as they exist in the different churches and secondly to say something about ecumenical basic communities.

BASIC COMMUNITIES IN THE CHURCH

Basic communities are necessary for the churches today. The churches of the future will be built up from below by basic communities formed by free initiative and association. Everything should be done, not to suppress, but to promote this development (which has already begun) and to keep it on the right lines. In order to understand what this means, we must consider the situation of the churches as it is to a large extent today and as it may come to be on an even larger scale.

Concretely and sociologically regarded, the churches will not exist as formerly simply in virtue of their ministry, their sociologically

[1] Action 365 consists in ecumenically constituted basic communities seeking to undertake practical responsibility for the world (action) in the light of daily Scripture reading (365 days a year). The main fields of activity are ecumenism in practice, Christian publicity work, fraternal service, and third-world work. In this way a renewal of the churches is meant to be brought about. The address of Action 365 is Kennedyallee 111a, D-6000 Frankfurt 70. Tel. 0611/632063.

firm structures and in virtue of an awareness of being taken for granted by public opinion, nor will they recruit new members on this basis simply because children adopt and continue the life-style of their parents and are baptized and indoctrinated by the Church. The Church will exist actually and not merely theoretically only by being renewed again and again by the free decision of faith and the formation of conscience on the part of individuals in the midst of a secular society which does not from the outset bear a Christian imprint. The fact that this is one description (more sociological than theological, at least under certain aspects) of the Church's continual self-renewal and that this renewal must always adopt and recognize in historical fidelity the traditional message of the Gospel and the ministry derived from Jesus does not alter anything in the new form (as distinct from the old) in which the Church comes to be today and will come to be in the future.

Faith in Jesus Christ, which is always necessary if someone is really to be a Christian in virtue of his free decision, was formed at one time in a situation which, even from the secular sociological standpoint, was more or less homogeneously Christian; today this faith must itself form and sustain its own sociological sphere. If in this way several or many individuals become Christians and join together, despite the pressure of a secularized society, they form basic communities, set up a community Church, as distinct from the people's Church of past centuries (that is, a Church which was sustained and in which the individual was sustained by a consensus of the people as a whole, institutionalized in all its sociological dimensions and thus not living in a diaspora).

Such basic communities must not be seen as contrasting with or opposed to the traditional Church and its institutions. Basic communities, if they are Christian, do not merely adopt the Gospel, the faith of the Church. They do not merely respect authority in the Church and, despite all conceivable individual conflicts (which, of course, can always occur again and again), seek to live in peace and as far as possible positively recognized by ecclesiastical authority, expecting from the latter at least a benevolent toleration, even if authority by right (real or assumed) feels that it is not yet in a position to approve or recognize a particular basic community. Genuinely Christian basic communities also remain positively open to the whole wealth of tradition of spiritual experience, of theological reflection, of liturgical practice, of socio-political theory and practice which the history of the Church offers to us.

A genuine basic community is not to be understood as the opposite of the parish. But not every genuine basic community needs to be identical with a parish; in this respect it can also be sociologically disparate from a parish or it may belong to the latter's substructures, since no one can maintain that everything Christian on the plane of local sociability must or even can be organized only in parishes properly so-called. The churches have always recognized in principle that there can be free associations from below which pursue specifically Christian aims and yet do not spring from the direct initiative of authority in the Church and are not subject to the control of this authority. But, on the other hand, none of this excludes the possibility that a parish institutionalized in the first place from above could and should also be at the same time a living basic community from below. The more this happens, the better it is for the Church. For in this way as much as possible may be transferred into the Church of the future from the older Church with its wealth of history, experience, and rootedness in broad strata of the people. This is something to be attempted, since even the Church of the future (which is actually built up from the communities which are most alive) must not try to become a Church of elitist groups, a Church of a holy remnant without any secular sociological significance. Even if it patiently accepts its actual future from God's decree in history, of itself it always has the task of becoming the Church of as many as possible, the Church rooted as widely as possible in secular society, to be and (again) to become a Church of the people.

None of this means that even in an ideal situation parish and basic community are in all circumstances identical with each other. Even a parish as official institution, which is or is becoming a basic community, can have under itself and alongside itself differently structured, living basic communities which in the light of their origin, their objective, and their charism are not simply merged in a parish, however much the latter is sustained from below by the living faith and love of Christians. This, of course, is not the place to discuss the legally and practically feasible forms of a deliberately planned coexistence of living basic communities with a particular objective, on the one hand, and of parishes, on the other hand, which are themselves basic communities. In this connection we may say only that where such a basic community with its own particular objective is so developed that it integrates into itself alone more or less the whole Christian life of its members in worship, prayer, love, responsibility for society, proclamation of the Gospel, and so on, it must be understood either as a parish already recognized or seeking recognition by the greater Church or as a development which cannot be recognized ecclesiologically as legitimate, since it would then have become a cancerous structure in the total organism of the Church. In practice this means that basic communities in the ordinary sense of the term should not seek to suppress parishes, unless they are themselves recognized as parishes (in the old style, as 'personal parishes') by the greater Church.

Basic communities, as they are actually formed today, are an experiment. This statement has a number of implications. First of all, very diverse forms of basic communities are conceivable in principle. Such forms in their legitimacy and variety cannot simply be deduced from a theoretical ecclesiology. In the last resort these forms are based on the underivability of history in general and of the history of secular society in particular, which is the presupposition for these basic communities and their concrete forms.

Hence it is also implied that these basic communities are an experiment in the strict sense of the term. That is to say, in the last resort they are not authorized or refuted by *a priori* ecclesiological theory, but only (despite the legitimacy of theoretical ecclesiology and despite all fidelity to the history of the Church) by experience and the future. This means that concrete basic communities (now understood as distinct from officially institutionalized communities) are always a venture of hope. But this again means that such living basic communities may not be accepted or at least tolerated by the institutional Church only if it is certain that the venture has actually been successful.[2]

These basic communities obviously have a duty to maintain unity with the diocesan greater Church; for this reason they must also be established as members of the greater Church, even if this requires

[2] Cf. K. Rahner, 'Mut und Mühe den Glauben zu bezeugen' in *Entschluss* 1 (1980):7–10.

certain 'sacrifices' and some renunciation on their part alone; they have to observe the laws (which are legitimate and can be concretely fulfilled) of the Church as a whole; despite their (even theological) singularity, they may not develop a sectarian and heretical theology of their own; they must remain open in a spirit of self-criticism to the life of the Church as a whole in truth and love and also make a concrete contribution to this beyond their own frontiers; their singularity must not go to such extremes that certain necessary functions, the fulfillment of which is under the supervision of the diocesan Church, simply collapse or wither away. But none of this prevents a basic community from having its own marked peculiarity, from giving itself a certain structure and what we might call a constitution, from really demanding from members who have freely joined it something that goes completely beyond what a parishioner is expected to do today for his own parish. The 'constitutions' of such basic communities can be considerably different in individual cases. In it the sustaining function and 'right of co-determination' of lay people may be considerably greater than that to which we have hitherto been generally accustomed, although, of course, in the past also, behind apparently very 'authoritarian' official structures, lay people very often had a much greater share in decision making in the parish. Hence there is no reason for not recognizing legally what often exists in fact.

ECUMENICAL BASIC COMMUNITIES

I propose to add a few remarks on ecumenical basic communities, since Action 365 is concerned with these.

First of all it must be said that such ecumenical groups of Christians are legitimate and necessary. All Christians and all churches have a mandate and an obligation to work for the unity of Christians and of the churches. This mandate is more urgent today than ever. But it cannot be fulfilled if the authorities alone in the churches are working from above for unity or if this work merely takes the form of academic discussions by theologians on points of controversy and ecumenism. It is at the base of the churches that people must get to know one another, must come more closely together; it is here that strangeness and mutual misunderstanding must be broken down, here people must pray together, exchange spiritual experience, and jointly undertake responsibility for the world, for secular society.

When, therefore, the groups of Christians of Action 365 are formed, aware of their socio-political responsibility in the light of their basic Christian attitude, it is possible and appropriate for them to cross denominational frontiers and come together to form ecumenical basic communities. This is particularly appropriate and even indispensable when it is a question of undertaking social responsibility for justice, love, and freedom, when there is not merely talk of this responsibility, but action in the light of it in concrete everyday life, so that the liberating power of the Gospel is attested in deed and truth before the world. In this field of social responsibility to the world on the part of Christians, however, a common task is possible for Christians of different denominations and must be undertaken jointly, because it is likely to be better and more successfully achieved in this way. Ecumenical groups with an objective, as in Action 365, are legitimate and necessary today. Otherwise, Christians do not fulfill effectively enough their common task in regard to the secular world, and the ecumenical task remains pure theory which adjourns the actual unification of Christians to the Last Day.

The special task of a socio-political character which Action 365 undertakes for its own (admittedly modest) part does not exclude but in fact includes the meeting of such groups together, even for religious and for Christian activities, for prayer. For these groups want to undertake their specific task, not in a merely secular, humanitarian spirit, but in the spirit of Christ, in the power of his death and his resurrection, in the Holy Spirit. Hence it is justified and necessary for such groups themselves to guard and continually secure afresh the innermost centre of their motivation by which their real task is sustained.

In this connection it would take us too far to enter into the problem of actual and mutual intercommunion. We can only say that in principle there can be and are legitimate wishes and attempts at the base and that, on the other hand, such intercommunion cannot be put in practice impatiently and hastily in a form which dismisses the still existing separation of the churches as simply negligible in religious and Christian terms. The exact and concrete conclusion from the dialectic of these two principles cannot be further considered at the moment.

Nevertheless, there is one thing more I would like to say in this connection. It is that ecumenical basic communities like those of Action 365 must beware of the danger of becoming a kind of third denomination. I do not, of course, assume or presume that Action 365 has even a remote intention of doing anything of this kind. But there are also unforeseen dangers. A third denomination, even if it results from the intention of overcoming denominational limits, will not in fact overcome but only intensify the divisions in Christendom. Ecumenical basic communities like those of Action 365 cannot have any hope merely from their own resources, independently of the authority and the historically and sociologically existing institutions of the Church. If such basic communities were to cut themselves off in an elitist and ghettolike form from the actual churches and attempt to integrate autarchically the whole of Christian life in themselves, they would in practice form a third denomination and would therefore only increase the misery of a divided Christendom.

In such ecumenical groups, Christians belonging to particular denominations, if they are not to compromise the very thing about which they are most intimately concerned, must remain in vital contact with their own churches, must help to sustain the life of these churches (and not merely their own as communities), in patience, inward participation, and unselfish love; they must be a leaven in the churches, not seeking to remain in isolation, but intermingled with the whole mass of the Christian people. Even if it is difficult, ecumenical basic communities must share the historical burden of the old churches, maintain and cherish a living union of integration and trust with the authorities in the churches; at once humble and proud, they may perhaps regard themselves as the vanguard of the Church on pilgrimage through history, but not as an army that can be seen more closely to be fighting only for its own victories.

With all the freedom that rightly belongs to a community from below, ecumenical basic communities must always regard themselves as incorporated in the churches to which their members actively belong and want to belong, not merely accepting this situation as something to which they have been doomed by the past; they must in this way seek to serve the Church that is to come.

PART FOUR

The Future of the Church

13

ETERNITY FROM TIME

SCEPTICISM IN REGARD TO ETERNAL LIFE

There can be no doubt that belief in eternal life as a consequence of survival after death has grown weaker in the consciousness of modern people. This fundamental doctrine of Christianity, scarcely affected at first by the Enlightenment from the eighteenth century onward, is now questioned, or at any rate has lost its place among those things which mainly interest people today. It is true that at all times there have been some who thought (as they put it) that death is the end of everything; but the conviction that man lives on into a definitive permanent existence was generally taken for granted and firmly established in the public mind, at least among Christian nations, but also far beyond these, even though the ideas of this life after death were and are very diverse. Today, even among Christians, what was once a basic Christian conviction is largely threatened. There are Christians who are sure of the existence of God and who lead lives according to the tenets of their religion, but who do not think it necessary to show any great interest in the question of an eternal life that is not simply identical with life here and now.

Of course, the fact that this scepticism in regard to eternal life exists in modern society does not mean that it is justified. Faced by the essential and ultimate questions of human existence, we cannot hide behind the prestige and allure of popular opinion at the present time. The lofty and sublime persuasion of a few can be the truth that holds for all, even though there are not many who acknowledge it. The ultimate truths are not found in the popular press, nor are they established by thoughtless chatter in a public house.

Of course, it can readily be admitted by a Christian that the ways of presenting the idea of the perennially valid truth of eternal life are more inadequate than is necessary or avoidable, obscuring rather than elucidating the real meaning. Among these unsatisfactory ideas of eternity is that of a never ending time running on into infinity. Up to very recently preachers have too often made indiscriminate use of this idea with reference to the eternity of hell. But even modern physics knows that in order to express certain facts or realities of the physical world without getting lost in mathematical abstractness (which is also incapable by itself of bringing out what is really meant) we must work with very inadequate ideas, perhaps even with several apparently mutually contradictory ideas, which, however, can bring home to us only up to a point the meaning of the reality under discussion. If this sort of thing happens even in physics, people today ought really not to be put off (as they so readily are) by the fact that in the sphere of religion, also, more or less apt terms and ideas (for example, in regard to eternal life) can be worked out only imperfectly and arduously.

Within our present scope it is, of course, not possible even to a slight degree to make clear the existence and nature of the eternal life awaiting us. Here and now we are attempting to draw attention only to one point from this immense theme: that is, that we experience eternity in the present time in a way that constantly eludes reflection and can learn from this that the eternity which emerges through death out of the present time and becomes definitive cannot be conceived as a continuation of time into eternity.

THE TYRANNY OF OUR CONCEPT OF TIME

By way of preparation for our main reflections, it must again be made more clear what are the difficulties that arise if we understand eternity 'after' death as the unlimited continuation of time. If we understand eternity (which is the definitiveness of our life, emerging in time) as the running on of time with one section coming after another, each to be filled out in a new way and each different from the others, then, of course, all the semiclever and semistupid questions arise that tempt today's semiclever person to regard belief in eternal life as incredible, if not downright ridiculous. For then he can ask what is to be used to fill up these ever new periods of time. Will it not gradually become boring if, as devout people think, this never stopping conveyor belt of time has its individual parts stacked again and again with the same thing, with the eternal glorification of the infinite God by his creature's praise? Why then is there no opportunity in this ever continuing time for the damned to be converted, change their outlook, repent, and thus turn their hell into heaven? Are they prevented by a God who, in a final act of despotism, refuses to accept a change of mind on the part of the lost, although there would be place for such a change and it could happen at some point in these ever continuing times ('aeons', as they are called in Scripture)?

If eternity is conceived, then, as time open to infinity, have not the world, man and his history always ahead of them that which is not yet (in other words, that which can find its place only in a future space of time), and is not heaven the very thing that may not enter into this scheme of ever continuing, continual succession in time? But if it is to go on forever, if everything that exists is no more than the starting point for attaining what is to come, and so on and so on, is not the eternity of this kind of time the damnation of Ahasuerus, the wandering Jew, doomed always to roam, without ever finally arriving anywhere? Under the tyranny of this concept of time, is not the eternal heaven dissolved into an eternal hell, and vice versa? It is easy to see how dangerous and pernicious is the idea of eternity as an endless running on of time.

In order to get out of this difficulty we can, of course, in the first place say quite appropriately that a notion of eternity can be formed with the aid of a negation, excluding from the notion of the real, the permanent, and the definitive the element of sequence, of succession, of one thing after another. This method of forming a new concept by the negation of certain aspects of the present concept is not always illegitimate in principle. It is a method that is often unavoidable. With its aid a blind person, for example, can form an idea, if not a visualization, of colour and consequently gain the assurance that there are colours, even though he has never seen them; he can also hope, although blind from birth, that perhaps one day he will see. But it is a method that also has its problems. How are we to know in the concrete case whether what is conceptually grasped can really exist, even when a particular element of what is experienced is excluded by a negation of this kind? In our case can there really be something permanent, if we exclude from its notion the succession that exists in all the enduring things that we directly experience?

HINTS OF AN ETERNAL REALITY

In order to gain further confidence that there can also be something permanent and eternal which is not subject to the domination of endless succession, let us take a closer look at our experience of time and (so I think) discover there something 'eternal': that is, at least something that is not simply in the 'now', in the mere moment of time, perishing and giving way to something else that is different from what went before, replacing this, only to be itself replaced and thrust into nothingness. We are considering the paradox of time itself which lives in secret from an eternity.

A kind of permanency in time appears at three levels. There is the necessary permanency of any reality (what we used to describe as 'substance') which persists while sustaining the alternation of qualities, phenomena, and occurrences. There is mental experience which combines past, present, and future in a unity. There is free personal decision which, by its very nature, does not permit what it has posited purely and simply to disappear into the void of nothingness. Let us look again a little more closely at these three hints of something eternal in the world of our experience.

THE TOTALITY OF A HISTORY

Time appears to us in the first place as a chain of individual occurrences stretching forward and backward into infinity, with each occurrence replacing the one before it and itself disappearing to make way for what follows. But at the same time, even though we are much less attentive to the fact, we are sure that these changing phenomena replacing one another are nevertheless manifestations of something permanent which (at least for a longer or shorter period) persists as the same reality, sustaining the changing appearances, bringing them together into a totality, into a history, which is in fact one and does not disintegrate or crumble into a dust of pure individual moments. Something of this can be seen, for instance, in the history of a flower, continuing in varying stages from the seed until it finally withers. Or we may consider our own life history from beginning to end, in which every moment is different from the one before it and yet each is a determination of one and the same reality, which persists as the same throughout this changing history, and, as one and the same, claims for itself all these alternating moments. These identities, lying behind the alternation and contents of the moments of time and thus holding together the infinitesimally tiny elements of time, shaping out of the dust of these elements a greater, structured history, cannot as such share the quality of time itself as it divides and passes away, if they are to fulfill their task of sustaining and unifying time. If time is to make sense as a greater unity and more definite shape, as history, there must be something that we always take for granted in ordinary life and that is not simply the succession of moments of time flashing out and then fading again. There is in time something that is not identical with time itself. This something may perhaps need to expand over time if it is to be itself, but it is not identical with this extension in moments of time. Even what is properly temporal contains more than time: at least something that persists and gives a unity to time in historical temporal shapes.

MENTAL EXPERIENCE

This supra-temporal element in time becomes still more clear when we reflect on the way in which time is unified and shaped in the mental process of experiencing it. Time is not simply there; it is experienced by us, not by merely submitting to its sequence, but by confronting it, gathering together past, present, and future and mentally binding them into a unity and shape which is more than the pure succession of time where the next moment triumphs over the last by annihilating it. Someone observing this mental unifying of time, this interruption of time's course, might retort sceptically that this time so unified, in which bare succession is eliminated, this time that 'stands still', ceases to run on, and consequently does not run out, is nothing but an *idea* of time, and the subject reflecting on time in this way is hopelessly borne along and passes away in real time. But, if time as such is nothing but the flow of time atoms, each of which extinguishes its predecessor and is then extinguished by its successor, how can it be unified meaningfully and truly (even if merely 'in thought') into such instant time-configurations, into a history of meaning and structure, unless there is more to time itself than mere passing away?

And, even more importantly, how is the thinking subject, conferring unity and shape in time as it runs on, to be understood as capable of doing this? How can a thinking subject of this kind create a time that stands still, even merely in thought, if it is completely dependent on flowing time for its own true being, when thinking itself is also a reality, and thinking and what is thought are mutually dependent? No, if and insofar as there is a thought of time, something happens which does in fact occur in time's course, but as an event which has a peculiar superiority over time, an event intimating eternity, since the thought that thinks time is not simply time's subject.

FREE DECISIONS

Eternity is experienced in time itself most clearly when the intellectual subject in man makes a free decision which concerns and involves the one and entire person. We cannot analyze decisions of this kind in all their dimensions here. That would take too long. All that we can say is that there are free decisions in man, involving the person's total self-disposal, for which he bears an ultimate, inescapable responsibility, a responsibility which he cannot shift off to anyone or anything else, neither by a psychology seeking to break down the ultimate character of man as subject nor by social sciences seeking to reduce man to a pure effect of social conditions. But (and this in the long run is unavoidable and inexorably occurs at certain points, whether there is any very explicit and theorctical reflection on it or not) if someone says as he proceeds to act, 'I am inexorably and inescapably responsible for this, there is nothing in the last resort to which I can appeal to relieve me of responsibility', he can simultaneously think and say, 'Not that all this is so important or so bad. For when the end really comes I can always take refuge in the empty void where no one can reach me any longer, neither the voice of conscience nor world history nor any God.' No, ultimate personal decisions, at least when they involve a life in its totality, are irrevocable, they are truly eternity coming to be in time.

Of course, if we had time to do so, we would have to ask here about the possibility of repentance and conversion within the continuing course of the time and history of man, we would have to bear in mind the essentially dialogic character of human freedom, to which God assigns a decisive role in this history of freedom. But none of these things would remove the basic fact, rooted in the nature of this freedom and its inextricable responsibility, that freedom in the last resort (and, indeed, freedom alone) wills and posits finality and unrevisability, that this implies the finality, the eternity of the existence of this freedom and consequently does not permit this freedom any flight from responsibility into the void. Here time really creates eternity and eternity is experienced in time.

ACCEPTING INCOMPREHENSIBILITY

There may perhaps be some doubt as to whether our suggestions provide adequate illumination for the understanding of that eternity which we as Christians hope to reach as our definitive life after death. But I think that these suggestions at least show that it cannot be said that each and every thing within the range of our experience is so exclusively and solely temporal that we can think meaningfully of something as real only by thinking of it either as existing simply here and now and then disappearing into the void or as a reality consisting merely of an unlimited number of moments of time continuing always without end and incapable in principle of offering any scope for a decision of freedom that posits a real finality. Both these ideas (that is, of time as ending in the void or of time as never ceasing) are equally incompatible with the Christian belief in eternal life. And neither of these ideas can appeal to the actual experience we have of time if we unhesitatingly permit the *whole* experience to speak for itself.

These merely tentatively outlined considerations must, however, allow us to draw a few conclusions for concrete life. First of all, even in this way, it becomes evident that we cannot positively imagine here the concreteness of our eternal life. We know, it is true, that it will be an existence and life that has God himself in himself as its content, a life that implies love, limitless knowledge, supreme happiness, and so on. But how all this can be experienced in the concreteness of a state beyond time, what is the meaning of transfigured corporality, eternal fellowship with the redeemed, and so on: this is something we cannot concretely imagine or picture to ourselves here and now. We Christians need not be disturbed today if we can scarcely summon up the courage to see it all as depicted from Scripture up to Dante, and even subsequently. For we are actually going into the unknown, the unimaginable, and, properly speaking, know only that it is filled with the incomprehensibility of God and his love and that it is final. It is sufficient to accept for ourselves now the incomprehensibility of our eternal life and nevertheless to go on hoping and trusting. Our experience of time (which is always a mysterious experience of something more than time) certainly gives us the right not to hold suspect as empty speculation our 'no' to time in the concept of eternity; but it certainly does not relieve us of the decision to say this 'no' to time in our 'yes' to eternity. Thus it leaves our life one of faith and hope that must still wait for the definitive end and has no power triumphantly to exhibit it before the fact.

VICTORY OF GOD'S LOVE

In the third case of eternity in time, which we considered briefly, it becomes clear, if we look closely enough, that our eternal life, however much it will then be filled with God himself, will be the definitiveness of that moral and free act of our life in which (beyond all the dividedness of time) as one and whole, we made ourselves the persons we wanted finally to be. But if our eternity is thus nothing but the now definitive history which we ourselves freely made, then we can see with both horror and supreme delight the immense grandeur, depth, and density of those acts in which our whole life is involved. Of course, in our life there is a great deal of routine and superficiality that is unavoidable, in which freedom occurs without bearing any trace of finality or eternity. If, however, there is such a thing as eternal life at all, if it is not merely something different added to our temporal life and likewise stretching out over time, if it is truly the finality of this present life of freedom which fittingly comes to a final and definitive consummation, only then can be seen the unfathomable depths and the richness of our existence, of that existence which often gives the impression of consisting of nothing but banalities. Where an ultimate responsibility is assumed in obedience to a person's own conscience, where ultimate selfless love and fidelity are given, where an ultimate selfless obedience to truth regardless of self is lived out, and so on, at this point there is really in our life something that is infinitely precious, that of itself has the right and reality not to perish, that is able to fill out an eternity, that actually deserves not merely to be rewarded (a misleading expression, savouring of selfishness) by perpetual eternity but to claim this as its most authentic right, as its most intimate nature.

This is the dignity and potentiality with which we human beings are endowed—all of us, not merely the great geniuses of mankind, not merely a Buddha or a Socrates, but all of us, even though there are far too many who seem to be terribly mediocre, mayflies, as it were. But the truth proclaimed by Christianity is that in this time (apparently stretching out endlessly, in order to reproduce in an eternal recurrence always the same thing and always that which perishes in the eternal cycle of coming and going), whenever life is lived in faith, hope, and love, eternity truly occurs: eternity which does not come only to depart, which persists and (this is what matters) is such that its persistence means supreme happiness and not hell, since it has received God himself and thus is really worthy of being definitive and forever. Of course, in principle, it must be firmly maintained that man's history of freedom can also produce a person's similarly timeless definitive perdition. But what Christianity really proclaims as essential is not the equal possibility of these *two* ways of passing from time to eternity, but the victory of the love of God who bestows himself in and through our freedom: it points to the cross and resurrection of Jesus as to the event of this now manifest victory of God's love. This love is the cause and guarantee that our brief time, which passes away, creates an eternity which is not made up out of time. If it seems that we perish in death, since the dead do not become perceptible again anywhere where time goes on, this is merely a sign that eternity, born from time, is something other than what can readily be seen here and now.

PART FIVE

Sin and Suffering

14

PURGATORY

When people belonging to the same profession are talking together about their professional concerns they naturally use a highly specialized language not easily understood by outsiders. Not only has this language its own peculiar terminology but it is often spoken in a very casual and offhand manner. It is the same with theologians.

A short time ago one theologian said to another, 'The pope insisted again yesterday on the traditional doctrine of purgatory.' The other replied, 'I've nothing against that. But if I only knew what exactly I am supposed to believe in this respect! Do you know? Can you look into the pope's mind to see what he was thinking? I can't. Anyway, if you could, it would presumably still be doubtful whether what the pope precisely understood by purgatory in this declaration would as such be absolutely binding on me as a matter of faith.' 'But', the first theologian then said, 'You and the pope know the other doctrinal declarations of the Church to which this new exhortation refers, and, without looking into the pope's mind, you can see precisely what purgatory means by reading these older and lengthy declarations.'

'O Lord,' said the second theologian, 'if only it was as simple as you think. These older definitions in Denzinger—or am I to consult also as many theologians as possible?—must first of all be scrutinized to see to what extent they are regarded as binding by the teaching authority. This, in fact, varies. It can vary considerably. Think, for instance, of the ideas of purgatory formerly implied in declarations about the extent of "temporal punishment" remitted by indulgences: the kind of declarations which the Church today somewhat shamefacedly almost completely avoids. And if I examine critically and sift through these official teachings of the Church on purgatory (which is not only my right but also my duty as a theologian), am I then bound to believe in what Paul VI still described as "expiation in the fire" of purgatory, or can I be content with the Tridentine profession of faith, which states that there is a place of purification and that the souls detained there are helped by the intercession of the faithful? And if I do not feel particularly tied to the idea of fire and torment (St. Catherine of Genoa also had a different idea of purgatory) and consequently need not rack my brain to find a way of imagining this fire, without having to resort to mythology, what is the meaning in other parts of this teaching on purgatory of "souls" (if the term is not to be taken in a mainly Platonic sense)? How are they "detained"? By what means are they "purified"? Why is this purification a "penalty"? Can we say that what is apparently to be removed by this purification is an internal state produced in these "souls" by sins committed during life and not yet completely eradicated by turning to God and being forgiven? Or is it a question of penalties imposed as it were from outside by God's justice, penalties which quite simply have to be paid? But how are these penalties conceivable if it is assumed that they bear no relation to the internal moral quality of the "poor souls"? Must we regard purgatory as a process which goes on in a temporal succession which is more or less the same as the time we experience here in our history?

'These and similar questions cannot simply be thrust aside. If we are to believe the Church's teaching on purgatory, we must believe *something* that can be given formal expression. Or are we simply not to pursue these questions further? Can we answer them without going back to the complicated and obscure history of this doctrine? But how are we to do that if it only means that everything will become more obscure and more difficult than before and if the normal believer cannot by any means investigate these things for himself? There is not much to be got out of Scripture, whether of the Old or the New Testament, particularly if we may hold the opinion that prayers for the dead do not necessarily imply a doctrine of purgatory. If we turn to the Fathers of the Church, there are certainly not a few whom we could name as upholding some kind of doctrine of purgatory. But does this mean *ipso facto* that such an idea is part of revealed doctrine and binding as such or might it not be merely an ideal type which in the last resort remains without binding force and which enables us to satisfy our curiosity by finding answers to questions which we ought to leave unanswered in the presence of the silent majesty of death?

'Of course, people can always insist that the Church's sense of faith at least from the Middle Ages onward has clung stubbornly to the existence of purgatory, even though the emergence of this decision of faith came after an obscure earlier history, and, consequently, the essential question has in fact already been decided. But even if we leave aside the question of how precisely the nature of divine revelation is to be understood and how from that standpoint a material criterion can be established to settle the question of what can belong *a priori* to the real substance of revelation and what from the very outset cannot (a question which might lead to considerable difficulties when applied to the doctrine of purgatory), this kind of dogmatic positivism does not take us very much farther. For (as I have said frequently enough already) the question remains of what is the binding content of this official teaching of the Church on purgatory.'

The other theologian broke in impatiently, 'Can we not formulate this teaching in a way that, on the one hand, completely accords with the Church's older doctrinal statements and with Rome's exhortations at the present time and yet, on the other hand, permits us to see in this formulation something that seems "realizable", intelligible, credible, and compatible with the rest of our anthropology?'

'How, then?' asked the other.

'I shall try to do so as well as I can', was the answer. 'Of course, I assume here (without attempting to justify this belief) the permanency of the person in death. I say "permanency" because I think it will be a good thing to refrain from the outset from more precise suggestions as to how this permanency might be more concretely imagined, how it might be given more tangible form, if it were associated with the permanency that is realized in a sequence of events in time. For it seems to me that things cannot simply go on after death in temporal extension, since that would mean that the finality of judgment at death (at least for someone who has come to a radical personal decision in his earthly life) is no longer credible. Over and above this, the problems raised in regard to time in a modern metaphysics or even physics of cognition certainly permit me to think that what we know and take for granted as time is far from being a determination of reality that is always and everywhere valid. I have no intention of forgetting what I have just said in what I am about to say. I assume that the one human being, despite the unity of his origin and goal, is also an inwardly plural being, about whom, from the very nature of the case, diverse statements can rightly be made which are really true of *him* and yet determine him in different ways and refer to different realities in him.

'I am expressing myself in this roundabout way because I want to avoid the term "part", which is constantly liable to lead to the mistaken assumption that unity (even in man) must subsequently be regarded as made up of "parts", or (conversely) that we can quite naturally and simply discover and say something about one part of the one reality without qualifying the whole at the same time. But let us leave aside the difficult problems and paradoxes associated with an existent that is really one and yet plural in the sense that a determination does not affect everything about it in the same way, that opposites can be predicated of it, even though these contradictory statements cannot be made about it simply (as we usually say) in the same respect. This singular state of affairs can, of course, be "visualized" simply by regarding the contradictory statements as true of different "pieces" or "parts", but this is to forget that these "parts" are really those of an existent that is absolutely truly one. But again let us leave aside the metaphysics and epistemology of a plural "one" in which plurality and unity are really true in the same way.

'We assume that a human being has a history in which not everything happens at one and the same time, that something "about" him can be completed, without this completedness having to be or being able to be predicated immediately of each and every thing "about" him. In his normal self-understanding everyone makes this (abstractly formulated) assumption, not merely with reference to his body (in which a person's pain "in" his leg is not actually a pain "in" his arm, although in both instances it is "his" pain), but also in much more "existential" events and situations. He is perhaps sure that he loves God and yet does not venture to assert that he loves God with all his heart, that his whole existence is integrated into this love: he admits that in him are abysmal depths, a mass of instincts, a subconscious, an "id", etc., as realities of which it certainly cannot be said that they are all completely integrated into the personal decision of the subject that has decided or can decide finally for or against God. At this point, however, it must be noted that a Christian anthropology which upholds the fundamental unity of the one human being and takes this seriously cannot assume that these unintegrated realities of the person simply cease with death as the "separation of body and soul" and thus become irrelevant to the permanent existence of the personal subject, or that they are abolished by what can be regarded as a purely juridical decree of God. Under these circumstances death presumably opens up several possibilities. Perhaps the unintegrated elements in man are incorporated into the final personal decision, now become definitive in death, in a lengthy "process" which (while still maintaining what I said earlier about the release of the deceased person from our time) might nevertheless be seen as analogous to the present time in a way that by and large corresponds to the traditional idea of purgatory. With the aid of an idea of this kind it might be possible to see that death as a task to be accomplished within quite definite spatio-temporal limits does not necessarily mean a pure and simple departure from this material world as a whole, so that the subject now become definitive in principle in its personal decision can and must still continue in its own way to participate in the fundamental temporality and historicity of the world, even if it has reached its consummation in the immediate vision of God. It could also be pointed out that the idea of the lot of a "dead" person as a kind of process is so widespread in the history of religion that these convictions should not be too quickly laid aside in a spirit of modern rationalistic scepticism, particularly since (for the Christian) such convictions and ideas have also exercised an influence on Christian doctrine and its development and presumably had a good deal to do with the ready acceptance of Christian teaching on purgatory in former times.

'There is another way of looking at the question. Perhaps what happens is not, properly speaking, a process; but, nevertheless, this total integration in and through death, which comes to prevail in the whole length and breadth of the person's existence as the result of a final basic decision, can be seen at least analogously as taking place in time. Under these circumstances the notions of time used univocally or analogously in the traditional doctrine of purgatory would not refer directly to the properties of what is understood as real in the doctrine of purgatory, but would serve as vivid illustrations of the fact that a person is really a plural being, the total existence of which is not actually realized at one stroke from the very outset, and, consequently, that the actual realization of the totality of its existence is dependent in the most varied and indeterminable ways on preconditions which are not simply implicit in the "good will" of the basic decision. It is difficult to say whether I am not getting lost in this web of ideas that I have spun, whether I am not getting involved in contradictions or theological impossibilities. But are we simply to remain silent from the very outset in face of the majestic darkness of death, content with the assumption that the Christian sustained by hope falls through death into the incomprehensibility of God, to regard this as "beatifying", and thus to refrain from all further differentiations in regard to life "after" death? If, however, we want to take seriously the traditional teaching on purgatory, with its bold differentation, and yet not to picture the hereafter to ourselves as if we had already been there and were quite familiar with it (an impression only too obviously created by the doctrine of purgatory as traditionally formulated), then we are faced by the question of whether, without contradicting the official teaching on purgatory, we may take it to mean that everything happens in death itself, that the "purification" in purgatory is an aspect of death itself and can be made intelligible in the light of the different characteristics of death itself. Can we then say that the doctrine of purgatory is in fact a kind of thanatology presented with a different imagery and under different aspects, but uncurtailed and not oversimplified? Even if we attempt to eliminate all temporal elements in this imagery, we must still give some explanation of how the elements of the traditional imagery can be understood as realized in the very event of death.

'Why should that be absolutely impossible? Why could not the "duration" of the event of purification be identified with the (diverse) depth and intensity of the pain that man experiences in death itself, since there is a terrible difference between what he actually is and what he ought to be? Why should this pain (which is concretely identical with the individual character of dying proper to each person in accordance with his state) not itself be the purifying event which is supposed to constitute the essence of purgatory? Why could suffrages for the deceased in "purgatory" not be related to the occurrence of death? If we do not know even in the light of the traditional idea of purgatory whether the deceased for whom we pray are "still" in purgatory and if we nevertheless regard these suffrages as appropriate in any case, then it cannot be unreasonable to relate our intercessions to that death, no matter when precisely in our earthly time these prayers were said. (Jesus' prayer on the cross was certainly meaningful even for those people who had lived long before him.) It is not indeed particularly easy to see how it is possible on account of God's retributive justice to detain in purgatory someone who has already completed his true inward development (including, of course, the integration of his whole being into the love of God) and has still to suffer only outwardly through God's retributive justice, even though this suffering does not bring him to a greater maturity. But if we reject such an idea, there is really no longer any reason to deny that purgatory takes place in death itself. If someone were to introduce an element of time into the very occurrence of death (in the withdrawal from the present world), which need not be regarded as *a priori* unreasonable, then it would still be possible to avoid the idea of a time in "purgatory" "after" death and there would be no need subsequently to qualify this idea with the statement that time in purgatory is only "analogous" to the time with which we are familiar.

'But now', said the theologian, 'I have been talking far too long and not made the matter any clearer. To be honest', he said, 'it must be admitted that the doctrine of purgatory does not seem particularly important today even to the devout Christian. The latter (as he hopes) submits willingly to death and thinks that he falls then into the hands of an infinite, loving God who brings everything to perfection, even though (as far as our experience goes) we surrender ourselves to him as imperfect beings. We think, moreover, that we can pray with the Church for the deceased, that we ourselves can thus entrust those with whom we are united to eternal light and unending peace. Is that not sufficient? Does the traditional doctrine of purgatory really amount to more in existential faith? I don't know. But when I recall the modest statements of Scripture I am inclined to answer this question in the negative. This does not at all mean that I would blame for this reason the people who can see more clearly in the traditional doctrine of purgatory what we all certainly maintain and who therefore cling to this traditional statement.'

The other theologian had listened patiently to these lengthy explanations, without interrupting. But now he suggested that the whole problem should be considered again from a completely different aspect. 'All you have said up to now', he declared, 'is true enough. But you really ought not to take this doctrine of purgatory straight from Denzinger and then try to interpret it "speculatively" in isolation. This traditional teaching was not simply telephoned down from heaven just as it stands; it was not inscribed by heaven on our minds as on a *tabula rasa,* but has also at least historical roots in human thought and speculation which can be traced back long before the time of Christian revelation properly so-called. But if this doctrine has emerged out of a context and milieu of this kind, then we ought also today to reflect again more explicitly on this context. At the same time, what interests me here is not precisely the concrete form in which belief in a life after death was actually portrayed in the course of the history of religion. But the conviction that the human person survives beyond death and leads a life of a very definite kind is immensely widespread in the whole breadth and depth of the history of mankind and of religion. Has all this nothing to do with the doctrine of purgatory?

'Of the many questions into which this question could be split up, there is one that particularly interests me. I shall attempt to state and explain it. Christian eschatology tends basically to assume that the death of the individual directly and immediately involves the "particular judgment", that this person's history is definitively completed and (leaving aside the possibility of definitive perdition in "hell") that the beatific vision unites him to the primal ground of all reality radically anticipating everything in itself and thus any further development of personal history is superseded. But can we really admit that this description of the human condition after death tells the whole story? We can think also of a plurality of acts on the part of the blessed in heaven, we can portray the "communion of saints" as one in which individuals are involved with one another, etc. By and large we have few speculative misgivings as to why the most radical act of existence in the immediate vicinity of the one and absolute being of God should not have superseded from the very outset the development of any plurality of existence on man's part; nor does it matter very much or at all if we console ourselves with the thought that unity with the deepest source of all reality brings a person into immediate contact with all that emerges in continuous creation from this source. Christianity regards man's consummation as so radical that it leaves no scope for a pluralistic self-realization. In the beatific vision the variety of connections to the pluralistic world is already grasped in its originally single ground. It may then be thought that as we descend with this plural world set up by God in his generous love, we share in a way in its consummation. But if we express it in this way, in order to safeguard the closeness of the blessed to the world unfolded in its plurality, we are really saying that the relationship of the deceased person to the world is quite different from what it was before death.

'The doctrine of purgatory brings a peculiar qualification to this eschatological idea of Christianity, which sees survival as from God in the beatific vision and not as emerging from history. It places between death and radical eschatology understood in the light of God a (brief) intermediate state in which, on the one hand, man's radical consummation is not yet supposed to exist (whether this "not yet" is imagined or contrasted with our normal categories of time) and in which, on the other hand, things do not simply go on as before. What happens, then, in this intermediate state? The answer found in the traditional doctrine of purgatory is that through suffering, expiation for sin is made here and the soul is purified. But it cannot be denied that an answer of this kind is, first, terribly formal and abstract and, second, really has no connection with what such a "soul" inevitably is, what it has and does, since we cannot really imagine that its life and activity is nothing but "suffering".

'Here, I think, it might be helpful to recall the religious tradition of mankind on life beyond the grave. Complex, confusing, and in many ways contradictory as this tradition may be and however much our reservations in regard to ideas of time in this connection must be maintained, nevertheless in these traditions of mankind there are ideas of a further development of those who have died, partly even of wholly welcome further developments, of an enduring and active relationship with the world, the environment, and the milieu to which they formerly belonged. If and insofar as these ideas could be based on experience (and from a theological standpoint this ought not to be denied outright from the very outset, since it is a question of realities coming *before* a person's radical withdrawal from the world by the beatific vision), the question might be asked whether humanly speaking (even if not properly in the light of faith) we have not the opportunity and the right to introduce into the traditional doctrine of purgatory such ideas where they are appropriate and not mythological portrayals of the hereafter (which are completely useless today). The traditional doctrine of purgatory, reduced to what is really binding as a matter of faith, leaves ample abstractly formal scope for the use perhaps of some of the material derived from these traditions of mankind. In this way we might make a little progress. These traditions of humanity, in which there is in fact no trace of the absolutely radical doctrine of the immediate vision of God, would then not be opposed to this properly Christian eschatology, but would refer to the human dimension and the human consummation which are asserted in principle, even though very abstractly, by the doctrine of purgatory and distinguished from the beatific vision.

'What has just been said, merely by way of suggestion, may not seem particularly exciting to an average Christian. But perhaps what has been said might be grasped somewhat more "existentially" in the light of further questions. Are the eschatological statements of Christianity really binding as a matter of faith insofar as they refer absolutely to *all* human beings, to all who were human biologically and in their mental capacity? Or are they statements of faith only with reference to people who have fulfilled themselves and reached finality in a free decision? The traditional teaching assumes that the first of these alternatives is obviously true, as, for instance, the teaching of the Fifth Lateran Council on the immortality of the soul as true of any soul that ever existed, whatever its state may have been immediately before death. But is that certainly true? To put it more cautiously, is this doctrine of the final permanency of human spirit-persons and of their final destiny in the immediate possession of God or in eternal perdition true and binding as a matter of faith with regard to those who never reached finality as a result of self-fulfillment in freedom?

'If we accept this, we ought to admit (at least with further assumptions, which however are taken for granted in traditional eschatology) that the majority of heaven's inhabitants (at least if we include today, as opposed to the Augustinian tradition, children who die unbaptized) consists of people who never came to a personal decision, that eternal bliss must be regarded partly as the fruit of a free act (under the influence of grace, of course) and partly as the fruit of a merely natural happening. (But, despite Romano Guardini, it cannot be said that the eternal happiness of baptized infants demonstrates the free unmeritedness of divine grace, for freedom gained by salvation is itself supreme grace, since freedom and grace are not in competition.) It can, of course, be said that in the last resort we know nothing about all these things. But the traditional doctrine of limbo in particular and of the salvation of the baptized who died in infancy crosses this frontier, at which people would be glad to come to a stop, by regarding statements about the hereafter as absolutely binding only with reference to the person who has reached his consummation in the realization of his radical freedom. Would a midway solution (in the light of the doctrine of purgatory) be conceivable here, by seeing an opportunity of free personal decision as open to these others within the confines of "purgatory"?

'At this point, I think, we should not apply too hastily or too summarily the principle that with the death of a person his history of freedom is always and inevitably at an end, that he is definitively judged according to his works in this life. The principle is correct. But in the cases to be considered here this history of freedom has not even begun and the death to be considered here is not by any means death in the full theological sense as freedom made definitive, the freedom with which a person radically disposes of himself for finality. If there is such a state as purgatory which does not come into existence merely by an external decree and intervention of God, but is a connatural consequence of the nature of the plural human being, then I could imagine that it might offer opportunities and scope for a postmortal history of freedom to someone who had been denied such a history in his earthly life. To be honest, the thought of something like this seems to me more probable than the idea that there are people who continue to exist and to whom God has refused for all eternity to permit this eternity of theirs to be also the finality of their act of freedom. These "blessed ones" would be people who had never freely loved God for all eternity, whose eternal love had never passed into finality through the gate of their freedom. I find an idea of this kind dreadful.

'It may, of course, be asked if there is not some way of avoiding this conclusion other than the one we have suggested. But how? I cannot see any other distinct possibility. The theory put forward by Ladislaus Boros (that such a decision occurs "in" death, and even with "infants"), examined more closely, seems to be merely another way of expressing what was meant here. For this theory allows for an opportunity which is opened up *through* the medical exitus and does not precede the latter: that is, it comes "after" death, particularly since there is no solid empirical basis for the assumption that the people considered here have the opportunity of a decision of this kind before death. On the other hand, the intention in our reflections was to bring purgatory (if we may express it in this way) into the closest proximity to death.

'For my own part I really have little time for the theory of a "migration of souls", or similar ideas. But, if we consider how widespread is this idea in space and time, not to be found today only in some narrower cultural group, if we do not assume far too hastily and as a matter of course that our Western attitude alone is the correct one, then we may wonder whether there may not be some truth in this theory of the migration of souls. Then, however we may want to modify this theory from the standpoint of a metaphysical and realistic anthropology, we might raise the question as to whether there could not be a place in the light of the doctrine of purgatory for such a modified theory of the transmigration of souls even within the scheme of Christian dogmatics. I say "modified", since the doctrine of purgatory could be understood as providing an opportunity for *those* who did not reach a final personal decision in this earthly (or, first) life and, of course, not for others. Christianity, it is true, rightly presumes that such a definitive personal decision is certainly made in the normal case of *one* human life, even though it is a life that has to be lived in a very primitive way, and, conversely, a tolerable theory of the migration of souls also assumes that the eternal cycle of a person's birth and death can be brought to a halt: in other words, there is that decision which Christianity assumes as normally happening in every life.

'The traditional teaching on the lot of infants, however, also assumes without hesitation that these children, if baptized, enter into their eternal happiness without a personal decision in freedom, since it has no doubt about a happy lot of such baptized infants. Even according to traditional Christian teaching then, there are cases in which a personal decision in freedom does not take place: in other words, the question cannot be avoided as to whether and how something can still happen that was not possible in a particular life. If someone does not, in the light of a Western mentality, for metaphysical or existential-ontological reasons regard the migration of souls as *a priori* absurd, he might, I think, raise the question of whether an Eastern person could find it possible to tolerate a modified theory of the migration of souls without contradicting Christian dogma.

'Once more, this theory would have to be modified for a Christian, since the latter in any case has the opportunity (and indeed the presumption) of a definitive decision for or against God and consequently may not raise doubts about the end of temporal history, and, of course, must also reject a reincarnation in subhuman creatures. At the same time, after all, it must be remembered that in any case the Christian (despite the presumption just mentioned) and the advocate of a theory of migration of souls know nothing that is absolutely certain about how many cases there are of human beings for whom there is not an absolute decision for or against God in a particular life. The former cannot deny that there are such cases, according to traditional doctrine; the latter cannot know if such a case is normal in relation to the totality of human beings.'

'It seems to me', said the first theologian, now more or less exhausted, 'that we have terribly little exact knowledge when it comes to eschatology. Whenever we reflect more closely on what is really meant by the traditional formularies, we get involved in obscurities and uncertainties.'

'What do you mean, obscure and uncertain?' retorted the other. 'If, when I pray, I say that I hope and believe in eternal life, I know what I am saying and all the obscurities and uncertainties surrounding this statement amount for me only to the assumption that I am surrendering myself unreservedly but in hope to the eternal mystery which is called God and says yes to myself.'

15

WHY DOES GOD ALLOW US TO SUFFER?

Why does God allow us to suffer? is the question with which we now propose to deal. It can scarcely be denied that this is one of the most fundamental questions of human existence. Here and there perhaps there may be a fortunate few who do not appreciate its importance. But most people are not so fortunate and it is certain that those who are will sooner or later be faced with suffering and then they, too, will be unable to avoid this question which is universal, universally oppressive, and touches our existence at its very roots. At the beginning, then, we need say only that this is not an easy question, prompted like many others by idle curiosity, but we are not going to approach it from the outset in a spirit of world-weariness or to talk about its terrible import in terms of sentimental lyricism.

PERMISSIVE SUFFERING

Why does God allow us to suffer? This does not seem to me a bad way of formulating our question. If, for the moment, we understand the term 'God' as referring to the one and primal reality which sustains everything and which, as such, can authenticate the question of the unity and meaning of all realities experienced or open to experience by us (so that we are not forbidden from the very outset to raise the question of the unity, meaning, and goal of all realities, as if it were pointless), then it is clear from the outset not only that we can and must ask whether there is suffering, what it is, and where it comes from, but that we also may and must immediately ask why

God allows us to suffer in this way. Although this is an absolutely fundamental question, it is not by any means settled in advance from the very outset that we are bringing an absolutely firm notion of God to our question of suffering; the possibility remains entirely open that we shall gain a more or less correct idea of God only when we attempt to answer this question of ours and that the idea would not be accessible to us at all apart from our question.

Why does God *allow* us to suffer? This, too, seems to me an appropriate way of formulating the question, since it embraces deliberately in summary form without discrimination the different real or conceivable possibilities of God's relationship to our suffering: in other words, in this connection it does not make the traditional distinctions, for instance, between permitting and causing. And rightly so.

Obviously, the legitimacy, or in other words, the objective justification of such a distinction (especially that between causing and permitting), is not to be questioned, since respect for God's absolute holiness and goodness forbids us to attribute to him the sin of the free creature and the resultant suffering simply in the same way as we attribute that suffering which does not arise in the first and last place from a creaturely sin and nevertheless is present in the world. But, even if the legitimacy of this traditional and inevitable distinction remains unaffected, it can and must be said at once here that in the last resort the distinction is of secondary importance and does not forbid us to ask in one and the same question and at the same time about God's relationship to all suffering in every form. For what does 'permitting' mean when we are talking about a God who is purely and simply the ground and cause of all reality, who, moreover, in the absolute sovereignty of his freedom and power, in no way restricted by anyone or anything, encompasses all creaturely freedom and does not come up against any limit there? All this (perhaps regarded as more obvious than it really is) was stated in particular by all classical schools of Christian theology from Augustine onward more radically than would be assumed by popular thought on the relationship between God and the world. What does 'permitting' mean, if according to the theology (particularly of the classical schools) on the relationship between divine and human freedom there can be no doubt that God, without in any way infringing or diminishing the freedom of the creature, in his predestination could so forestall creaturely freedom that in practice sin as 'no' to his holy will did not occur in the world; if in the last resort it is contrary to classical theological metaphysics to assert (as a widespread popular apologetics asserts) that God *must* 'permit' sin in his world if, as is his right, he wants to have creaturely freedom in his world?

On this point it is irrelevant in the last resort whether this classical theological metaphysics has grasped the situation accurately enough or in fact has overlooked something. Particularly from this standpoint, it *cannot* be said that there is an indissoluble connection between this freedom willed by God in the world and the actual sin of the creature. If there is not this connection, the distinction between God's permitting and his causing something may still be meaningful. But the distinction does not itself provide an answer to the question of how and why God can permit sin and consequently the suffering that sin incurs. Having regard to God's omnipotent freedom, which knows no bounds, causing and permitting seem to us to come so closely together that we can ask quite simply why God allows us to suffer, without having to distinguish *a priori* in this 'allowing' by God between permitting and causing. We are still only at the preliminary stage of scrutinizing our question as such.

It must be asked whether the question makes sense if everything that can be described as suffering is reduced to one concept or covered by a single word. If this happens, utterly different realities are subsumed under one notion: a procedure that is always extremely dangerous. Without denying the interconnection of the most diverse realities in the world, we must certainly make a clear distinction between the suffering, on the one hand, that is involved *with* and *in* man's free act of sin or arises directly out of it and, on the other hand, all the incidents that involve suffering but cannot be ascribed on the basis of our ordinary experience to man's freely committed sin and nevertheless constitute the greater part of the suffering in the world, particularly since they are largely very obviously partial causes and preconditions of that moral evil in the world which is itself suffering and produces suffering. Since, then, sin arising from creaturely freedom (which is never absolute) is itself by its very nature interwoven in an indissoluble and undelimitable way with other suffering; since, in other words, it is not by any means self-explanatory on its own account; since (and this will have to be stated more precisely later) it points to the mystery of God and the mystery of other innocent suffering and since for this reason, of course, an appeal to *other* creaturely freedom (for instance, of the 'angels' or of the 'devils') in the last resort does not get us any further, even though it might be justified in itself, our basic question is then justified if it concentrates on suffering in its entirety without for that reason denying the distinctions involved: How can God let us suffer?

ATTEMPTS AT A THEISTIC ANSWER

If we want to consider how this question might be answered, we must first of all scrutinize the answers usually given. In accordance with the question as stated here, we are, of course, at the moment scrutinizing only answers that come within the scope of a *theistic* world vision. We are therefore not interested in what a convinced atheist or a sceptical positivist would say, in what would be the attitude of a thinker for whom the world from the outset and also in its ultimate roots exists in an absolute dualism of good and evil or for whom the co-existence of light and darkness, day and night, good and evil, is something simply to be taken for granted and requires no elucidation or justification; for these, what we call 'evil'—as a *necessary* dialectic to the good—could not by any means arouse that protest which the theist in particular raises against suffering in the name of an infinitely good God. Within the scope of a theistic basic conviction there are always several possible answers to our basic question. None of them, it should be stressed, need be pointless or absolutely exclude a different answer. The only question is whether these traditional answers are sufficient in the last resort or whether they simply do not provide any solution to the basic question. Let us see.

Suffering as a Natural Side Effect in an Evolving World

A first attempt to answer our question, more or less distinctly articulated, tends to see suffering as a practically unavoidable side effect in a pluralistic and evolving world. If we look more closely (it is claimed) the world is not a particularly bad place; it consists in fact of many complex realities which do not *a priori* fit in smoothly with one another. The struggle for existence is part of biological development: it is unavoidable and there is no reason to sing sad dirges because the pike swallows the young whitefish or because the female insect sometimes devours the male after copulation. To interpret biological activity as suffering is merely stupid: it is a simple fact and in no way open to an interpretation of this kind. What we call pain and death in this sphere are no more than a ruse of nature, an artifice, to gain more life.

According to this theory, in the last resort moral evil and the suffering that it involves must also be understood in the same way. These, too, are frictional phenomena which necessarily accompany mind, freedom, and moral development. Evil is no more than the good that is not yet perfect or the inescapable tribute which the finite mind must pay to its material foundations on which it rests and which it has to use. In the last resort, evil is to be ascribed merely to what is otherwise known as suffering in the material world, to be explained entirely as a consequence of heredity, social conditions, psychological misdirections, bad education, etc. An adequate elucidation might well lead to an understanding and explanation of physical and moral suffering of such a kind as to show up a serious protest against it as a foolish exaggeration of the demands which a materially conditioned mind can properly make on reality. We must see without illusions the limits of the possible and not to be too demanding. Then it becomes immediately clear that God created a really good world and the question of whether it is the best of all possible worlds can be left aside.

What is to be said about this first attempt to interpret suffering in the world and at the same time to provide a justification of God the Creator? As outlined here it is certainly not to be regarded as superficial or stupid. It is also an answer to be considered more seriously by some of those who indulge in self-torment with their protests against this dark world and their own terrible existence; they might perhaps wonder whether their protest is not permeated by an exaggerated self-esteem which only creates further suffering by its implicit complaint about an injury done to itself. But in the last resort this answer is in fact unsatisfactory and superficial. In view of the limited scope of the question as formulated here, let us leave aside the problem of how pain and death are to be viewed within the dimension of purely biological existence as such. Strictly within this dimension many a protest against suffering may well be inappropriate. We shall refrain from any judgment about this here, even though the groaning of the nonhuman creature, of which Paul speaks, can provide food for thought and suggest a degree of caution. But this first answer breaks down as soon as we see how these physico-biological contradictions are projected into the dimension of spiritual personality and freedom.

Of course, there is a great deal in the realm of freedom and personal history that is determined or co-determined by material or biological conditions and, in fact, to an extent that can scarcely be exaggerated. But the observation of the fact that the realization of the spirit, of freedom and personal decision, is thus materially conditioned does not as such solve the problem of this conditioning. There ought to be freedom, self-determination, unrepeatable uniqueness. When the attempt is made to realize these things, it can only be by coming up against the anonymous constraint of biological necessity and universal law; what is meant to be spirit in unique freedom becomes matter under universal compulsion. Under these circumstances pain could be eliminated and explained only if it were possible to regard spirit as a secondary manifestation of matter. But that is impossible. Moreover the history of freedom does not permit suffering to be played down. It is not sufficient to ascribe suffering to the hardships arising from the material world as such. Freedom as such itself produces suffering and pain and death.

It is possible to imagine freedom and its dignity existing without suffering in paradisiacal harmony. But in practice, freedom as such has produced immense and indescribable suffering that cannot be blamed on material and biological conditions. Responsibility for the march into the gas chambers of Auschwitz cannot be spread over the phenomena leading to the plunge of a swarm of migratory ants into an abyss. Evil is not merely a complicated case of what is biologically unpleasant or of death prevailing everywhere. The vast protest rising up from world history is not simply an intensification of the noise that always and everywhere accompanies a life and death that can basically be taken for granted; to play down in this way the pain in world history is a betrayal of personal dignity, of freedom, and of the absolute imperative of morality, and it is possible to cope on these cheap terms with suffering and death in the history of humanity only as long as this suffering touches a person merely from a distance. There are certainly stoics who uphold a theory that minimizes the importance of suffering and death and yet go calmly and with dignity into death. But, whether they reflect on it or not, they are then living in the light of a deeper understanding of existence than is implied in this theory.

Suffering as Effect of Creaturely, Sinful Freedom

There is a second interpretation of suffering in the world that is not adequate in itself. This seeks to derive suffering exclusively from creaturely freedom and to explain it in this light. Suffering, pain, and death are said to be always and everywhere and in every respect the effect and manifestation of the evil decision of creaturely freedom and nothing else. A bold theory. It is then not *a priori* absurd to take into account a creaturely freedom which is not identical with human freedom and which has created a history prior to the history of the biological nature of this earth, thus co-determining *a priori* the peculiar character of this history of nature and the history of humanity and marking it with suffering. Without this hypothesis, which has often been adopted in different variations in the history of Christian thought, an adequate derivation of all suffering from creaturely freedom alone would not be possible. Admittedly an attempt has also been made to deduce at least all human suffering from human freedom alone, without recourse to a supra- and pre-human history, in the sense of the traditional claim that, prior to a human free decision at the dawn of history, man did not have to die and existed in a paradisiacal immunity from suffering. In this way it is possible to maintain the theory that, in the last resort, all our human suffering arises entirely from freedom (that is, from man's freedom).

If, in the first place, we leave aside the problems created by the assumptions behind these two varieties of the basic theory, the latter seems to have something very seductive about it. Facing, as it were, God's glory and goodness, it tells man (or the free creature as such): You alone, you entirely alone, are responsible for all the horror of creaturely history. You, through your freedom, are to blame:

through the freedom with which you made a decision that by its very nature could not be shifted off to anyone else and least of all to God. Creaturely freedom is thus set up as somehow purely and simply absolute and underivable in its decision. Then it is clear that the blessed radiance of God's holy grace is not imperiled by the cry of despair that inevitably follows the evil decision of creaturely freedom.

But (we touched briefly on this problem at the very beginning) for a really Christian understanding, the creature's freedom is not so absolute and underivable as is assumed in this arrogant conception, which refuses to admit that in the last resort there cannot be something in the world that is independent of God, that even this free decision of the creature cannot be made by the latter entirely alone and with an absolutely undivided responsibility. According to Christian understanding, freedom of this kind simply does not exist. The freedom of men and angels is a *created* freedom, sustained in its existence and nature always and everywhere by God's supreme providence, in its power and action, in its capacity and concrete decision. We may not be able to see how true creaturely freedom can so exist with the inalienability of its decision *and* at the same time with the inescapability from God's sovereignty, in which God sustains this creaturely freedom and places it in its freedom, but for that very reason does not share his sovereignty with the creature's freedom; this in no way alters the fact that our freedom is completely embraced in God's supreme providence.

Distinctions can rightly be introduced into the permanent origination of our free decisions in the light of the way in which these decisions on each occasion turn out to be good or bad; within the scope of Catholic theology it is possible to work out the most diverse theories of the way in which this attribution of our free decisions to God's disposition is to be conceptualized and interpreted. Or it might be decided *a priori* and in principle to refrain from all attempts of this kind and to assume that it is fundamentally impossible for us here and now to get any nearer to a solution of this problem. None of this in any way changes the basic conviction of all Christian theology that to regard our freedom *in this way* as absolute and autonomous is contrary to the Christian understanding of God.

We are free, we cannot shift on to God the responsibility for our free decisions, but these very decisions of ours are in fact completely embraced solely by God's disposition, which has its ground in him alone and in nothing else. As is evident from all attempts of the different permissible Catholic systems of grace, it is impossible to reconcile into a higher synthesis the statement that we cannot shift on to God our freedom decisions as our own and the statement that these also come within the scope of God's disposition (whether this disposition is to be understood as causing or permitting). But this in no way alters the fact that even our free decision as such is nevertheless in every respect and in its whole reality dependent on God.

If, however, this is the situation in the light of the Christian idea of God, the statement that suffering arises from freedom is not a final and definitive conclusion, but a hint that, important as it may be, again disappears into the mystery of the sovereign freedom of God himself. And if in truth we have to admit that we are responsible and may not escape from this responsibility, it also remains true that this permanent responsibility of ours must be and will be assumed by God himself, even though we do not know how that is possible. If, then, we point to our freedom as an answer to the question of why God allows us to suffer, this answer is largely true and is not to be dismissed, but it is not final. We are not permitted to be content with this answer, but neither are we permitted to assume that there is an answer going beyond this which would be completely comprehensible to us.

In these circumstances, how far suffering in the world is to be ascribed to man's creaturely freedom and eventually to that of the angels and the devils, and how far suffering exists that is truly man's suffering and yet does not spring from an evil use of freedom, is more or less merely a question of theoretical curiosity, the answer to which in no way alters our existential situation. Whatever form the answer takes, it remains in any case provisional and in the end is lost in God's incomprehensibility and in his freedom. Consequently there is no need to discuss at greater length here all the questions with which we were faced at the beginning. As far as our question is concerned, it is irrelevant in the last resort whether our cosmos bears the traces of a disaster occurring in the course of the angels' history of freedom, whether and how humanity lived in paradise before its sin, in what sense death can be understood as the price of sin, etc. These are questions which may be imposed on us by a

Christian self-understanding. Here, however, they can be left aside, since they certainly cannot yield the final answer to our essential question.

Suffering as a Situation of Trial and Maturing

A third traditional answer to our question suggests that God allows us to suffer in order to test us and bring us to maturity. Suffering, it is claimed, is the necessary situation in which alone a mature person can grow in patience, hope, and wisdom, and in the pattern of Christ.

We need not examine the implications of this third answer more closely here. It contains an important truth which is certainly not to be minimized or obscured here and, taking for granted the fact that suffering comes to everyone and occurs in every milieu, this third answer can and must be seen as a true imperative, binding on each individual: Live in such a way that the suffering affecting you and your milieu does not in the last resort turn your attitude to God into one of despair, but perfects you, even though the process of maturing leads through all the abysses of dying and death with Jesus. Nevertheless, this third suggestion still does not provide an answer to our real question. And this is not only because there is such a terrible amount of suffering in the world, to which only a fraudulent and unrealistic piety could ascribe such a humane effect.

The children burned to death by napalm bombs were not going through a process of human maturing. Elsewhere, too, in innumerable cases there is suffering which is destructive in its effects, despite all good will to endure it in a human and Christian way, which simply demands too much from a person, warps and damages his character, leaves him preoccupied solely with satisfying the most primitive needs of existence, makes him stupid or wicked. In desperation it might almost be said that suffering as a means of human and Christian maturing is something that can be endured only by a noble mind untouched by any real distress, practising spiritual massage in an ivory tower.

This again is a one-sided and unfair way of expressing it and fails to appreciate the range of opportunities of coping with a terrible existence in faith, hope, and love. But all this in no way alters the fact that there is infinitely diverse, terrible suffering in the history of humanity (including the uncertain lot of children dying in infancy and old people in senile decline) which cannot be integrated into a process of maturing and personal probation, so that this third attempt at an explanation also remains inadequate. The question might also be raised quite plainly and sincerely whether humanity might be better enabled to reach moral maturity in a situation less fraught with suffering. How could it be proved that really genuine happiness must necessarily soften and corrupt man?

In principle, a situation free from suffering would seem to be as such morally better. On this point Christian ascetics are not always completely consistent. They say that suffering springs from sin and extol emphatically (and somewhat theoretically) this situation of suffering as the authentic climate in which the Christian virtues can flourish. Of course, accepting the fact that suffering exists, such Christian imperatives are wholly appropriate and salutary and rightly call for the imitation of the crucified Christ. But this does not answer the question of why God allows us to endure sufferings which simply cannot have this humane educative function (and there are innumerable examples of these). The most appalling sufferings have no such function at all; they are cruelties of nature which far transcend our moral resources.

Suffering as a Pointer to Another, Eternal life

A fourth attempt to answer our basic question consists in referring to eternal life after death and after our history of suffering. This suggestion should certainly not be dismissed with the stupid claim that it contains only a dubious analgesic, opium of the people and for the people. As Christians we certainly cherish a courageous hope, which only God's grace can give us, looking for eternal life without death, pain, and tears. But this suggestion is not an answer to our basic question. For no one can prove that this suffering is the absolutely necessary means for attaining eternal life, that death under any circumstances is the sole gateway to eternal life. In fact, Christian tradition tells us that death did not have to be. But neither can it be said that sin, which is supposed to be the cause of death, is itself unavoidable or that it does not in the last resort represent an unanswered question to God himself.

If, moreover, eternal life cannot simply be used as a way of brushing aside the history of cruelty, then a crudely understood future state of happiness does not justify the horrors that preceded it. And how is eternal life to be conceived, if we can be happy there looking back to the torment of history? *This* question, at least, still remains open. How are we to avoid the temptation to return the admission ticket to eternal life, if this eternal life cannot consist in forgetting history to such an extent that the identity of the person now in bliss with his existence in history is canceled? In brief, since it is possible to think of an eternal life achieved without suffering, it can indeed be seen as a conquest of suffering but not as an authorization of the latter.

The Incomprehensibility of Suffering as Part of the Incomprehensibility of God

What then are we to say? Is no justification to be found of suffering in man's history? Must we simply leave our basic question unanswered? Let us begin our reflections once more from a quite different starting point. Christian faith declares that God is the incomprehensible mystery. This he is now and for all eternity, this he will be even when we see him face to face. Even then, the terrible radiance of the incomprehensible God will remain, unveiled and eternal. It will be, we might say, endurable only if we *love* God and exist unconditionally and selflessly in *this* love that affirms God as he is; the never comprehensible and never transparent mystery of the infinite God can be our eternal bliss only in the act in which we selflessly affirm him. Apart from a love of this kind, in which man forsakes himself, never really to return to himself, the sole appropriate basic act of our existence would only be the act of a radical protest that we are not ourselves God and also that we cannot cope with him: the act which constitutes hell. This love, dispossessing man until he is absorbed selflessly into the mystery of God, has no justification outside itself any more than the mystery of God to which it surrenders man.

This mystery of God's incomprehensibility, however, is not merely the mystery of a being to be understood as static, but is also the mystery of God's freedom, of his underivable disposition, which has not to be justified before any other authority. It is to *this* that man surrenders himself even when he loves God face to face in eternal life and abandons himself unconditionally to God's incomprehensibility. God is loved in his freedom, God himself and not only what we have grasped of him in what must remain eternally no more than a fleeting glance. Only the knowledge which is itself dissolved and transfigured in love, which, in the last resort, is not acquired as knowledge is otherwise acquired, but which is surrendered, lovingly lost in God's incomprehensibility and sees there (and not elsewhere) its fulfillment, its true nature: this alone is the knowledge that saves us and makes us free by the very fact that it is turned into unselfish love, the incomprehensible miracle demanded from man who seems to be the subject that by its very nature is egoistic and wholly self-centered. When we consider all this, our basic question can be seen from quite different aspects. What was hitherto regarded as its unanswerability is then no longer the scandal in our existence, to be removed as quickly as possible, which must be elucidated as clearly as possible, but an element in the incomprehensibility that penetrates, challenges, and lays claim to our whole life.

The incomprehensibility of suffering is part of the incomprehensibility of God. Not in the sense that we could deduce it as necessary and thus inevitably as clarified from something else that we already know of God. If this were so it would not be at all incomprehensible. But the very fact that it is really and eternally incomprehensible means that suffering is truly a manifestation of God's incomprehensibility in his nature and in his freedom. In his nature because, despite what might be described as the terrible amorality of suffering (at least on the part of children and innocent people), we have to acknowledge the pure goodness of God, which needs no acquittal before our tribunal. In his freedom, because this, too, if it wills the suffering of the creature, is incomprehensible, since it could achieve without suffering the sacred aims of the freedom that wills suffering. Suffering, then, is the form (as such, again, underivable) in which the incomprehensibility of God himself appears.

Without wanting to introduce a logical system of assumptions and conclusions, it might be said at most that, concretely, within our existence which can be realized only historically in freedom, suffering is unavoidable insofar as its absence would mean that God would not be taken seriously as the incomprehensible mystery with which we have to cope here and now, but would remain an abstract theorem giving us no further trouble in the concreteness of our life. In the actual course of our existence the fact is that the acceptance of God as the intractable mystery and the silent acceptance of the inexplicability and unanswerability of suffering are one and the same event. Theoretically it might perhaps be said that the impossibility of tracing back a free disposition of God, which is understandable only in itself and in its loving acceptance by us, without being ascribed to something else, understandable in love and not in theory, is itself an exercise of absolute surrender to the mystery of God, even if this free disposition of God does not really involve suffering. But it might just as well be said that the very fact of such a capitulation to freedom, without expecting it to be justified by anything other than itself, involves pain in a sublime sense, compared to which suffering in a more physico-biological sense must ultimately seem insignificant, particularly since for us, at least at the present time, subjective assessment of a pain and its real depth, superficiality, or radicalness are not identical. Thus, the ecstatic outburst of the creaturely subject from itself, in order to surrender unconditionally to God's freedom, in truth might also involve pain in a sublime sense: pain with which in any case the bliss of escaping from oneself has to be paid for, so that what we otherwise regard as suffering is no more than its counterpart on a lower plane of being. However that may be, in our present concrete state, the acceptance of suffering without an answer other than the incomprehensibility of God and his freedom is the concrete form in which we accept God himself and allow him to be God. If there is not directly or indirectly this absolute acceptance of the incomprehensibility of suffering, all that can really happen is the affirmation of our own idea of God and not the affirmation of God himself.

Walter Dirks tells of a visit to Romano Guardini, when the latter already bore the marks of his fatal illness:

> To hear what the old man confided on his sick bed was an unforgettable experience. At the Last Judgment he would not only allow himself to be questioned, but would also in his turn ask questions.

> He firmly hoped that the angel would not deny him the true answer to the question which no book, not even the Bible, no dogma and no teaching authority, no 'theodicy' or theology, not even his own theology, had been able to answer for him: Why, God, these fearful detours on the way to salvation, the suffering of the innocent, why sin?[1]

All that we want to say here and now is that Guardini rightly could not discover any answer to this question, that the question can certainly be answered only by the angel at the judgment, and even then the true answer must still be only the incomprehensible God in his freedom and nothing else. In other words, this answer can be heard only if we surrender ourselves in unconditionally adoring love as answer to God. If we do not achieve this love, forgetting itself for God, or, better, if we do not accept it as given to us, there is nothing left but naked despair at the absurdity of our suffering, a despair which is really the only form of atheism that must be taken seriously. There is no blessed light to illumine the dark abyss of suffering other than God himself. And we find him only when we lovingly assent to the incomprehensibility of God[2] himself, without which he would not be God.

[1] Cited in E. Biser, *Interpretation und Veränderung* (Paderborn, 1979), pp. 132–33.

[2] Cf. K. Rahner 'The Human Question of Meaning in Face of the Absolute Mystery of God', *Theological Investigations,* vol. 18 (London/New York, 1983), pp. 89–104. See also K. Rahner, 'Ignatius of Loyola Speaks to a Modern Jesuit', in K. Rahner, P. Imhof, and H. N. Loose, *Ignatius of Loyola* (London/New York, 1979), p. 17.

PART SIX

Mary and Woman

16

MARY AND THE CHRISTIAN IMAGE OF WOMAN

The Church from the beginning never regarded Mary merely as a person who inevitably appears, like many others, in a biography of Jesus. Mary has her proper and unique function in salvation history as such and the Church accordingly in its liturgy and piety pays special reverence to the Blessed Virgin, whom it acknowledges as Mother of God. The Church sees in Mary its own image in pure perfection, the image of the nature of the Christian in its purity and fullness and therefore also the perfect image of woman.

This image of woman must not be lost sight of today. It is this image that has enabled the Church in past centuries, perhaps without any very close reflection, to prevent society (with which it often enough too uncritically identified itself) from setting up a purely male domination. The Church itself had also to learn slowly and painfully, amid the changes in secular society, to give woman what is due to her by nature and by right: an historical process which is still far from complete. But in its understanding of faith the Church has a starting point of its own and a dynamism of its own for this process. And what is its own is in fact present as an archetype in its image of Mary.

Like the Christian faith as a whole, the image of Mary has obviously a history in the Church. Consequently, the image of woman, as available to the Church in Mary, also has its history which is not told and elucidated simply by presenting the history of the Marian dogmas from the Council of Ephesus (431) to Pius XII and up to chapter 8 of the constitution *Lumen Gentium* or to the Apostolic

Exhortation of Paul VI on Marian devotion (1974). This is right particularly since it was only at the Second Vatican Council and in the teaching of Paul VI that the process began explicitly of seeing in the image of Mary the image of woman as such, even though, of course, Christendom had at all times (perhaps occasionally not very discreetly) stamped its knowledge of woman on to the image of Mary. The image of woman in the image of Mary has a history which still continues today and is as unfinished, incomplete, and unforeseeable as anything that belongs to history.

CHANGES IN THE IMAGE OF MARY

While we talk of changes in the image of the Blessed Virgin as image of woman, the fact must not be overlooked that there is something permanent about this image. For the faith also of the Church of the future, Mary will remain the believer who, with and in her existence, in her faith, and in her person, received the eternal Word of the Father as God's irrevocable promise to the world, Jesus, the blessed fruit of her womb. She will always be recognized as the person whose existence from the beginning—despite the sin of the world, which she also had to endure—was encompassed by the victorious grace of God which preserved her and her freedom by its unobtrusive power as 'immaculate'. The Church will always confess that Mary with her whole existence ('body and soul') has 'already' reached her consummation, whether or not this is regarded as a 'temporal' privilege for her alone. The Church will always see in Mary the one who had a unique function in salvation history, who reached her eschatological goal in Jesus Christ, crucified and risen, however this unique function is described more precisely in its different aspects ('first of the redeemed', 'co-redemptrix', 'mediatrix of grace'). At the same time, the Church will neither obscure the nature of Jesus and his function as mediator of salvation nor give way to a pseudo-democratic resentment, unwilling to accept a situation in which everyone does not have the same task in history. It will confess that man receives from others and has himself the whole fullness of being human (by nature and grace) only because in unselfish love he sees it as present in all others together.

If we ask about possible and conceivable changes in the image of the Blessed Virgin today or in future, some basic considerations must first be put forward. In the first place, Christian dogma also has its history. Its truth is always present only in an historical form and particularly when we are not reflecting on such an historical form of truth. Perhaps we cannot do so adequately because this form is that of our own time and, consequently, there is lacking the distance at which we recall in historical reflection forms of truth other than our own. This is true also of Marian dogmas. Historically there has been an historical development up to the definition of the assumption of Mary with body and soul into her consummation (1950) in which individual Marian dogmas (divine maturity, immaculate conception, assumption into heaven) were added to one another, so to speak, to form the Mariology that we acknowledge today as part of our faith. These individual Marian dogmas have grown out of a single Mariological basic principle.

I do not think that Mariology will develop further in this 'quantitative' way (as not a few Mariologists hoped, even as recently as twenty years ago) so that in the foreseeable future there might, for example, be definitions of Mary as 'co-redemptrix' or 'mediatrix of grace'. After the events at the Second Vatican Council, linked with the controversial formulation of Mariology, this seems to me improbable. That is not to say that Catholic Mariology will have no history in the future. But presumably this will not consist (to put it crudely) in a 'quantitative' augmentation of Marian dogma. What is more likely to happen is that the old dogma will be both reconsidered and theologically assimilated under new aspects and against new backgrounds of understanding, which formerly were not so explicitly present. In what follows we shall reflect a little on these things.

Here is a second consideration. If we legitimately disregard sublime speculations on Mary's dignity in the light of her divine maternity which points directly to the incomprehensibility of the infinite God, Mariological statements refer to a particular individual, an historical and finite human being, who has a definite (albeit unique) place in mankind as a whole and in its history. This person's unique function in history does not permit us to see her in the light of what is ultimately a mistaken Platonism and to ascribe to her alone the whole fullness of human reality which can be realized only in mankind as a whole and in its whole history.

This is really obvious. But it seems to me that Mariology in the past did not always 'subcutaneously' take this obviousness seriously enough and was exposed to the danger of attributing to Mary, even as an individual human being, all those privileges (at least *eminenter*) which are at all possible in a human being, but in fact realizable only in the whole of mankind taken together. The individual Christian was thus bound to regard himself only as a defective repetition of what had been realized perfectly in Mary as an individual person. But this is not true. Just as (in Augustine's terminology) the whole Christ is present only in head and body (of the Church) together, and the body (of the Church) also helps the head to reach its whole fullness, so it is analogously with Mary. It is only the Church as a whole that gives reality to Mary and in its loving unity gives to this individual person her whole fullness, which she does not have when considered independently. This is true particularly when we consider Mary as the perfect woman in her relationship to all women in the human race. Only the whole—with Mary—is Mary.

NEW VIEW OF JESUS CHRIST

A first alteration of the horizons of understanding for Mary results from the change in modern Christology. Traditional Christology (despite the treatise *De legato divino* in fundamental theology) was a pure descendence Christology, a Christology from above, a doctrine of the descent of the preexistent Logos into flesh, into history. There was indeed always a fundamental theology of the encounter with the historical, concrete Jesus, but as a purely fundamental theological formulation of the question and as a presupposition to dogmatics it remained outside dogmatic Christology in the form in which the latter appeared as early as Paul's Letters to the Philippians and Colossians and more especially in the prologue to John's Gospel.

A dogmatic Christology today (notwithstanding the rights of an independent fundamental theology) must itself start with the historical Jesus and show that the self-understanding of the historical Jesus (at least when his resurrection is taken into account) justifies this descendence Christology which, as we said, is present even in the New Testament but needs a separate justification. Fundamental theology and dogmatic Christology must find a clearer internal unity. This, too, is attempted in recent Christologies, which are dogmatic Christologies and yet incorporate the questions of fundamental theology. We may recall, for instance, the works of Walter Kasper, Edward Schillebeeckx and, although to be read with reserve and critically, Hans Küng. They all practise an 'ascendence Christology', a Christology 'from below', not to suppress the older Christology, but to take it in and authenticate it before the historical conscience of modern man.

It is time for something similar to happen in Mariology today. Here, too, there must be something like an 'ascendence Mariology', a Mariology 'from below'. This means in the first place that the formulations of the questions, the methods of answering them, and the answers themselves, which refer to Mary and are usual in modern exegesis working historically, are taken into account by dogmatic Mariology. It must be asked, for example, what is really the precise literary genre of the narratives referring to Mary in Matthew, Luke, and John; other statements of Scripture which make Mary's role in the life of Jesus seem restricted must be evaluated more impartially than has hitherto been the case generally in Mariology. If the 'historical' element in these Marian narratives is cautiously and critically estimated as more slight than was hitherto thought, this need not turn out to the disadvantage of a dogmatic Mariology. Such narratives are not only reportage, but also theology, which as inspired scriptural statements are binding on us and set us the task of showing how these statements emerge from the experience which early Christendom had of Mary in connection with Jesus.

Under these assumptions of modern exegesis, a Mariology from below can be developed which, of course, must take in classical Mariology, but which sees it from new aspects and can purify it from pious exaggerations. The questions involved in the doctrine of the 'virgin birth' must be thought out afresh. Mary must be seen also as the woman of the people, as poor, as a learner, who lives in the light of the historical, social, and religious situation of her time and her people. She is to be seen, not as a heavenly being, but as a human person, as active and suffering for herself and others, as learning in the midst of many uncertainties, as accepting her function in salvation history in faith, hope, and love, and by this very fact, as model and mother of believers.

MARY AS IMAGE OF WOMAN

Mariology can be set in motion today from another aspect. Mary should be and remain for the Christian the pure image of woman, not merely a model for believers in general. Nor is an orthodox Christology subcutaneously monophysite or monothelite, but takes absolutely seriously the true and undiminished reality of Jesus as the one who confronts God in creaturely freedom. If at the same time it is remembered that he was a man, then, notwithstanding the unique importance of Jesus for both sexes, it can certainly be said that Mary represents the pure image of woman in her relationship to God in the same way that Jesus as man presents that image for man as such.

If we ask what exactly this means for Mary as model for woman, serious questions emerge which have not yet been adequately recognized. The various anthropological sciences of the present time (for all their fundamental equality, from which the Church's theory and practice have something to learn) say a great deal and much that is important about the distinction of the sexes and, thus, also about the peculiar nature of woman which determines all dimensions of her existence. In principle, therefore, there can be no doubt that woman even in her grace-given relationship to God is a woman and not a sexless being. But if we begin to describe concretely the religious character of woman, anthropologically and theologically (from human experience, from the Old and the New Testament), we are at once involved (not to speak too poetically) in great embarrassment.

Such concrete descriptions of woman's religious existence are based often and hastily on characteristics which really do not belong to the external, authentic nature of woman, but are historically, culturally, and sociologically conditioned. The charge might be made today that these descriptions purporting to be a theologically guaranteed understanding of her nature are really opposed to woman's emancipation. The danger then arises that Mary's image will be drawn with the aid of such an historically and culturally conditioned image of woman and then used theologically to sanction and perpetuate this older and today in many respects dubious image.

On the other hand, on closer inspection it becomes clear that many features (authentic in themselves) introduced into the image of Mary as woman in her relationship to God are by no means specifically and exclusively feminine. Is it not true that a man also in his approach to God must be able to be silent, be wholly receptive, commit himself, listen in humility and faith, serve and not dominate? In describing the religious existence we seize only too easily and too often on characteristics which are really generally human and can and must be predicated of both sexes.

If we add that such attributes of woman are present in a specifically feminine and not masculine form, the question arises of what exactly and concretely is meant by this. It does not seem very easy to give a clear answer to this question by attempting to characterize this specifically feminine way of religious existence with the aid of modalities which are sociologically and culturally conditioned and do not belong simply to woman's nature always and everywhere.

Mariology today and in future still has a great deal to do if it wants to have an image of Mary that will really be true also for the religious existence of woman as such. It is an image that can perhaps be produced authentically today only by women, by women theologians. But this means that Mariology, despite its autonomy as a dogmatic treatise, is caught up in that mental and spiritual history in which woman even today looks for the nature she always had and which nevertheless is continually freshly assigned to her. Mariology is not at an end. Even today it has a history stretching into the future, which has still to be found. In this history the Church is seeking the nature of woman, of Mary, and also its own nature.

17

MARY'S VIRGINITY

The following reflections are concerned simply with Mary's virginity as a single theme. Apart from possible exceptions, which we reserve to ourselves, this is a legitimate procedure in the light both of the material and of the apologetic and kerygmatic intention behind the reflections, since on the whole the questions of the origin, meaning, and binding force in faith and of the possibility of conveying these doctrines to modern man's sense of faith involve more or less the same difficulties in regard to *virginitas ante partum* (VAP), *in partu* (VIP), and *post partum* (VPP), and since Rudolph Pesch,[1] too, questions only the VPP, but by that very fact also raises the question of the VAP.

The reflections presented here are not directly concerned with the question of the meaning and the limits to the meaning of the doctrine of the virginity of Mary and the binding force of this doctrine in faith. In this connection nothing will be directly settled here, since an adequate treatment of *these* questions would require much more space than is available here and since the trend of these reflections does not seem to me to call for so broad a theme. In *these* reflections all that is to be asked is what group of questions would have to be kept in mind, considered, and possibly discussed if any representatives of the Church's magisterium wanted to comment on the questions raised again by Pesch. For only when we are clear about these preliminary questions can we decide properly the question of whether the Church's magisterium at the present moment should or

[1] R. Pesch, *Das Markusevangelium,* vol. 1 (HThk II; Freiburg, 1976), 'Excursus: Zur Frage der Bruder und Schwestern Jesu', pp. 322–24.

can comment on the problems raised again by Pesch, whether this is possible and opportune. What is to be said from the exegetical standpoint on the question as formulated here is explained elsewhere and cannot and need not be repeated here. This involves a further limitation of the task to be undertaken here. But the formulation of the theme as so restricted includes two things: it must not only be asked what preliminary theological reflections (in terms of systematic theology and history of dogma) are necessary today if we want to give an appropriate answer that is 'as such' correct and binding in faith in regard to the doctrine of Mary's virginity; it must *also* be asked what preliminary reflections of this kind are necessary if an authoritative teaching of the Church on this virginity is really to have any prospect of actually 'getting through' to the understanding of faith of *those* members of the Church whom the authoritative declaration is meant to reach. The Church has the duty, not only of saying the right thing, but also of saying this right thing 'rightly': that is, so that there is the greatest possible prospect that its right teaching will also actually be believed. These two aspects of our theme will be given equal consideration here, although they do not need always to be expressly distinguished.

PRELIMINARY METHODOLOGICAL CONSIDERATIONS

(1) If the essential problem (particularly as including VAP) is to be treated correctly today dogmatically and kerygmatically, the question of an objectively and apologetically correct understanding of a 'miracle' cannot be excluded, since VAP, at least in the traditional and 'biological' sense, includes such a miracle. Both from the nature of the case (that is, in the light of a correct and clear idea of God and of his relationship to the world) and from the standpoint of a modern mentality (which is not in itself a criterion of truth, but cannot be disregarded if proclamation of the faith is to be effective) the idea of miracle (in itself and with reference to its credibility) as a breach of suspension of the 'laws of nature' has become highly problematic, quite apart from the question of whether miracles in this sense can be proved empirically to be facts. (The resurrection of Jesus as a miracle cannot and may not be brought into the present discussion,

since this miracle as eschatological event is *a priori sui generis*.[2]) But in any case, an appropriate and apologetically and kerygmatically effective teaching on VAP cannot be established on the basis of a procedure that ignores the general problems in regard to a 'miracle' arising from the nature of the case and for the modern mentality prior to the question of VAP.

(2) If the doctrine of Mary's virginity is to be really effectively conveyed to the Christian (particularly the educated Christian) today, the conclusions of recent studies on the development of dogma cannot be disregarded; here, too, what has been learned at other points of the history of dogma and even from the New Testament itself must be kept in mind. But, among other things (which cannot be explicitly considered here), this means at least the following:

(*a*) With reference to its individual statements and expressions the Church's dogma cannot be set out today as merely the sum total of a number of individual propositions, each of which is presented simply as based on individual statements of Scripture, or of former declarations of the magisterium. Each individual statement must be made in its coherence both with the one totality of faith and with the original and unifying centre of the reality of faith. Otherwise, the teaching of Vatican II on the hierarchy of truths amounts to no more than empty talk and a feeble excuse. The original one and unifying event of the final revelation in Christianity is not a sum total of individual propositions to be simply accepted, arbitrarily communicated by God in their individual form, but the event of God's most intimate self-communication which finds its full historical tangibility and its eschatological irreversibility in Jesus Christ, crucified and risen. The Church's teaching on Mary, too, must be seen and made intelligible from this standpoint, even though this does not necessarily mean a simply logically deductive argument. This is true in particular of VAP, VIP, and VPP. If there is not a clear and explicit recourse to that event, the proclamation of this doctrine remains ineffective and the magisterium does not achieve what is unconditionally required of it today. We are speaking of no more than a

[2] Cf., for example, Karl Rahner, *Foundations of Christian Faith* (London/New York, 1978), pp. 264–85. The whole question of an idea of miracle in general that is possible and convincing today cannot, of course, be discussed here. On this cf. B. Weissmahr, *Gottes Wirken in der Welt* (Frankfurt, 1973).

postulate, and how it can be fulfilled remains obscure. But the realization of this postulate is obviously not possible here.

(*b*) An appropriate and effective proclamation of the doctrine of Mary's virginity (including VAP) must see without prejudice that the content of this doctrine (as correct and therefore to be more precisely defined) is not in itself alone a single primary datum, based on purely empirical observations, but a factor deduced from a previous conviction in regard to Mary and her function in salvation history. Even if and insofar as such empirical observations were possible and can or could be assumed to be established, they would not *ipso facto* yield the real content of the theological teaching. In the first place it is perceptible from the history of dogma that VIP is not based on such empirical (physiological) observations or on information given by Mary, but is a theological 'conclusion' (in the widest sense of the term and as such needing to be more precisely defined), which has become established only in the course of time in the Church's consciousness. But the same is true *mutatis mutandis* of VAP. The mere fact that, for example, the intervention of a male person is not perceptible in Jesus' coming into existence or that there might be historical information as given by Mary available in this connection could not on its own account authenticate VAP in the sense intended here, either in itself or as an object of a theological belief as such. Nor would an empirical observation of VPP, in the sense that Mary in fact had no more children, alone and independently authenticate the content of VPP as understood in the traditional sense. The fact remains, then, that this whole doctrine, insofar as and in the sense in which it can be an object of faith and binding in faith, must be a factor deduced from a more fundamental global understanding of Mary and her function in salvation history and can be justified only in this way in terms of the history of faith and the history of dogma. But how is this to come about? This is the question which the one Mariology of today cannot evade.

(*c*) If this question is really objectively and convincingly answered, then undoubtedly for our question, too, the result will be the same as that which can be observed in the history of dogma in regard to very many other doctrines and in these cases is impartially noted by the Church's magisterium today when it appears in the work of theologians. It can rightly be said that the development of dogma (that is, the explication of the original global experience of revelation in individual propositions) is a 'one way' course: that is, *if* and when such an explication leads on the part of the Church to an *absolute* assent to a particular individual proposition, it is no longer retrospectively revisable in the sense that such a proposition could later be declared erroneous. Nor is this the case even if this explication of faith, which has in fact taken place at an earlier stage, cannot be achieved conclusively in a purely logical argument. But this understanding of the development of dogma does not exclude, but positively includes, a recourse to the original understanding of faith. (Otherwise we would need, for example, to practise only Denzinger theology and could do without a biblical theology or see the latter as merely historical curiosity.)

Despite the 'one way' character of the history of dogma, recourse to the original understanding of faith, from which the later teaching developed, can be a criterion for the right understanding of the later dogma. It could, in fact, be shown from very many examples (accepted or even confirmed by the Church's magisterium) that recourse to the earlier understanding of faith as source of later teaching can be a criterion for the right and really binding understanding of faith. We ask, for example, what is 'really' meant when we speak of original sin, what is 'really' meant when we say that Jesus founded the Church, instituted seven sacraments, etc.; and we are then asking not *only* what people generally make of the answers of traditional theology, but *also* at the same time about the sources of these answers, whether they lead unambiguously to these answers *or* whether in such traditional answers, despite their genuine origin as a whole from these sources, there have been amalgamated indiscriminately also ideas and interpretations which are not part of the binding content of the article of faith as so established, but have not hitherto been eliminated from it in traditional theology or in the Church's dogmatic pronouncements and for historical reasons could not hitherto have been eliminated.

Not everything that was actually and implicitly assumed at a particular time to be necessary for the clarification of the meaning of an article of faith is really and in principle an inseparable part of this article of faith itself. If, for instance, it is shown historically that the Fathers of Trent in practice had something in mind that they took for granted and did not eliminate from their understanding of the term 'substance', this is far from saying that their notion of substance is binding for the present-day interpretation of transubstantiation. Or if Augustine thought that libido is the necessary means of transmitting original sin and *in this way* explained original sin as Catholic dogma, this is far from saying that we must or even can regard this understanding of original sin today as dogma. If Pius XII still thought that monogenism was an indispensable and unrenounceable element of the Catholic doctrine of original sin, we may nevertheless hold a different opinion today and, while maintaining the doctrine of original sin and its essential meaning, eliminate a monogenistic interpretation of this doctrine as an historically conditioned amalgam, even though theology hitherto and the magisterium never thought and could not have thought of such a possibility. Pius XII declared that it was part of Catholic faith (DC 3896) that the human soul is directly created by God. But as can easily be proved historically, in making this statement (correct in itself) he had in mind a conceptual model of the immediacy of this act of creation that is no longer shared by many theologians today,[3] without thinking of the possibility of distinguishing between what was really meant and the conceptual model that could be eliminated.

Perhaps the most important and almost startling example in the history of faith and the history of ideas lies in the unity and distinction between the imminent expectation of the historical pre-Easter Jesus, on the one hand, and what the Church today believes to be really meant by this imminent expectation. Here is a process beginning as early as the New Testament and not really closed even today, and which is nevertheless legitimate. Because of the historically changing horizons of understanding of people and the Church, this critical recourse to the ultimate origin of particular theological propositions is constantly necessary in order to cope with new queries about the really binding sense of these theological propositions; but it then provides the opportunity of preserving what is really binding in faith, even though amalgams have to be eliminated or distinguished from its previous formulation as no longer possible or as not binding in faith. At the same time, as we said, such opportunities of distinguishing need not have been explicitly grasped as possible in earlier theology. The claim that these distinctions are or can be legitimate is then reinforced particularly today by the proof that

[3] Cf., for example, B. Weissmahr, pp. 31–39.

the original understanding of faith did not explicitly contain these amalgams, nor can the latter be conclusively deduced from that understanding. It is not an argument against the partial theory indicated here of the development of the history of dogma that practical difficulties and conflicts arise in the concrete history of the Church's faith as a result of such processes of distinguishing between what was really meant in a later proposition in the history of dogma in the light of the earlier global sense of faith and the concrete conceptual model with the aid of which the later proposition hitherto presented what had really been meant. This is clear precisely from this history of faith. Once such an individual process is closed, it usually does not create any great emotional or existential difficulty for the believer or the theologian. We may recall, for instance, the teaching of the Council of Florence (DS 1551) that all those who are not Catholics at the time of their death are lost and then compare this teaching with that of Vatican II and the mentality corresponding to it in the Church today. But as long as such a process of fresh interpretation of theological teaching goes on (even while preserving what is really meant by it and what is binding), conflicts and differences of opinion are simply unavoidable and must be endured with patience and tolerance.

In the present reflection the question is not whether a new insight and of what kind might emerge in regard to the doctrine of Mary's virginity if it were thought out afresh from the standpoint of the history of dogma and of systematic theology, while keeping in mind the above-mentioned conclusions from the history of dogma and the development of the Church's sense of faith. Possibly nothing 'new' would 'come out' with the use of such a method. But it is also possible that very important new conclusions might emerge on the sense in which this doctrine is binding in faith. None of this is material for discussion here. The important thing here is to stress urgently the absolute necessity of a confrontation of the doctrine of Mary's virginity with present-day ideas of the possibilities of development of dogma. In principle this dogma, too, is open to further development. It cannot be said that the Mariology of the last centuries has allowed precisely and impartially enough for this fundamental possibility.

(*d*) The systematic theologian in his Mariology needs to ask the exegete and biblical theologian what the latter's investigations have shown to be the exact literary genre of the infancy stories in the New Testament, especially those in Matthew and Luke. If this question is to be answered according to the principles of modern exegesis, very many distinctions will certainly be required. The alternative of historical account or legend is certainly too simple. If we allow for midrash-like narratives and do so in principle even when the theological tradition in Mariology did not hitherto allow for this, the question raised here is still far from adequately answered. The intention of the statement and the mode of the statement in the account of the infancy of Jesus must be more closely defined and distinguished from each other. It can be asked if and when an evangelist transmits narrative traditions (since in any case they have a theological meaning and point) without *ipso facto* ascribing to such a narrative an absolute binding force in faith. Something of this kind is possible in principle. When, for example, Luke makes Jesus eat after his resurrection, it may be asked whether something of this kind belongs simply and without interpretation to the dimension of historical reality. It is only when questions of this kind have been answered by the exegete that the systematic theologian can consider what conclusions to draw for his Mariology. This is a difficult question.

It is then possible that the subsequent history of faith on Mary will state more than New Testament Mariology alone suggests, if it is considered merely in the light of the hermeneutic of the definition of such a literary genre. (If and why this 'more' is conceivable is something that cannot be further discussed here.) But in principle the opposite is possible. Tradition transmits the account of the Gospels, referring purely and simply to their authority, without itself considering separately in a strict sense the meaning and limits of what the Gospels report, and without considering independently the exact literary genre and thus the hermeneutic in the light of which the Gospel accounts must be read today; it must be defined quite precisely what they are meant to convey to us as binding in faith and what is not so binding. This second possibility, too, exists in principle. When, for example, Paul, according to Luke (Acts 17:26), says in regard to the narrative in Genesis that all mankind stems from *one* man, or when Paul spontaneously assumes the same thing in Romans 5, this does not mean that we are forbidden ourselves to define more precisely the literary genre of the narrative in Genesis and from that standpoint to appreciate the fact that monogenism in the biological sense is not a principle that is binding in faith. Collaboration of this kind between exegesis and systematic theology in a relationship of mutual dependence and reciprocal questioning is necessary today. We may get the impression that this collaboration has not yet gone far enough in the field of Mariology and could bring further results, if it is impartially and seriously attempted.

(*e*) What has been said or suggested up to now could perhaps be recapitulated and at the same time generalized by saying that Christianity has been engaged from the Enlightenment onward in a vast process of fresh interpretation of its dogma: that is, of the transposition of this dogma from the horizons of understanding of antiquity and the Middle Ages into those of the present time. Such a transposition contains, of course, a lot of individual dogmatic questions, even though this transposition also amounts to a single and entire task which aims at the innermost and real core of the nature of Christianity. The particular tasks involved in this transposition vary greatly with the content of the individual dogma, are undertaken sooner or later with a certain historical fortuitousness, are accomplished quickly or slowly, unobtrusively or with obvious conflicts. But it would *a priori* be wrong to see and to interpret this transposition process as a kind of demolition or reduction (described as 'demythologizing' etc.). Even when it is achieved courageously and impartially, step by step, considering the detail and the whole, the process can in fact convey to the believer and the theologian the experience which, as such, seen purely historically, is by no means obvious, but is part of the believer's hope in faith: that is, this transposition process does not cancel the identity of the Christian faith and the Church throughout all the radically changing epochs of the history of ideas, but confirms the fact that the new faith is the old and the old faith is continually becoming new.

Certainly it cannot be maintained *a priori* that Mariology is not also involved in this transposition process. Until the middle of the twentieth century, among theologians and devout Catholics there was a certain feeling of pride and gratification in the way that Mariology was explicated into materially continually freshly articulated propositions (a process that now seems to have been brought to a halt), while today a new task must be historically assigned to Mariology if it is not to become sterile, to be a museum piece, kept in storage as part of the Church's official teaching but with no role to play in the present-day Christian's life of faith. Mariology, too, must be seen today as part of this transposition process in which the old becomes new in order to endure. What all this means concretely has, of course, not by any means been sufficiently considered and here we cannot even give a hint of it. But these connections between a history of Mariological doctrine and the present rapidly moving history of faith of the Church as a whole must be seen and made relevant: what has been learned from the history of dogma in general, the modern conclusions of a hermeneutics of statements of faith, of a theology (and philosophy) of religious language, and the results of historically critical exegesis must be brought to bear on and made relevant to Mariology, if the latter is to remain as a theological discipline and retain a religious significance for life.

(3) If a position established by a purely exegetical and historical effort is perhaps assigned a merely 'greater probability' than its opposite, the systematic theologian must be careful to avoid exploiting such a situation too quickly and thoughtlessly by declaring as a result of a purely formal logical reasoning that the exegetically slighter probability in virtue of his own premises and reflections has turned out to be the truth, even though historically there is a greater probability (but no more than that) opposed to it. In terms of formal logic this is correct. But such an argument must be handled (if at all) with the utmost caution. In the first place the question must be asked quite strictly and straightforwardly whether the systematic theologian in the light of his own principles can really be so unambiguously and exclusively certain of his position that he can declare the historically more probable to be false and the historically less probable to be true. In such cases it must also be remembered that in many questions of fundamental theology it is possible only to reach historical probabilities and yet to regard these as an existentially adequate fundamental-theological basis for an assent of faith directed to the same object, to assign, that is, to greater probabilities in existential decisions a considerable weight that cannot simply be dismissed by the above-mentioned operation in formal logic. In the end however, as far as it is possible, we must try to the best of our ability to avoid a kind of schizophrenia in which a person gives an assent of faith precisely to what he regards as historically less probable.

(4) Finally, what follows may be put in the form of a question. Is it really necessary, after all, always to give an unambiguous answer

immediately to all questions which arise in faith and in theology? Even in the dimension of faith a space may be left open for what is uncertain and unanswered, if this space is devoutly respected by all sides and no one side attempts immediately and decidedly to fill it with an answer with which the other side is not satisfied in the light of faith or intellectually. In all fields of theology there are in fact open questions, different schools, theological controversies. History teaches us that questions of this kind are by no means always and *a priori* regarded by theologians and believers as such, that is, recognized *as* open. In the famous controversy on grace, the great majority of the papal commission was decidedly of the opinion that Molinism should be condemned as heretical; in other words, that the alternative between the two systems was certainly not an open question. Nevertheless, it has remained so for centuries, although Paul V acted as if the pope would decide the issue before long. The question of *Humanae Vitae* likewise is still open, although Paul VI did not expressly admit this.

There are then open questions in theology, even though this openness often creates difficulties of conscience for the faith of believers and theologians; people call impatiently for a settlement of these questions and there are those who declare that a decision is of considerable importance for their faith and its clarity and can and must be made quickly and unambiguously in a definite form. Where this is possible it may or should be done. But we should not be too impatient and as a result of weakness of faith be too ready to think that a decision is always and everywhere possible and required. In regard to our question of Mary's virginity, we are all certainly convinced in faith that Mary was incorporated with her whole body-soul existence into the historical salvific mission of Jesus. Have we not then jointly a basic understanding of what her 'virginity' means for all of us, even though we do not think that we all know with equal certainty and clarity what exactly this integratedness means 'biologically', particularly since we are all sure that this absolute integratedness must also include Mary's participation in the ordinariness and lowliness of Jesus' human existence?

CONCLUSIONS

What follows then from these reflections in regard to the concrete purpose for the sake of which this expert report was requested?

(1) In the first place it seems wholly inopportune for the episcopal magisterium in Germany to comment expressly, directly, and solely on the positions taken up by Rudolf Pesch in regard to the question of the 'brothers of Jesus' in his commentary on Mark. His theme is not expressly *virginitas ante partum,* but *virginitas post partum,* and even then only to the extent that this question is to be answered solely by the methods of exegesis as such and at the same time without any attempt to do more than establish a greater or lesser probability. What then is the magisterium to say about these positions of Pesch as such, if it seeks to restrict itself to these? If it were to say that other theological sources and studies in other fields of theology would establish as certain and as an object of faith the position opposed to that adopted by Pesch as exegetically probable, then in order to teach, not only correctly, but also effectively, the magisterium would have no alternative but to expound and justify at length its teaching on the virginity of Mary, taking into account the aspects of the question to which we referred in the first part of these reflections. But we would then be faced with the difficulties of such a declaration (which are to be discussed below). Obviously, too, it is not the business of the magisterium to judge the greater or lesser exegetical and historical probability of Pesch's position as such.

It is also to be remembered that the magisterium today must make clear in its procedure that it allows adequate scope and maintains respect for the freedom of theological studies. There will, of course, be Christians (conservative members of the clergy, for example) who demand an unambiguous reaction to our question as quickly as possible on the part of the magisterium, since these theological controversies make them feel insecure in their faith. But a *brief* comment by the magisterium on traditional lines, on the one hand, in practice would not clear up this insecurity and, on the other hand, would plunge more and other Christians into the opposite kind of insecurity and would be too brief to provide the latter with any real aid to their faith. In particular the German magisterium which is involved here, from the nature of the case, does not possess an authority such that its declaration could add any considerable weight to the traditional teaching. Such a brief declaration, issued directly against Pesch alone, as a matter of what we might call 'intellectual policy', therefore would not be of much help against 'insecurity' on whatever side this is mainly to be found. This situation in regard to intellectual policy is such that it cannot be substantially changed by brief declarations of the magisterium, but must certainly continue to be endured for a considerable time in patience and hope, since a really effective clarification in the Church's sense of faith would also require time.

(2) Could the German Bishops' Conference perhaps regard Pesch's study as providing, not indeed the essential and comprehensive theme, but an occasion for issuing a lengthy instruction on the question raised here? From a practical standpoint this suggestion, too, must be rejected. However desirable it may be in itself, who is to compose this instruction? Where are the theologians who want and are able to take on this task? It would mean taking into account all those aspects (and more) which were mentioned in our first part. Definite positions would have to be adopted in regard to too many individual theological questions. Could both these things be achieved so that the instruction, composed in this way, would reproduce the joint and binding teaching of the episcopate and would thus be more than a theological treatise the importance of which depends entirely on the force of its arguments? In the light of these and similar considerations it has to be said that an official instruction of this kind, if it is to be both correct *and* effective, is not possible at the present time. This negative answer does not mean, of course, that the episcopate has no task and no possibility of exercising an influence in regard to this question as a whole. It can encourage theologians to apply themselves more urgently than in the last decades to this group of questions, it can perhaps supply technical and material aids, it can help to make sure that such theological work is carried out in a climate of seriousness, of mutual respect, and with due regard to the mentality in matters of faith also of the average Christian, and so on.

(3) If, however, the German episcopate's commission on faith or the episcopate itself felt that a declaration on the outstanding question could not be neglected, then in order to be effective it would not only have to consider the aspects indicated in our first part (and many others). It would seem expedient to go beyond this and for the instruction regarded as unavoidable to choose from the outset a more general theme as a continuation and amplification of the former instruction of the German episcopate on the Church's magisterium and incorporate into this the question raised here and similar current questions of a concrete character (as raised recently by

Hans Küng, for instance) which might then serve as examples and illustrations of the more general theme. In such an instruction of a more general and fundamental character it would be possible to discuss a great deal of what is disturbing, explicitly or implicitly, the sense of faith of the (educated) Christian today: the permanent identity of the Christian teaching on faith despite and in its historicity, the problems of development of dogma, the change of horizons of understanding in the history of faith, the consequences of the doctrine of the hierarchy of truths, the diversity of degrees of binding force of official doctrinal pronouncements of the Church, the meaning and limitations of the magisterium, the latter's real existential location in the individual's sense of faith, etc.—all themes that can only be indicated here and not exhaustively enumerated. Within this larger framework questions raised by Pesch, Küng, or others can be mentioned as examples of a concrete character which can both elucidate the general theme and conversely be correctly answered in the light of this theme itself. Since Pesch's question can certainly be answered appropriately and effectively (in a form that can be assimilated) only in the light of this more general theme, it seems that the latter must also be the theme of an instruction, *if* such an instruction is regarded as objectively necessary and opportune in the situation. Of course, the objection can be raised that it is much more difficult to cope with the comprehensive theme than with the more restricted theme (although doubts were expressed above about the possibility of coping with the latter). But again it must be said on the contrary that the narrower problem of Mary's virginity today compels us to face the more general problem and that this general problem (particularly in the light of experiences of the past history of dogma) can lead to fundamental solutions, which can then be helpful to the still continuing process of the history of Mariology.

PART SEVEN

Angels

18

ON ANGELS

After the existence of the devil and of demons had been taken for granted in the teaching and practice of Christianity as a whole in all denominations for almost two thousand years, it has today become an acute problem. For obvious reasons, interest centres on the devil and on demons, but the essential question is inevitably about the existence of nonhuman, created, personal beings: that is, a question about the existence of 'angels', whether these are understood as good and finally perfected, or as bad and lost. It is to this general question that we shall devote some reflections here. Our reflections will not be related to all the questions that as such are involved in the problem of the existence of 'angels'. While presupposing the present state of the question in Catholic theology, we are attempting only to put forward some considerations which perhaps have not been very explicitly examined in the course of the controversy up to now.

The present state of the controversy can be briefly and simply indicated. Angels and demons appear in the later parts of the Old Testament and in the New Testament (these include the devil, who is seen in some sense as representative and head of the demonic realm, although there is a difference in origin and nature between Satan and the demons which may not simply be overlooked). In the light of the history of religion this teaching in the later part of the Old Testament and in the New Testament is not the original teaching of these inspired Scriptures of Christianity, but has entered into it from the religious milieu of late Judaism and early Christianity, although this observation does not in principle imply anything decisive about the exact meaning and the binding force in faith of this teaching, since it is not *a priori* impossible for a doctrine accepted 'from outside' to be binding in faith. This teaching of the New Testament assumes as a matter of course the existence of angels and demons and for that very reason the real purpose of the New Testament statements is not to insist on this existence, but to show that these 'principalities and powers' will finally be deprived of power by Jesus Christ and his Spirit; the familiar teaching on angelology and demonology is merely reproduced in a more developed form and its practical consequences indicated (devotion to guardian angels, exorcism, possession).

This traditional teaching amounts to an attempt to contribute to the understanding of evil in the world: the latter is not merely the effect and consequence of man's freedom, but has a previous, more general causal ground in the sinister domination of evil powers and agencies, even though these do not eliminate man's free responsibility. The speculative angelology of Christian theology has, of course, been enriched (especially in the Middle Ages) by many philosophical ideas and theories which are certainly not binding in faith. The doctrine of demons has certainly led in practice in Christian life to terrible abnormalities, including the horrors of the witch trials. The most important statement of the traditional teaching by the magisterium is found in the profession of faith of the Fourth Lateran Council of 1215, where it is said that God

> by his almighty power from the beginning of time created from nothing both the spiritual and the corporeal creature, the angelic and the earthly; then the human creature as belonging to both orders, being composed of spirit and body. For the devil and the other demons were created by God as good by nature, but became evil from themselves. Man, however, sinned at the prompting of the devil.

This teaching, which can also be found in many other documents of the magisterium, was repeated by Paul VI in an address on 15 November 1972.

In the present controversy within *Catholic* theology (which is all that we shall consider), three positions can be distinguished.

The *first* view is that the doctrine of created (definitively) good and (definitively) evil personal spiritual beings, alongside and above man (including their influence on the calamitous history of the human world), is a strictly binding truth of faith which must be unconditionally upheld even today. At the same time in the last resort it is irrelevant whether this teaching (which, however, is clearly present in the New Testament, in Paul's writings and also in the words and practice of Jesus himself) can be deduced with purely exegetical methods from Scripture as a real statement of faith, or whether this 'literal' interpretation of Scripture becomes the object of binding faith only by the Church's dogmatic definition which is not open to doubt. But, even admitting the correctness of this first position, there can be no doubt that it has had to be curtailed in the course of history and has in fact been curtailed without protest. No one today will maintain that the space between the earth and the moon is the real and essential locality of the demons. Even the defenders of this first position will be more cautious today in the interpretation of certain illnesses as demonic possession and will be glad that there are no witches or witch trials today, which were formerly regarded as obvious conclusions from the traditional teaching. The defenders of the first position will also refrain from producing bulky theological treatises on demonology, such as those formerly composed, especially in post-Tridentine theology up to the present century (the two volumes by von Petersdorff appeared as recently as 1956). It can be said even at this point that the defenders of the first position will have to proceed cautiously and modestly, since the tradition they invoke is not entirely credible in each and every aspect that it presents.

The defenders of a *second* position today deny forthrightly and unequivocally the existence of the devil and the demons. They insist that the doctrine of the devil has entered into Scripture from outside, that an exact historico-critical exegesis shows that Scripture does not teach but only assumes the existence of the devil and demons (and angels), and in the light of this hypothesis makes statements the real content of which persists if the hypothesis is dropped. If and insofar as the permanent binding force of definitions of the magisterium is maintained, these declarations, in the sense that they are supposed to remain binding, are interpreted in this second position like the statements of Scripture: the existence of demons (and angels) is not defined, but all that is said is that, *if* and insofar as they exist (which is spontaneously assumed, but not really taught), they are created good by God and are evil only through their own fault, they do not represent any absolute and original power of evil, but remain subject to the greater power of good, to God's salvific will and to his grace. This second position does not make use merely of historico-critical exegesis in an attempt to relativize the statements of Scripture (together with those of tradition drawn from Scripture and those of the magisterium), but tries with the aid of psychology, parapsychology, and sociology to show how it was possible to reach a theory of the devil which of its nature is no more than a projection and personification of evil in the world, experienced by man as overwhelmingly powerful and ineradicable. These personifying projections are meant to help man to understand the existence of evil everywhere present in the world and at the same time to relieve him of responsibility for it. When evil appears in a particularly terrifying form, it is said to be due not really to man, but to the activity of the devil; when a human being in the midst of conflicting impulses feels almost schizophrenically the tendency to evil, it is a question of a diabolic whispered temptation. In defence of this second position attention is also drawn to the harmful effects of belief in the devil on the life of the individual and on society.

At this point, however, the defenders of the second position need to be reminded that it is very difficult epistemologically to prove the nonexistence of an entity by showing the inconclusiveness of the arguments hitherto adduced to establish its existence. They need to be warned against an innate temptation to trivialize the evil in the world and to interpret it as an inevitable and ultimately innocuous irritating phenomenon and as an unavoidable drawback in a changing world, evolving from the very outset toward its consummation and *unable* actually to plunge into final perdition. In regard to this second position (which is easily linked with a denial of 'original sin'), the question needs constantly to be asked whether it upholds the seriousness of sin and guilt as revealed on the cross of the Son of God; the question must constantly be asked what *the evil* and the demonic, permeating all dimensions of existence and the world and not to be eliminated in a spirit of naive bourgeois optimism, really is, if we are not to elucidate it with the aid of the traditional teaching on demons.

A *third* position admits that there is something that is still not clear about this question: it is not unequivocally certain that the traditional teaching of Scripture and the Church asserts absolutely and not merely hypothetically the existence of nonhuman, created, good and evil personal beings, that it upholds absolutely (over and above the doctrine of the createdness of all things other than the one God, of the creaturely finiteness of evil, of the rejection of a manicheistic dualism) the existence of these angels and demons. This third position, therefore, represents a certain neutrality between the other two positions and entrusts the problem to the future history of faith and theology. Those who hold it cannot admit to being clearly convinced by the arguments of either the first or second position. In the light of what has been learned from the history of dogma, a position of this kind is not surprising. In the course of this history views and doctrines have continually been put forward (not as definitions in the strict sense, or only as definitions open to a variety of interpretations) by the magisterium in its ordinary or extraordinary teaching (also with an appeal to Scripture) which later turned out to be mistaken and which the magisterium eventually tacitly or expressly withdrew. Cases like this (which do not need to be presented here) have constantly occurred, in which a considerable time had to elapse between the appearance of a new problem and its settlement in one way or another, a period of time that could be of varying length depending on the peculiar nature of the particular problem and the preconditions of its solution. Those who hold this position cannot therefore be blamed for cowardice or laziness in seeking an easy way out by simply refusing to express a clear view on this question, particularly since what is involved here is not merely the expression of a personal opinion, but a decision as to how the two first positions are judged by the sense of faith of the whole Church—a question that can be answered only with difficulty, since this sense of faith is difficult to grasp and is continually developing in the course of history.

It is to be hoped that the present *status quaestionis* in regard to this problem has now been defined up to a point, although, of course, the essential objective arguments supporting the three positions were not developed in detail. In what follows the theological problem of the existence of angels and devils will not be investigated further from all the aspects hitherto mentioned in this controversy. There will not be any exegetical investigations or studies in the history of religion here, nor will the declarations of the Church's magisterium be examined in regard to their content and their binding force, although all these inquiries are obviously indispensable for an answer to the actual problem. Instead of this, we want to point to a few questions which have not hitherto been discussed or at most only marginally discussed in this controversy. These questions, selected from the total complex of problems, cannot individually decide the problem as a whole, since even a clear answer to any one of them leaves the main problem unsettled and since they raise further problems which are perhaps more obscure and have been less considered hitherto than their own immediate object. With the reservation that the reader may endure patiently the somewhat high-sounding nomenclature, we would like to distinguish three questions which will occupy us here: an epistemological question, an existential-ontological question, and a question of the theology of the cosmos. What is meant by these questions will become clear without more ado in the course of the discussion.

1. THE EPISTEMOLOGICAL QUESTION

We come to the first, the epistemological question, which is seen here as a specifically theological and not a universally philosophical question. We are asking what can fall in principle and *a priori* in any way into the sphere of an actual supernatural revelation, and (if this general question can be and has been answered) whether the existence of the angels can in any way be among the objects belonging to *this* sphere. The general epistemological question—in the light of which the question is to be decided whether the existence of the angels is or is not (can be or cannot be) a revealed truth of faith—is a very obscure question and one which perhaps has never hitherto been sufficiently clearly formulated. This general epistemological question of the possibility of defining in principle and *a priori* the field of reality which comes into question at all for a supernatural divine revelation obviously therefore cannot be thematicized and answered *here* with the detail and the theological precision with which the question of the existence of the angels as object of revelation could be clearly answered. (It will in fact become clear, even assuming that the general epistemological question has been answered and assuming the existence of angels, that there are still two possibilities on which the answer to the general epistemological question alone cannot throw much light.) It is, however, possible to raise this general epistemological problem, and it undoubtedly has an importance for the question of the existence of the angels. And, consequently, some suggestions at least should be put forward in regard to this general problem of theological knowledge.

Is it possible to answer the question of whether there is a formal principle permitting *a priori* a distinction between objects that from the very outset simply cannot be regarded as an object of revelation and those which can be the object of a supernatural revelation? Is it possible perhaps to say of certain propositions on the existence and nature of particular realities that they could never be revealed because their content from the very outset could never be the object of revelation? Unless we are completely mistaken, this is the sort of question that is scarcely or never raised in Catholic theology. (This assertion may be due to my own ignorance; apart from touching on the question elsewhere in my own reflections, I have come across it in Catholic theology only in P. Knauer's fundamental theology;[1] without my knowing it, of course, the question may have been dealt with elsewhere, from different aspects and with a different terminology.)

The absence of this formulation of the question is easy to understand. We start out tacitly and as a matter of course from the assumption that God is omniscient, can communicate himself 'externally', is free in this communication; thus any truth, if God wills it, can also be the object of his supernatural verbal revelation. It seems therefore from the very outset that there cannot be an axiom that excludes *a priori* and in principle certain propositions from the area of possible divine revelation. In addition to this consideration, assumed tacitly and as a matter of course, the fact is that Catholic theology (clearly, for example, at Vatican I) assumes that there are propositions within the scope of revelation which are really part of revelation (for example, on the existence of God, of a natural law, etc.), but which can also in principle be established by 'natural' reason without the aid of supernatural revelation, so that the revelation of such propositions only gives them a greater clarity and certainty for man in working out his salvation. In textbook theology

[1] P. Knauer, *Der Glaube kommt vom Hören: Ökumenische Fundamentaltheologie* (Graz, 1977).

there has scarcely been any consideration (over and above what has been indicated) of how revelation of facts and truths, as such accessible to natural reason alone, is related to the revelation of mysteries of faith properly so-called, which in principle can be known only by personal supernatural revelation: for this very reason (it seems to me) it was assumed quite generally and without further reflection as a matter of course that God, if he only wants to do so and regards it as appropriate (as important for salvation) in particular situations, can reveal any conceivable truth. This belief was confirmed by the impression commonly gained from the history of revelation: since all bearers of revelation (from Moses and the prophets up to Jesus and his final revelation) were regarded tacitly as formally equal in status, distinguished only in the content of their revelation and not in the event itself of revelation (although this did not exclude the use of 'revelation' as a merely analogous common generic term), and since the most diverse contents (from the political maxims of a prophet to the eschatologically victorious communication of the Spirit to the world) were observed in the history of revelation regarded in this way as formally leveled down, it was really quite impossible to think of the question of whether the content of one proposition or another could be *a priori* excluded from the field of revelation properly so-called. In practice the only question recognized was that of whether one thing or another (for example, the existence of angels) had actually been revealed (not the question of whether one proposition or another in the light of its content measured against the nature of divine revelation *could* be revealed at all or must from the very outset be excluded from this field).

Here the view will be maintained that there is such an *a priori* axiom to determine the possibility of such a revelation. The axiom runs (with the reservation that further qualifications will be introduced at a later stage): in a supernatural revelation (in its unity, here assumed as necessary, of communication of the Spirit and word, by which alone a verbal revelation can in any way be God's word and not merely a word about God) properly and primarily only God himself (in his self-communication) can reveal himself. Everything else (that is, everything as created distinct from God) can as such by no means be the original object of an actual, supernatural revelation and thus an original object of faith. (At a later stage special consideration must be given to the question of whether and how there can be secondary objects of revelation, dependent in event and content on revelation properly so-called as God's self-communication, which are not God himself.) This basic axiom ought really to be self-evident and immediately comprehensible. If we do not think anthropomorphically of the relationship between God and the world, if we admit that God is the free cause of the world and not a particular part of reality, any special intervention of God inside the world, which is both distinction from world realities and yet in some way belongs to them, must be rejected as a merely mythological idea or this 'particularity' must consist in the fact that God himself as such communicates himself by himself directly to the world and that the history of salvation *and* revelation in *one* consists in this. The fact that God cannot really become a particular element of a partial character in the world and its history does not amount to a limitation of God, but is precisely identical with a rightly understood and radically seriously accepted divinity of God. What is meant here can also be seen from the opposite standpoint. If God, revealing and communicating himself, were to communicate himself through *something else*, created by him and distinct from him, because this other created thing would carry with it a reference to him, if then God's revelation were established by something 'creaturely', this created reality would in principle be accessible to man's reason, since the formal object of this reason cannot exclude anything finite from its range, since reason as unlimited transcendentality can in principle comprehend all that is finite, and consequently nothing finite can in principle be an absolute mystery. Revelation properly speaking can have as its object only God himself as such.

Of course, this basic axiom is bound at first to rouse bewilderment and protest. It is indeed easy to see that the three fundamental mysteries of Christianity—Trinity, incarnation, and imparting of the Spirit—are covered and summed up in their formal solidarity by this axiom. It is also possible to see comparatively quickly that the mystery of the Church as such can be traced back to the mystery of God's self-communication established by God irreversibly in Christ. But it cannot be denied that there are apparently other articles of faith which, on the one hand, are understood as mysteries properly so-called and are accessible only by God's revelation, and which, on the other hand, since they at least give the impression of expressing a finite reality, seem to contradict the basic axiom as formulated (we may recall, for example, the dogma of transubstantiation). This difficulty, of course, cannot be cleared up here, if only because the task would presuppose that we are clear about which and how many real mysteries of faith exist and are to be distinguished. We simply assume here that our basic axiom can be compatible with the Church's conviction in regard to articles which it regards as real mysteries of faith, while admittedly also assuming that these other mysteries of faith are themselves correctly interpreted in regard to their character as mysteries, which is by no means so simple in individual cases. But with all this the real difficulty which must occupy us here in regard to this basic axiom is not even envisaged. It seems, that is, to be simply obvious that the Church's sense of faith is aware of propositions which are understood as real revelation, although they express a finite object and by no means raise any claim to be mysteries properly so-called. There seems to be a whole lot of such truths of faith, although it seems that no effort has been made hitherto to distinguish these truths of faith in their diversity and to arrange them formally in a lucid system.

It is impossible here, of course, to undertake a systematization of such propositions which on the one hand are supposed to be revealed and on the other hand do not contain any real mysteries and thus create much greater difficulties in regard to our basic axiom than do those possible mysteries which are not *a priori* compatible with this axiom. On this problem a few hints must suffice. In the first place there are certainly propositions the content of which amounts to a precondition, immediately perceptible and understandable as absolutely necessary, on man's part for the possibility of revelation properly so-called as God's self-communication. That man is a being who really can have something to do with God is a proposition that directly expresses a finite reality and one in fact that can be known 'naturally' (or can be regarded as so knowable), but which on the other hand is guaranteed by the event of actual revelation as its precondition. Such propositions can certainly be regarded in a secondary and derived sense as revealed statements, since and insofar as their content is inevitably perceived as God's self-communication *in* the event of revelation. Rightly understood and interpreted, these propositions do not conflict with our basic axiom but confirm it. We may well take the view that the majority of revealed statements, which do not contain any absolute mysteries, can be interpreted in this way and thus do not contradict our basic axiom. But can this be said of all propositions that the Church's sense of faith sees as revealed?

This question is difficult to answer, if only because there is no complete register of propositions likely to emerge clearly set out and immediately understandable. If, for example, a prophet in the Old Testament proclaims a political axiom for a particular historical situation as the 'word of Yahweh', as a word of revelation, even if his claim is recognized it is still by no means clear what exactly is the sense in which this word is revelation. (As compared with the medieval theology of prophecy, it is in fact striking how little attention is paid by modern fundamental theology to the concrete happening in the prophet's consciousness, to the claim made that his word, which is primarily a datum of his own consciousness, is God's word. In modern fundamental theology attention is fixed too hastily on the external authentication of the words of the bearer of revelation, on the miracle as distinct from the event of revelation itself, without closer reflection 'psychologically' on the very event of revelation in its bearer, even though the latter has no recourse at all to miracle to support his conviction that he has received inwardly a divine revelation.) In any event such propositions ought to be more closely examined and more clearly distinguished in their content and in their psychological and sociological origins, so that even the assertion that they are divine revelation might and should take very diverse forms. Although it is impossible to go into all this here, the embarrassment arising with regard to this basic axiom cannot simply be concealed; therefore a basic solution of the problem facing us may be briefly outlined, so that it can perhaps be made clear that we can insist on our basic axiom, without on that account simply denying that there are propositions which on the one hand directly express a *finite* truth and yet on the other hand claim to be revealed.

With regard to this suggestion we assume that revelation can always be approached only in faith and that such a faith always and at all times, even though completely unthematically and without verbal objectivation, must be sustained by God's self-communication (by what we are accustomed to call 'uncreated grace') and that (even though implicitly and unthematically) it always affirms the actual self-communication and self-revelation of God in the sense of our basic axiom. On this assumption, it can certainly be said that a finite reality and the proposition related to it can be affirmed as revealed when and insofar as their being sustained by faith properly so-called as immediacy to the absolute God and their synthesis are thus directly and conclusively experienced. When (to put it somewhat boldly) the mysticism of the transcendental experience of grace is encountered in an indissoluble synthesis (not distorting the openness of this mysticism) with a categorial experience, this, too, may be understood as willed by God, as the will and sign of God, as revealed. But this is always in the light of the actual experience of grace, in which a person submits in faith to the absolute mystery of God, to the latter's actual revelation in the sense of our basic axiom, even though this experience of grace as such may itself remain merely implicit in many instances and depending on the particular situation in the history of revelation, while the attention of the recipient of revelation is fixed on the categorial content of his experience.

It seems to me that a Catholic theology cannot really reject the theory above outlined if it admits that revelation, if it is to be understood as revelation no matter what its particular content, must be accepted in *faith*, and that in the last resort faith always and everywhere has the same nature and cannot be defined solely in the light of its individual object where there occurs God's self-communication as such in the Holy Spirit. This theory might be elucidated and supported by a theology of mysticism and private revelations, although the distinction between public and private revelation would have to be made clear, while admitting that in the last resort they have the same fundamental nature. There are certainly instances in the Church's ordinary theology and practice when we cannot do without the theory outlined. The obligation of an assent of faith, which a Catholic admits in regard to an *ex cathedra* decision of the pope, is in fact dependent on the legitimacy of the election of this pope and on the certain knowledge of the promulgation of that decision. These things and the knowledge of them seem to be purely natural, historical, and contingent, not in themselves amounting to an object of faith, nor belonging to the group of those truths and facts of which we spoke above and which must necessarily also be involved in the acceptance of revelation properly so-called, and which nevertheless are supposed to be the foundation of a decision of faith.

Although in textbook theology in the *analysis fidei* an attempt is generally made in a somewhat different way to provide help in regard to this problem, the solution offered here still seems to be the most intelligible, even for these cases. The Catholic's experience in the Holy Spirit of faith directed toward the immediacy of God authenticates and confirms for him also the categorial starting point and mediation of his own actual faith, in this case the actual legitimacy of the election of the pope, etc. In the last resort, however, it seems unimportant whether we describe a proposition about an historically contingent reality as a revealed article of faith or as a proposition that is affirmed absolutely only in a decision of faith, whether it is regarded as the content of a *fides divina* or of a mere *fides ecclesiastica* (if the latter exists at all), particularly since today this traditional distinction between divine and purely ecclesiastical faith seems to have little support. If we understand and interpret in this way truths of revelation, whose content seems to be finite and historically contingent, without necessarily having been implicitly affirmed in the former sense in the act of faith, then we are compelled to adopt a differentiated view of revealed truth as it normally exists, but we must not deny a rightly understood revealedness of such truths and need not see them as contradicting our basic axiom in this question.

After these circumstantial and yet far too brief preliminary reflections, we can now return to our proper question. *Can* the existence of angels (and demons) be revealed at all? If our basic axiom and the qualifications subsequently added are correct, then the answer to this question must be: Since the existence of angels (if it is a fact) involves at most a finite and creaturely reality which can in no way be a mystery of faith properly speaking, this existence of angels cannot be understood as more than a content of revelation of a secondary and derived character, *if* it can be proved that this reality as such is known naturally *and* at the same time has such a religious significance that we can seriously assume that this existence can enter into a synthesis with the proper reality of faith and its expression, such as we demanded for a secondary and derived object of faith of this kind. Before we can inquire whether this condition is fulfilled, we must draw attention also to the fact that not every reality of a finite and knowable character *about which* a statement of faith can be made or which might be known by faith can *ipso facto* be regarded as such a secondary and derived object of faith. If a person enjoys a glass of wine, for instance, and regards it with gratitude as part of God's creation, he is not making the creation of wine an object of faith by making a statement (perhaps of considerable importance) in the light of faith *about* what remains a secular object of natural knowledge. If, then, we assume that the existence of angels as such is the object of natural knowledge, we can and must make theological statements about this fact (that they are created and finite, that as such they are created good, that they can have become evil only through their own freedom, while remaining subject to God's supreme decrees).

Such a statement can be of great religious importance; but it does not for that reason necessarily turn its object into an object of faith, in the sense that the denial of the existence of this object would be an offense against faith itself; the statement can certainly be made hypothetically, that is, its object as such can be left to a purely natural appraisal. But this does not mean on the other hand that such a finite object, which in itself is accessible to natural knowledge, can never and under no circumstances become an object of faith, even though of a secondary and derived character. Whether the one or the other alternative applies is decided by the question of whether this object enters into a synthesis with the actual realization of faith and its original content in such a way that the Church's sense of faith as a whole sees that in practice the original realization of faith can be concretely achieved only while affirming this secondary object. (What is meant by these admittedly not very clear or familiar propositions may be illustrated by an example. The legitimacy of Vatican I was dependent on the legitimacy of the election of Pope Pius IX, a legitimacy which is certainly a finite, contingent fact accessible to natural knowledge and not derivable from the nature of the Church; and yet the concrete act of faith of the Church as a whole, in which it accepts its concrete nature together with its historical continuity throughout the ages, must assume as absolute this legitimacy of Pius IX, that is, as a secondary object of faith and not merely as a hypothetical presupposition for a judgment of faith. Of course, from the very nature of the case more ought to be said and in more exact detail about this synthesis; perhaps the peculiar character and even the distinction of *various* syntheses of this kind ought to be worked out. But this is not possible here.)

What we are asking is: When the existence of angels is mentioned in Scripture and tradition, when at the same time, according to our basic axiom about possible objects of revelation, there can be no question of a primary and original object of faith, is this existence merely assumed hypothetically as the object of natural knowledge, about which the statement of faith (that they are created, etc.) is made while allowing for the permanently hypothetical character of its object (*if* there are angels—of which we are convinced naturally, but not as a matter of faith—*then* they are created, etc.), *or* does the natural knowledge of the existence of angels enter into a synthesis with faith (in the createdness of everything outside God) in such a way that this existence (although in itself of a natural and hypothetical character) becomes a secondary and derived object of faith? After all that has been said up to now, this statement of the question forbids us to work purely and simply with the straightforward dilemma that the existence of the angels is either an object of revelation (of a primary, undifferentiated character) or a mere assertion of natural knowledge which in itself can be mistaken, the origin of which can be explained psychologically, sociologically, and so on, and in regard to which faith makes a purely hypothetical statement. It is not as simple as that. The claim that something is 'revealed' must be distinguished, and in regard to the term 'natural knowledge' it cannot simply be assumed that its object can never and under no circumstances enter into the sphere of derived and secondary objects of faith.

If, however, these distinctions are introduced into the formulation of the question, it must be said that it cannot be answered unambiguously here and now at the present stage of the controversy. Certainly it can be said that, if angels exist, they are as such and primarily the object of a natural knowledge, while the term 'natural' can leave entirely open the question of whether such a 'natural' knowledge would be possible on the assumption of the existence of a 'nature' existing purely as such as understood in the scholastic distinction between nature and grace. All that 'natural knowledge' need mean here is that it has emerged outside and independently of the history of revelation of the Old and the New Covenant and remains valid, but as such it does not have the guarantee of being divinely revealed. That the existence of angels is the object of natural knowledge in this sense (while the question of whether this is true or false remains, of course, completely open) can certainly be disputed. For not only must the supporters of the first position admit that the doctrine of angels came into the Old and New Testament from outside and did not originate there, but the supporters of the second position also affirm such a natural knowledge, which, however, they regard as false and are thus able to deny the revealed character of this doctrine.

Two questions thus arise for us. First, can the origin of such a natural knowledge of the existence of angels not only be made intelligible in the light of psychology, sociology, and the history of ideas, but also be proved to be objectively true and still valid today (or at least shown to be probable and meaningful), or is this not the case, and is therefore the existence of the angels for us an absolute mythological notion? Second, if the existence of the angels can be proved to be the object of a natural knowledge which remains correct even today, is it then an object of faith in Scripture and tradition or merely an object of natural knowledge *about* which faith makes a hypothetical statement, without raising it to the level of an object of faith and thus without forbidding its denial? The first of these two questions must be considered further in the third section of our reflections. But if we assume a positive answer (that is, the opinion that the existence of angels can be affirmed and shown to be probable even today), the second question mentioned above still remains open; it would still be necessary to ask whether this existence of angels remains hypothetical or is made into a secondary object of faith in statements about it. But this question must obviously remain open. For on the assumptions made with our basic axiom it would have to be proved that in Scripture and tradition faith really finds inescapable that synthesis which must exist between the original faith oriented to God himself alone and a finite object which is not an original object of faith, if such a finite reality is supposed to be a secondary object of faith. It will not be asserted apodictically here that such a synthesis (of a kind that needs to be more closely described) certainly does not exist in our case. But it can be proved only with difficulty or not at all convincingly that such a synthesis, conceivable in itself and necessary for a statement of *faith* in this connection, certainly does exist.

In an intellectual and historical milieu in which belief in superhuman spirits was taken for granted (which is evident in any case from the arguments for the second position), Christian faith naturally entered into a close and obvious symbiosis (which has remained a matter of course for many people, even up to the present time) with belief in the existence of such spiritual beings, a symbiosis which can certainly give the impression that it is identical with that peculiar synthesis which sets up a reality of natural experience as a secondary and derived object of faith. This is all the more likely since, for reasons arising from the sociology of ideas, such a symbiosis is liable to persist in the consciousness of official representatives of the Church's mind when it has begun to break down elsewhere. But it is still far from being clearly established that this symbiosis really amounts to the synthesis we are seeking. Parallels are not hard to find. The existence of witches was still affirmed unambiguously and without embarrassment in the churches in the seventeenth century and this affirmation was certainly regarded as a consequence or as an undoubted concrete expression of Christian belief in demons. Up to the present century the Mosaic authorship of the Pentateuch was regarded in Catholic circles as an obvious concrete expression of belief in the inspiration of Scripture. It would be possible to cite many more of such and similar examples of the breakdown of a unity at first accepted unreservedly between real faith and transitory human opinion. Of course, these examples do not prove that whenever and wherever there is such a connection it is a question merely of a transitory symbiosis and not of a synthesis in which the Church's sense of faith seizes on an essentially natural truth as a secondary and derived object of faith. Whether there is a mere symbiosis or a genuine synthesis in our case is not to be decided at the present moment; it will have to be seen whether in the near or more distant future the Church's sense of faith will abandon a transitory symbiosis of this kind, or even explicitly affirm a synthesis in which the existence of angels is accepted as a secondary object of faith.

At this point in our reflections, the view may perhaps be tentatively expressed that we now seem to have reached a stage in the history of the reflective awareness of faith in regard to our question at which an explicit intervention of the magisterium scarcely appears to be opportune. Not that the justification in principle of such an intervention need be disputed. But what is the use of it at this point? In practice and concretely it cannot take the form of an *ex cathedra* decision on the part of pope or council, since the preconditions for such a decision are lacking. This is evident from the fact that Vatican II nowhere pronounced new definitions, and after the council Paul VI, even in questions where he considered a new declaration of his magisterium appropriate, did not put forward any *ex cathedra* decisions. But if nondefining albeit authentic declarations of the magisterium are issued, they do not, as the experience of recent decades shows, bring the discussion to an end. The discussion and, consequently, the history of the Church's sense of faith continue. In regard to our question it is possible, of course, to appeal to former definitions and to explain that the question now facing us was definitively settled there. But even if we have no wish to deny to the Fourth Lateran Council the character of a general council of the Church, there is still a question about what was really defined there and what was not. This remains a matter for serious argument. The appeal to the Church's universal sense of faith and to the ordinary magisterium certainly does not bring a clear ending to the discussion. For the history of dogma shows that even defined truths of faith were amalgamated in the minds of the Church's members with opinions that were only later clearly and explicitly seen to be different from the dogmatic statement as originally understood and only then could this amalgam be eliminated.

These lengthy reflections do not seem to have taken us very far, for we are still discussing the third position as described at the beginning. But, with the reservation that many reflections of an exegetical character and on the history of dogma would need to be added, it can nevertheless be said that the path to be trodden in order to get back from this third position to the first has now been more clearly indicated. We may then (and this is the result of the previous reflections) not merely attempt to assert and to prove that the existence of angels and demons is an object of faith; we ought also to attempt to define the peculiar character of this object of faith as now understood and from that standpoint perceive how exactly an object of faith of this kind can be proved.

2. THE EXISTENTIAL-ONTOLOGICAL QUESTION

In our reflections we have now reached the second of the themes announced above. Even if it is assumed that angels and demons exist and that this existence is asserted by revelation (direct or indirect, as original or derived and secondary object of faith), there remains the great question of what appropriately is to be understood today by these angels and demons. The question could, of course, be answered satisfactorily only by a complete angelology and demonology and this is something that cannot be developed here. But neither can the question be settled by referring to a few Scripture texts. For even in regard to these texts it must be asked what in them is a time-conditioned conceptual model and what is the content really asserted and intended to be binding. But this question requires a criterion for distinguishing between the conceptual model and the actual content of the statement, which is scarcely or never provided by Scripture itself. Nor is it easy to expect a clear answer from tradition to this question of the nature of the angels. For traditional angelology and demonology is itself a very odd conglomerate of biblical passages, philosophical assumptions and views, and popular ideas laboriously worked up into a system. The controversy about the existence of angels and demons ought not be conducted as if it were clear *what* angels and demons are and as if the controversy were only about their existence. The popular indignation of many, especially of devout, Christians at any questioning of the existence of angels and demons is undoubtedly often and to a very considerable extent based on primitive ideas about these beings which are urgently in need of a 'demythologization', even if we want to maintain the existence of angels and demons as an object of faith.

In this second section of our reflections we propose to offer one or two modest suggestions for a demythologizing of a folkloristic, primitive belief in angels and demons. These critical reflections will not by any means start out from ideas that are particularly new and controversial. We shall appeal instead to principles that really cannot be questioned in Catholic theology or at any rate must not be questioned from the standpoint of positions clearly established in the light of faith. Even if the existence of angels and demons is admitted, these suggestions for a necessary demythologization of angelology and demonology are perhaps somewhat arbitrarily selected without any intention of a comprehensive and uniform replacement of these fragments of traditional theology.

In the first place, we may be allowed to register a protest against the generally accepted view in angelology and demonology that these created 'spirits' must be seen as 'pure' spirits without necessarily possessing an essential relationship to matter. These beings may be 'pure' spirits insofar as they neither are merely material realities nor possess *that* materiality which belongs to man in virtue of his bodily nature. But to go beyond this in describing the angels and demons as 'pure' spirits may be Neoplatonic philosophy; it is neither the Church's teaching as binding in faith nor logically implied in the fact that these beings have no body in the form that we ourselves know it as human beings. An assumption of this kind is completely unproved and arbitrary. Here, of course, it is impossible to argue in detail and with philosophical exactitude for the opposite view: that is, for an essential relatedness to matter on the part of personal subjectivities such as angels and demons (if they exist and if we are able to say anything at all about them). For then we would have to go into the question of what matter is in a philosophical sense; it would have to be shown that, particularly in a Thomistic understanding, matter as such cannot really be split in itself into many pieces of matter, but is the original albeit precisely the differentiating unity, the one 'field' of the cosmos, the condition of the possibility of the separatedness and the interaction of the individual concrete realities. It would also have to be shown (perhaps in a critique of the traditional textbook philosophy in the Church) that the internal dualism in a finite entity necessary for the understanding of its createdness is reflected twice in that philosophy: in the dualism of essence and existence and in the dualism of matter and form, two dualisms which are understandable and cogent in their duality only if it is assumed as a matter of course, as in Neoplatonism or in the philosophy of Aquinas (contrary to the intrinsic tendency of his system), that there are immaterial beings, *formae separatae*. But even if we leave aside such metaphysical reflections as impossible to pursue here, it can be said that the idea of good and bad angels as purely immaterial beings is contrary to the basic trend of the biblical teaching on angels. For traditional angelology contains in itself an odd contradiction which can only be scantily concealed in words. In the first place, in traditional angelology the angels are set up as Leibnizian monads which can draw the content of their existence (apart from its relationship to God) purely from their own internal resources, since as *formae separatae* they are always aware of themselves from the outset without the mediation of another being; and yet these monads (according to Scripture) are then suddenly supposed to be powers and authorities of this material world of ours, are supposed to have something to do with winds, fire, and water, are localized in this earthly world, in the last resort form together with human beings one and the same history of salvation, can be angels of individual nations, and are understood as effectively helpful and seductive in this world and its history.

It is possible to cope with these internal tensions and contradictions of traditional angelology only by resolutely discarding Neoplatonic ideas and assigning *a priori* to the angels (if they exist) an essential intrinsic relationship to *that* matter which is the sustaining ground of the finiteness of the world, of the unity of the cosmos and its history of personal beings. It is, of course, difficult to say *how* exactly this 'materiality' of the angels is to be understood as distinct from the materiality of that personal consciousness which is man. Nevertheless, it can be imagined that the kind of mastery and formation of space-time reality which comes about through the human body and the personal entelechy corresponding to it is not unique, that there can be greater and more differentiated unities of space-time reality than that of a human body and its synthesis and interiorization of materiality. The idea of a form related to matter producing a greater material unity and configuration than that of the human body is not more difficult to conceive than the idea of a *forma separata*, to which traditional angelology has become accustomed and thus finds understandable, without perceiving the tensions and (to be honest) the contradictions in it. In any case, the idea of such a superhuman principle establishing unity and interiority is more capable of being grasped by natural knowledge than are the monadic angels of a traditional angelology. But as was shown in the first section of our reflections, we cannot give up the possibility of a natural knowledge of angels, if these are not to be suspected *a priori* of being merely mythological figures. These reflections, however, must be continued in our third section.

Even if the existence of demons is assumed and upheld as a fact, the concrete ideas of them in popular theology and more especially in the ordinary piety of Catholics need a decisive demythologization. This is something that must be considered for a while here. As such, this demythologizing has no need of any particularly modern insights. It is sufficient to apply to the ideas of the demons those fundamental and universal insights on evil which were long ago developed by a Christian metaphysic of finite freedom, of the nature of the good and of culpable evil. There is no absolute evil. All evil is finite; it is not a positive reality in itself, but a want of good in an entity that remains good in its substance as coming from God and indestructable. In its origin, in its possibility of becoming definitive, in its co-existence with an absolute God and his unrestrictedly good freedom and power, freely posed wickedness is certainly a mystery which resists a rationalistic solution and cannot simply be understood as merely the unavoidable reverse side of the good, as an irritating phenomenon in the coming to be of the good. But this need not prevent us from seeing the wickedness of the wicked, the guilt of the guilty, even in its possible finality, as deficiency (although freely posited) of the good in a good entity, as something that would not and never could be evil if it were not and did not still remain good in very many respects and dimensions of reality. We can be evil and do evil only if we remain good and behave well (even though in a defective way). Even in an evil action of freedom of the most radical kind the good is affirmed as condition of the possibility of freedom and goodness and realized in a positive sense, although not to the extent and in the radicalness possible and required in the particular concrete situation. If we do not want to be Manichees and if we do not want to see evil and good as consisting in an absolute dualism of two equal powers, we must always and everywhere keep in mind the fact that even evil lives by the good and always continues to realize the good, that evil as absolute and forthright corruption would utterly destroy as an entity this entity that had become evil.

All this, however, is true of the devils and demons, if they exist. They have a nature that is good and created by God, that is not removed, but, again, posited, even by their free and definitive decision against God. Not that the finalized decision by these demons against God can be seen as a superficial patina clinging only externally to a reality created by God, so that the question might be asked why this patina is not swept away and the reality created good by God preserved. Wickedness freely chosen is certainly a determination reaching to the very heart of the personal reality created by God. But it is a determination of this reality created by God and therefore good and remaining good in its substance and self-realization. A popular idea of devils, however, is that they are beings consisting of nothing but opposition to God, of hatred and negation.

This popular idea confuses evil with what has become evil, *malitia* as such with actual *malum*; it identifies evil beings with the pure essence of evil, with what is nothing but wickedness. But there are not and cannot be any such evil beings. If the demons reject God, their rejection is a defective mode of their always positive nature and its realization, which always has a positive meaning and positively contributes only to the goodness of the world. Even more mythological would be an idea of demons as impish, malignant spirits whose action and behavior really contain in their substance nothing but a destruction of positive realities, although that action can be understood only as a realization of what is positively good. It is a mythological idea to suppose that in order to realize their nature in the world, with the good necessarily involved in it and with the negative present in and about this good through their decision, these evil spirits need a 'permission', understood up to a point juridically and legally, from God who permits them in one place and forbids them in another to inflict damage, without this having anything really to do with the nature and the cosmic function they possess, whether good or bad. If and insofar as events in the cosmos and its history are also conditioned by the existence and self-realization of such powers and authorities, these events are not properly to be understood as effects of new initiatives on the part of these demons, oriented only to evil as such, but as consequences of their nature and their cosmic function, which are always the expression of an essentially good nature *and* determined also by the evil decision. When the effects produced by these demonic cosmic powers are regarded *merely* as purely destructive, we are involved in principle (whether we notice it or not) in a kind of Manicheism, or we adopt a childish attitude and ascribe to the demons behaviour like that of small boys throwing stones at the windows of their school. Mythological, too, is the idea of a conflict and opposition between God and the demons, with God and the devil struggling against each other as more or less equally matched partners, engaged in an absolute antagonism. The demons (if they exist) are radically dependent on God, sustained entirely in their activity by a positive collaboration of God, planned from the outset in their activity together with the evil involved in it by God's providence totally independently of any other influence; in a properly metaphysical sense there cannot be a struggle between God and the devil, since the latter from the very outset, always and at every moment, in all his powers and in all his activity, is completely dependent on God.

The difference between the demons and God and their dependence on him are, in any case, as great as the difference and dependence on our part: that is, infinite. Compared with one another, they and we may display considerable differences in knowledge and power. But the difference does not place the demons in the role of an anti-God. And if, in particular with traditional textbook theology, we ascribe to them a superhuman measure of intelligence and power, we should certainly not regard them as present in almost childishly trivial manifestations which are of little importance either to world history or to salvation history. And if with traditional textbook theology we take seriously into account the intelligence and power of these agencies, we shall not suspect that they are involved when a saint falls down the stairs or some poor girl shows symptoms of schizophrenia or epilepsy which in other cases are certainly due to natural causes and are not interpreted there in terms of demonology. If we recognize the existence of such nonhuman spirit-persons, particularly if we regard them as belonging to a higher order despite their relationship to the world, we simply cannot conceive their activity as a sporadic interference intended *only* to do harm in the chain of causes and effects otherwise perceptible to us, but must see it as the effect of this higher order as such, which does not cancel the essential achievement and connection of the lesser orders, but takes up the latter intact into the higher order.

We no longer assume today that the biosphere can establish its power and its own internal laws only by partially abolishing and disturbing the normal course of the sphere of the physical and chemical. Higher systems do not remove the lower ones, but incorporate the latter while preserving them in their own existence. If there are superhuman created-and-personal realities, they form within the unity of the one cosmos a higher order in the world as a whole. Nor is this structural system, produced from the unity of all created realities in the one cosmos, removed by the sin of personal realities within this system of the one cosmos as a whole; for whole 'evil spirits' by their decision can give a false direction to other individual realities (or, if the latter are personal in character, at least can attempt to do this), and they can realize these evil intentions of theirs only in a positive affirmation of their nature and function. If we wanted to continue with such speculations within the scope of a traditional Catholic angelology and demonology, we could point to the vast intelligence and great freedom of these beings which mean that their radical and definitive culpability makes sense only as a result of wanting to be like God in the sense of rejecting such a deification through *grace*. But if this is assumed, it becomes even more clear that the natural cosmic function of the demons (like that of the other angels) must not be seen as canceled, but only as determined also by their refusal of God's offer of himself out of free, gracious love. Then the really demonic element in the world would be that fainthearted despondency in which the creature fears for itself and will not venture freely to entrust itself to the absoluteness of the love in which God seeks to bestow, not something befitting the creature, but himself. In brief: if we want to pursue angelology and demonology at all, we must remain on the level of the first initiative for such a theory and not degrade these cosmic powers and authorities to goblinlike, ghostly, malicious spirits who are more stupid and more wretched than feeble human beings.

3. THE QUESTION OF THE THEOLOGY OF THE COSMOS

We come to our third section. In the first section we came to the conclusion that if the existence of good and bad angels must be affirmed in theological terms, this proposition as revealed assumes both a natural knowledge of angels and also that synthesis between a natural knowledge and the original act of faith which not only makes this object of natural knowledge as such into one *about* which a theological statement can be made, but also elevates it to be a secondary and derived object of faith itself. In the first question, then, the question remained completely open whether the angels can be an object of natural knowledge, particularly since the supporters of both the first and the second positions outlined at the beginning start out today more or less from the assumption that the existence of the angels is either directly and solely an object of revelation or is not demonstrable at all. In the second section of our reflections we worked simply on the still-unverified assumption that there are angels, and the only question was how, *if* they exist, they are to be understood in the light of a Christian monotheism. In this third section, then, we have to ask if it makes sense to allow for the existence of angels as coming within the scope of natural knowledge. The new question is formulated cautiously, since we do not want to venture here on our own account and at our own risk to assert more than that the acceptance of the existence of angels is not inconsistent with natural reason. It cannot be denied that a statement of this kind does not mean that we have clearly reached the point which must be reached if we want to elevate this natural perception to a properly theological level. And even if it were claimed that the existence of the angels had been established with adequate natural certainty, the question would still be completely open as to whether faith makes a statement *merely about* this object of natural knowledge or synthesizes it as a secondary object of faith. The third section, therefore, does not aim at a conclusion which would amount to a decision between the first two positions outlined at the beginning. After these reflections, the third position still does not seem to have been eliminated. But perhaps our reflections in this third section may serve to upset somewhat the self-assurance of the supporters of the second position and thus to elucidate a little the justification of the third position as against the second.

In our reflections we are starting out from the assumption that if there are angels, they are to be understood, not *a priori* as Leibnizian monads, but as cosmic powers and authorities for which, with all their subjectivity and personality, a cosmic function (that is, one related to the world) is an essential constituent. If we could not make this assumption, then obviously there could be no talk of a primarily natural knowledge of the existence of angels.

It may certainly be claimed, particularly at the present time, that a theology of the cosmos is very undeveloped. Of course, elements of such a theology of the cosmos are to be found scattered in a traditional textbook theology. The createdness and temporal nature of the world as a whole are mentioned there; an angelology of the traditional kind can scarcely fail to include some cosmic aspects; a defence of the unity of the human race must include some consideration of the biosphere, particularly if there is no longer any attempt to defend traditional monogenism; in anthropology a substantial unity of mind and matter is maintained with reference to man, even though the older metaphysic of *materia prima* scarcely appears in textbook theology and consequently little can be seen of the unity of mind and matter as a cosmic unity; in eschatology there is usually a brief mention of the new heaven and the new earth, but it really does not become very clear whether, why, and how the definitive consummation of created spirit-persons and of their history carries with it also the consummation of the material cosmos or has little to do with this material cosmos. Perhaps all the questions that ought to be raised in a theology of the cosmos are so obscure in themselves that it is easy to understand the ineffectiveness of such a theology. The fact remains that in theology man and his relationship to God are at the centre of attention and it is in this light that all theological statements must be understood in their meaning and validity. This corresponds to the nature of revelation and theology and to an absolutely fundamentally legitimate development of the philosophical understanding of man, in which the latter gradually came to be seen, not so much as part of a cosmos, but as a transcendental subject with a world of his own which he projects in thought and action. But this development of the history of ideas in modern times was also coexistent with a contrary tendency: the earth moved away from the centre of the cosmos and became an insignificant particle in an immense cosmos which continually became, and is still becoming, greater for human knowledge; but man himself became increasingly clearly perceptible as the product (intentionally or accidentally) of a history of nature of the material cosmos. From this standpoint, too, a theology of the cosmos is required, particularly since the doctrine of the substantial unity of mind and matter in man (with all its consequences: salvific importance of history as such, incarnation of the Logos, resurrection of the body, etc.) simply forbids us to pursue an absolutely acosmic theology and anthropology.

Such a theology of the cosmos would have to work out the theological significance of the interpretation of the cosmos as a world continually *coming to be*. The older premodern world on the whole understood world and earth as static factors created by God once and for all, offering for all time a fixed stage on which man and man alone could carry on his history. Today we rightly speak of a history of nature, we are aware of a world that is always and everywhere coming to be and we understand the history of humanity also as a part of this history or at least as conditioned by it, even though a serious and cautious metaphysic of grades and orders of being (taking really seriously the differentiatedness of the world) recognizes essential differences between entities in the cosmos and is consequently aware of qualitative leaps, of real self-transcendence of one grade of being into a higher grade, which is possible only as a result of God's creative dynamism in the world. The recognition of essentially different grades of being (from real subjectivity, personality, and transcendentality to being as a whole) does not, however, imply a denial of the one material cosmos and its evolution taking place in a continually new self-transcendence of an inferior grade.

In the light of such a basic conception of the world (in which man is no longer seen without more ado as the centre of a world constructed statically around him, as the one who is absolutely and in every respect underivable, but in which he represents a peak and an effect of a world evolution), the question can no longer be avoided as to whether that subjectivity rooted in materiality which we know as man is the only one toward which this world evolution of the material cosmos has developed in continually new self-transcendence. This question must be raised in view of the vast immensity of the material cosmos as a world coming to be. If we imagine the cosmos as a world coming to be, and as oriented in its becoming to subjectivity, then it is really not to be taken for granted that this aim has been successful only at the tiny point we know as our earth. At this stage in our reflections, admittedly we should not forget what has been learned from this history of man's subjectivity. A personal and free subjectivity oriented in unlimited transcendentality to being purely and simply (and, consequently, to the ground of being which is God) is the centre of the cosmos, even though this human subjectivity rests on a materiality which as such cannot be regarded as the centre of all that is material, even if it made sense at all to speak of a material centre of this material cosmos. But even if we do not forget this human subjectivity, through which *everything* is the world of man, the world he has, however great it may be and however great it may still come to be, the question in fact remains open as to whether the immense growth of the material cosmos has served only for the emergence in particular of human subjectivity. Traditional theology especially, with its conviction of the existence of angels (of angels who have a common salvation history together with human beings), cannot start out from the axiom that in regard to God there can really only be human subjectivities. The question, then, can seriously be raised even if we have not or would not have any opportunity of answering it unequivocally.

If this question is raised, it does not mean (although this perhaps is possible and justifiable) that we are asking here about beings existing on other 'stars' as subjects with more or less the same biological corporality as that which we know as our own. It is true that the latter question could also be raised, because it cannot be regarded simply and absolutely as improbable that somewhere else in such an immeasurable cosmos there are the same chemical and physical preconditions as with us for the 'chance' of the emergence of life and that this life then develops according to the strict laws of evolution (with and in qualitative leaps) toward something essentially like ourselves. This question about 'human beings on other planets' is one that has recently been raised afresh and more urgently because it inevitably also brings up theological problems. But it is a question that will not be pursued further here, since at the present time it is not only unanswerable, but refers to living beings which at least up to now have not been incorporated in our own existential and theological sphere of life and thus existentially and theologically have no more relevance for us than any sort of 'dead' star anywhere in the universe.

The question will, however, be raised here as to whether this general starting point of a world coming to be, oriented to subjectivity, might not lead to some conclusions about the conceivability and probability of angels. If we speak of 'angels', it is assumed from the outset that (1) they have an essential connection with the world and (2) they have for us an existential relevance that we denied to possible 'human beings on other planets', since the existential sphere of life of the latter (at least up to now) does not overlap with ours. If there are such 'angels' who fulfill this second precondition, their relationship to matter, essential as it must be, is to be understood as different from ours and from that of the hypothetically assumed 'human beings on other planets'. Such an essential relationship of subjectivity and matter must by its very notion be understood always as a limited regionality of matter, which is interiorized and (if desired) organized and subjectivized by this finite subjectivity. But this limited regionality of a subjectivity need not be understood as like that of a human corporality. This material regionality can be understood as much more plural and more differentiated, more complex, and as embracing more material individual realities than is the case with human corporality, *and* this greater and more comprehensive, subjectively interiorized regionality ought also to be able to incorporate into itself as partial elements those individual realities that we know as human beings. It would be wrong to regard such an idea *a priori* as too abstruse. A free subjectivity of man, open to the whole of reality, which at the same time is the ultimate organizing principle of a peristalsis of the digestive organs, is not *a priori* more probable than the idea envisaged here.

As already pointed out, such a higher principle of unity and order of a material regionality, greater and more differentiated than the human body, does not mean that the individual realities incorporated into this more comprehensive system are in any sense suppressed by this principle and no longer realizable in accordance with their proper nature. A higher principle of order respects the essential nature of the individual realities it organizes and gives them a further determination only in the directions in which they are ambivalent and open. Nor is it inconceivable from this standpoint that such a higher principle of unity and order of a material regionality should incorporate into this unity and order also realities which are themselves already subjectively polarized and interiorized. In other words, even a human reality which itself represents a corporeally limited system of matter and subjectivity can be conceived as integrated into such a higher system, if and insofar as this corporality itself has a potentiality for a higher and more comprehensive order. If two subjectivities are thus understood as graded principles of unity and order, with one above the other, then, of course, such a gradation and sub- and super-ordination is originally present in connection with this organizing function in regard to matter as such only insofar as these two principles extend to a smaller ('body') or greater material area ('angelic region'), but not (as is obvious) insofar as both principles as intellectual subjects of freedom have an infinite openness to being as a whole and to God: that is, they are distinguished in the light of the range of their starting point within materiality and not in the light of their goal (God).

It can readily be admitted that we seem at first sight to have become involved in our reflections in a consideration of the nature of the 'angels' and have apparently moved away from the question of their existence, returning to points already touched on in the second section. But in the last resort this apparent deviation is justified. For the question can now be more clearly stated: If angels are understood in this way, can they be thought of as existing in the light of the conception of an essentially material world, moving progressively toward increasingly higher subjectivity and a genuine unity of plural material realities? We might think in the first place that a continually advancing subjectivizing and interiorizing of the material cosmos is also man's task, going beyond the area of his biological corporality in his knowledge and activity into the world as such (and not merely set in his environment as fixed by his corporality), thus subjectivizing and interiorizing the cosmos in possibilities and ways which he is only now beginning slowly to discover (astronautics, for example). The question, of course, might also be asked whether the time of the world must now be regarded as having lasted so long and being so far advanced that those more comprehensive subjectivities to which the evolution of the world is tending must already exist, or whether they belong to a future still to come. (By analogy with some other theological problems it might then be said that the angels are perhaps not protological, but eschatological beings.) But man's destiny of activating in deed and thought a greater subjectivizing and interiorizing of the cosmos does not exclude the possibility that this goal of the cosmos can and should be attained in other and higher ways, particularly since man's somatic starting point imposes on the fulfillment of this task limits which (as can easily be understood) cannot in fact be surmounted, although they are prior to the absolute fulfillment of this task.

The question of time seems more difficult to us. It might be asked whether the evolution of the world has 'already' arrived at 'angels'. Our conception of angels seems to see them mainly as the end product of an evolution of the world, while traditional theology regards them as (also cosmic) principles at the beginning of the world. Here there are certainly difficulties and obscurities which are not to be denied or minimized, but it can admittedly be asked whether that finite physical time which begins according to currently accepted ideas of modern physics with the 'big bang' (which can certainly not itself be simply identified with the beginning of the world in a theological sense) is the very time in which the material cosmos evolves under the necessary and already present principles of order which we call 'angels'. Whatever we think exactly of the way in which such angels come to be, they have in any case an essential relationship to matter, and, consequently, the history of the latter is also their own history, so that they do not become acosmic if we place them as principles of unity and order at the beginning of the history of the material cosmos, the history that we know as that of our material cosmos. In this history, then, angels, too, would reach the fulfillment of their nature as organizing and unifying regional principles of the material cosmos. It might then be asked if they could not (without any inconsistency) be both at the beginning and at the end of a material history, in a way similar to that in which the human intellectual subject is at the beginning and end of a history of the body, without implying that the 'soul' (which must be seen as present at the beginning of this corporeal history) had no history itself. Over and above all this, in principle, the possibility cannot be *a priori* excluded that the history of nature in regard to matter may develop toward such more widely ranging regional and interiorizing principles more rapidly than it did toward the emergence of man. It could certainly be assumed that subjectivity on the narrow basis of our biological corporality is attainable only with greater difficulty and more slowly (and also more 'casually') than on the basis of a more comprehensive materiality, that nature's feat of subjectivity within a small corporality (known as man) needed a longer start (called the biosphere) than would be required for cosmic subjectivity as a whole. It cannot then simply be claimed that 'angels' in this sense must be no more than goals still to be reached in a cosmic evolution. Nor can it be claimed, in the light of their nature and existence, that world evolution (with qualitative leaps) has already reached those subjectivities with a greater material regionality which we can call angels.

All our reflections hitherto in this third section seem to have made the existence and nature of 'angels' *conceivable*, but no more than that. Are there in fact in the world of our experience any indications that this thing, whose nature and existence can be conceived and expected, actually exists and makes itself known? With our conception of these 'angels' in particular we certainly do not expect the existence of such 'angels' to be made known by their effects, suddenly and unexpectedly interposed in isolation at certain individual points in the natural and normal course of material events. *A priori* we do not count on this sort of miraculous intervention of angels at purely individual points in space and time to make known their existence. But, we might ask, can the existence of such principles of the cosmos become known only in this way or is there a possibility of such an experience which does not necessitate the interruption of the material course of things and which is described and investigated by physics and chemistry? A possibility of this kind seems conceivable if the negative criterion just mentioned is kept in mind and in the light of the nature of angels as understood here. If man becomes aware of unities and orders of a greater, but particular, kind, which, on the one hand, are conceivable in the light of the individual elements of such a unity and order and are sustained by these elements without detriment to their own immanent laws, and which, on the other hand, exist without being required or necessitated by these structural elements themselves, so that in order to 'explain' them we would need to have recourse to mere 'chance' or even directly (which is unlikely) to a creative institution by God alone, then man has the right to think of organizing and unifying principles of these unities and orders, whose existence is not adequately explained by that of their elements.

Man seems to have always had and to be able to have today such experiences of unities and orders in the world of nature and the history of humanity, to be interpreted and explained in this way; in fact, it seems that in the course of the history of humanity such experiences have been the real although less obvious reason for belief in angels, and not only those dubious 'spiritistic' experiences with which supporters and opponents of the existence of angels are usually occupied. Both in nature and also in human history, and, moreover, in the interconnection and unity of nature and history, there are experiences of unity and order, experiences which seem to be adequately interpreted only if such principles of unity and order are presupposed and if it is understood that the materialities out of which these unities and orders are constructed do not themselves provide an explanation of these orders. *Non enim plura secundum se uniuntur*, as Aquinas rightly says.

At this stage of course, even before we catch sight concretely of these particular orders and unities, the old problems emerge from the debate between hylomorphism, holism, reduction of the biological to cybernetically interpreted chemical systems. For all these and similar theories are meant to provide the right answer to the question of exactly how complex unities are to be understood, when they seek to prevail against their 'environment' and thus to make their unity clear. But, although it might seem appropriate, we cannot, of course, go into all these difficult problems here. The problems are particularly difficult in the field of theology, since theology *of itself* cannot defend the principle of a fundamental essential difference between the purely material and the biological, but must remain neutral on this point and leave it entirely to the free discussion of the philosophy of nature. For theology as such, this kind of essential difference (despite all the unity of evolution and self-transcendence) is certainly present only when it is a question of man's intellectual subjectivity in unlimited transcendentality toward being as a whole and so toward God. Which of these systems of the philosophy of nature (apart from anthropology) is right is a question on which theology cannot have an independent opinion in the light of its own principles. But since the interpretation of those greater unities and orders (which are more comprehensive than any of the particular, material, living, individual human realities taken in isolation) is supposed to be a matter of natural knowledge, this incompetence of theology in regard to the theories mentioned is not simply irrelevant for our question.

It can, however, be said that if and insofar as a theological anthropology accepts as a fact the existence of material systems (at least in man) whose unity and order is at least partially determined by a unifying substantial principle, it cannot appeal to interpretations available in the philosophy of nature of the order and unity of individual biological realities, excluding holistically or cybernetically any higher principle for this order and unity, and then assert *a priori* that there cannot be higher and more complex unities within the material cosmos established by higher substantial principles. This should be obvious particularly because we must certainly distinguish in principle between the structure of a complex entity on the one hand and the unifying ground of this structure on the other and cannot assume *a priori* that the elements of such a structure alone in their diversity themselves contain the ground of the unity of this structure.

Of course, it is impossible, particularly here, to deal terminologically and objectively with the complex of questions coming ontologically under the heading of substance and structure. These two terms may offer an immense field for debate; but if the term 'structure' is understood in its traditional sense (that is, as the result of a unification, and not as the principle of this unification and unity), if, moreover, we at least leave open the question of whether a synthesizing 'from below' is not for us a concretely tangible process of a self-transcendence (in the sense indicated, of creating something qualitatively new), then we cannot regard structure at any rate as an unequivocal alternative to substance, substantial form, etc., and claim the right to go back from the structure to the real principle of this structure.

Where then, we ask finally, is it possible to discover concretely such unities and orders of a particular but greater kind, for which a proper principle of unity, order, and structure can be postulated: a principle which, since the unity and order it establishes are more comprehensive than those of the human body, possesses at least that subjectivity and transcendentality which is proper to the intellectual principle of man? It is, of course, possible here to do no more than hint at an answer to this question, since more concrete and better substantiated answers would lead us into the whole length and breadth of the particular sciences, and since, in view of the technically rationalistic mentality of modern man and the mathematically-quantitatively operating sciences involved in this, a mystagogy would be required for the genuine experience of such orders and unities—a mystagogy correcting the modern mentality and thus making effective the experience of these unities and orders. Nevertheless, both within the history of nature as such and also in the history of mankind, as well as in the interconnection of the history of nature and human history, embracing a variety of material realities in space of time, there are unities distinguishable from one another and containing in themselves a unity and order which at least gives the impression that it is not explicable purely and simply by the casual assemblage of its formative elements and preconditions, although, of course, quite definite circumstances and conditions must be present in these elements for such an ordered unity to be able to emerge in a particular form within the cosmos as a whole. The necessity of such conditions 'from below' may not, of course, be disputed or obscured. But it would not really contradict the explanation of this ordered unity envisaged here if it were clearly proved that such an ordered unity always and necessarily emerges if these conditions are fulfilled from below. (The theologian, for instance, will not deny that, if the biological preconditions and factualities are present for human procretion, a human being will necessarily emerge, although the 'human soul' thus emerging qualitatively transcends the event of such a biological procreation as much as the intellectual subjectivity of man always surpasses his biological reality as such, although the latter is incorporated into the former as an intrinsic constituent.)

In the history of the evolution of life, it seems that there are such ordered unities, complexes of plural meanings, which go beyond the biological individual realities. At the particular stages of evolution of flora and fauna, together with their mutual interdependence, unities delimitable from one another can be distinguished; a particular period of evolution is characterized by a uniform style which is common also to those individualities in such a period which are not directly derived from one another; by and large in an individual period everything is coherent, although this common physiognomy of an epoch cannot be interpreted merely as our own subjective impression. Many causes can be suggested, of course, for the rise and decline of such an epoch in the history of the evolution of life, just as the most diverse individual causes can be assigned for the death of a human being; but the impression is given (despite all these possible external causes) that in the last resort such a period dies from within itself, outgrows itself and *wants* to die, just as with the individual human being (despite his external breakdown) death is his own death coming from within, and what we call 'chance' is the executor of an internal necessity. If someone considers such a period in the history of nature with its unity, its common style, and its one destiny and does not think that he has understood the one totality as such when he has grasped its elements and their 'accidental' coordination, despite all the positivism of the sciences at the present time, he can have the courage to perceive a unifying principle in such a unity.

The same can certainly be said (and more emphatically) in regard to the periods of the history of mankind and in regard to the histories of individual nations and other historical unities that can be observed. Here, too, things do not go in utter shapelessness; here in particular there are unities clearly distinguishable from one another, each with a particular style of its own; here, too, each period of universal history, of the history of a nation, or of a particular civilisation has its internal drama and dialectic, its beginning and its end, has a common physiognomy, although this entire unity and peculiarity cannot be made intelligible solely by human beings, who directly carry on this history and realize throughout time unities of meaning that they themselves had by no means foreseen. These historical structures of meaning, extending in time over several generations, have, of course, their preconditions from below in all the individual empirical causes (geographical, biological, meteorological, sociological, etc.). But the very fact that these causes from below are really plural in character and mutually independent may lead us to wonder whether their blind, casual concurrence alone can explain the historical structures of meaning emerging from that concurrence. If the Christian in face of such a question is inclined to find an answer promptly and directly in an appeal to God's providence ruling over and in history, this answer is not wrong but raises the further question of *how* this providence of God is to be understood as concretely *carried out*, whether it does not itself come to prevail through real principles, created by God, establishing order and unity, principles described in the Book of Daniel as angels of the nations. When we observe that such unities of meaning of a greater even though particular spatio-temporality emerge in history, when we learn that they are not wholly and ultimately due solely to shortsighted historical planning by human beings or still less have their ground in 'chance', in the unplanned coincidence of subhuman causes, but when at the same time in seeking for the sufficient reason of such unities today particularly it is impossible to appeal to a 'direct' intervention of God's providence, the presumption at least of such 'angels of the nations' is justified.

Man in history need not regard such an assumption as degrading him as a historical being in freedom. For, within the framework of such a principle of unity, he still remains free in his history of freedom even in its earthly character, his relationship to God is not threatened; and, without these principles of unity and order, man's scope for freedom would not be wider, but more disorganized and diminished in meaning. At the same time it should not be forgotten that the meaning and function of such principles of unity and order are not intended properly and primarily to influence man's freedom, but to establish a unity and order (within a particular region) in the material world, although they can take the form of a temptation for man, if and insofar as such orders may in their principles imply a rejection of God's gracious self-communication, carrying in themselves a tendency to be closed up, to become absolute.

Another kind of such a unity and order and of the principles lying behind it may be seen in a singular unity (obvious, however, to a contemplative gaze) of nature and culture in certain areas developed by man in which the peculiar character of nature and the peculiar character of a culture created by man converge in an odd way, while this convergence is not entirely explained by an accidental concurrence of its elements of a natural and cultural character, particularly since there are natural areas for human habitation in which such a synthesis of nature and culture has evidently not been achieved and where man remains without roots and nature remains inhuman.

The existence of these cosmic powers can be experienced from another aspect: in the antagonism in which greater ordered unities encounter one another, as, for instance, in the conflict between the angels of the nations in Daniel. By the very diversity of their individual elements, the individual cosmic realities in the different spheres of this cosmos are in opposition to and in conflict with one another; but it looks as if greater, more differentiated unities, containing within themselves many individual elements of the most diverse character, each for their own part have a tendency to unity and permanence (like an individual living being), and nevertheless are in opposition to and in conflict with one another, presenting a threat to one another. It does not look as if all antagonism in the cosmos could be reduced to the mere diversity and mutual interaction of the ultimate rudimentary particles which form the cosmos. The world does not seem to be merely the regular drift and thrust of these rudimentary particles; there seem to be greater unities and orders which, on the one hand, are not the result of the fortuitous concurrence of these individual rudimentary realities, but which, on the other hand, by their diversity are in an opposition and antagonism toward one another that is more fundamental than the opposition between the rudimentary details. This at least is true from the biosphere onward and continuing into the human sphere, in the history of which there are antagonisms and struggles for existence that are prior to any properly moral decision and that establish between the greater human unities a state of real war or of real peace.

The question, then, is whether such antagonisms can be ascribed solely and directly to their institution by the Creator, in the sense that he sets up in their own nature the realities through which the antagonisms arise. It can be said, of course, that if we ascribe such cosmic antagonisms (in the biosphere and the history of humanity) to 'angelic powers and authorities' in order in a sense to take away the responsibility from God (who seems in his unity and inner concord not to be sufficiently effective in the world), we are merely shifting the problem, since in the last resort God must have created these antagonistic powers and authorities. But, when we experience such terrible antagonisms as struggles of life and death in the cosmos, we are led to postulate the principles necessary as preconditions for these things. Not in order to take away the responsibility from the God of eternal peace and of infinite concord in himself, but simply in order to give a name to the causes of such conflict in the cosmos which would not be present or visible if we were to think only of those rudimentary basic structures of the cosmos, even though these by their very diversity (which, admittedly, is itself an object of metaphysical astonishment and terror) contribute to these cosmic antagonisms. It is certainly a part of the nature and freedom of the infinite God, in whom all conceivable reality is always from the outset rooted in harmony as in its ground, that he can institute a cosmos of conflict and discord. But this very creative power of instituting conflict and discord in a cosmos coming to be (even prior to possible conflict and possible discord brought about freely by the creature's own fault) must be given an object, must create antagonistic realities. But the assumption that these consist first and last in the diversity and fortuitous concurrence of the rudimentary structures of the cosmos, or were introduced into the cosmos only by the deliberate fault of creatures, is an idea that does not seem to do justice to the greatness and radicalness of such antagonisms, of such cosmic conflicts, which still have to be settled. The higher 'powers and authorities' seem to exist and (prior to any possible fault which, if it exists, intensifies such antagonism) to be placed by God himself in a state of bellicose opposition to one another.

What has been said, of course, has not produced either conclusive evidence of the existence of angelic powers or a differentiated mystagogy into the experience of them. All that has been done is to indicate regions of possible experience in which man's natural knowledge might encounter (if it is possible at all) something like angels, without giving to these experiences an incredible or mythical interpretation as experiences of realities interposed between the experiences with which modern empirical sciences in accordance with their own method are occupied. Insofar as this evidence and the mystagogy to be presupposed for it cannot really be offered here, the third position (which we defended at the beginning of these reflections) has not yet been eliminated in favour of the first position. If we have achieved anything at all, it can consist in the last resort only in a number of warnings: in the warning not to adopt a biblicistic fundamentalism and too quickly and too naively be persuaded of the existence of good and bad angels; in the warning to take seriously the hermeneutic principles arising from the actual nature of a divine revelation, which must be observed if we attempt to prove theologically the existence of angels, although the latter cannot be part of the primary and original object of revelation; in the warning not to adopt a primitive rationalism and to think that *a priori* no creaturely subjectivity can be conceived in addition to and 'above' man, or that such a subjectivity is purely and simply outside the field of possible experience or must be imagined in the way in which it frequently occurs in popular opinion.

LIST OF SOURCES

Volume 19: Faith and Revelation

FOUNDATIONS OF CHRISTIAN FAITH
Lecture on 28 February 1979 in the Historische Kaufhaussaal, Freiburg im Breisgau. Previously unpublished.

ON THE RELATIONSHIP BETWEEN NATURAL SCIENCE AND THEOLOGY
Lecture on 15 July 1979 in the Protestant Academy of Tutzing. Previously unpublished.

THE CHURCH'S REDEMPTIVE HISTORICAL PROVENANCE FROM THE DEATH AND RESURRECTION OF JESUS
Lecture on 12 November 1976 at the Philosophical-Theological College of St. Pölten. Published in *Zeit des Geistes*, ed. J. Reikenstorfer (Vienna 1977), pp. 11–26.

BRIEF THEOLOGICAL OBSERVATIONS ON THE 'STATE OF FALLEN NATURE'
Composed in commemoration of Enrico Castelli.

CONSECRATION IN THE LIFE AND REFLECTION OF THE CHURCH
Lecture on 14 November 1976 in the Catholic Academy in Freiburg im Breisgau. Previously unpublished.

PASTORAL MINISTRIES AND COMMUNITY LEADERSHIP
Published in *Stimmen der Zeit* 195 (1977): 733–43.

THEOLOGY AND SPIRITUALITY OF PASTORAL WORK IN THE PARISH
Lecture at the Austrian Pastoral Conference of 28–30 December 1976 in Vienna. Published in *Pfarrseelsorge,* ed. J. Wiener and E. Erharter (Vienna 1977), pp. 11–25 (questions to the lecturer, pp. 25–30).

THE SPIRITUALITY OF THE SECULAR PRIEST
Lecture at the Catholic Academy of Bavaria (Munich), end of November 1977. Published in *Mitten unter den Menschen*, ed. F. Wulf (Düsseldorf 1979), pp. 27–42.

THE SPIRITUALITY OF THE PRIEST IN THE LIGHT OF HIS OFFICE
Lecture at a conference on the theme 'Spirituality of the Priest Today', 6–8 July 1976, in Eisenstadt. Published in *Priesterliche Spiritualität heute*, ed. S. László (Vienna 1977), pp. 101–32 (questions to the lecturer, pp. 133–42).

ON THE THEOLOGY OF WORSHIP
Published in *Tübinger Theologische Quartalschrift* 159, no. 3 (1979): 162–69.

THE SUNDAY PRECEPT IN AN INDUSTRIAL SOCIETY
Published in *Entschluss* (1979), no. 1, pp. 26–32.

BASIC COMMUNITIES
Lecture delivered under the title 'Ökumenische Basisgemeinden' on 14 June 1975 at the Federal meeting of Action 365 in Frankfurt am Main. Previously unpublished.

ETERNITY FROM TIME
Published in *Entschluss* (1979), no. 4, pp. 7–11.

PURGATORY
Published in the Festschrift for H. Stirnimann on his sixtieth birthday.

WHY DOES GOD ALLOW US TO SUFFER?
Previously unpublished.

MARY AND THE CHRISTIAN IMAGE OF WOMAN
Published in *Stimmen der Zeit* 193 (1975): 795–800.

MARY'S VIRGINITY
A report for the session in Frankfurt am Main of a subcommittee of the Commission for Faith of the German Bishops' Conference, 27 July 1976.

ON ANGELS
Previously unpublished.

Volume 20: Concern for the Church

COURAGE FOR AN ECCLESIAL CHRISTIANITY
Published in *Warum ich Christ bin*, ed. W. Jens (Munich 1979), pp. 296–309.

ON THE SITUATION OF FAITH
Previously unpublished.

WOMEN AND THE PRIESTHOOD
Published in *Stimmen der Zeit* 195 (1977): 291–301.

THE CHURCH'S RESPONSIBILITY FOR THE FREEDOM OF THE INDIVIDUAL
Previously unpublished.

THEOLOGICAL JUSTIFICATION OF THE CHURCH'S DEVELOPMENT WORK
Published in *Misereor—Zeichen der Hoffnung* (Festschrift for Gottfried Dossing), ed. Episcopal Commission for Misereor (Munich 1976), pp. 71–79.

BASIC THEOLOGICAL INTERPRETATION OF THE SECOND VATICAN COUNCIL
Published in *Zeitschrift für katholische Theologie* 101 (1979): 290–99.

THE ABIDING SIGNIFICANCE OF THE SECOND VATICAN COUNCIL
Published in *Stimmen der Zeit* 197 (1979): 795–806.

THE FUTURE OF THE CHURCH AND THE CHURCH OF THE FUTURE
Lecture on 23 September 1977 in Offenburg. Previously unpublished.

STRUCTURAL CHANGE IN THE CHURCH OF THE FUTURE
Published in *Gesselschaft als politischer Auftrag,* ed. E. Braun (Graz 1977): 245–66.

DREAM OF THE CHURCH
Radio lecture of 28 May 1977 (Sudwestfunk) under the title 'Vision und Wirklichkeit der Traum von der Kirche'. Published in *Ich habe einen Traum*, ed. M. Krauss (Stuttgart 1978), pp. 77–78.

THE SPIRITUALITY OF THE CHURCH OF THE FUTURE
Lecture on 20 January 1977 at the Catholic University Chaplaincy in Münster. Previously unpublished.

UNITY OF THE CHURCH—UNITY OF MANKIND
Lecture on 18 May 1977 at the Catholic Academy of Hamburg in collaboration with the seminar of the Protestant Theological Faculty. Published in *Einheit der Kirche—Einheit der Menscheit* (Freiburg 1978), pp. 50–76.

THE INEXHAUSTIBLE TRANSCENDENCE OF GOD AND OUR CONCERN FOR THE FUTURE
Radio lecture of 27 September 1978 (ORF Studio Salzburg) in connection with the ninth Salzburg Conference on Humanism, held under the title 'Hoffnung in der Überlebenskrise?' Published in *Zugänge zur Theologie* (Festschrift W. Joest) (Göttingen 1979), pp. 201–14; also in *Hoffnung in der Überlebenskrise* (Graz 1979), pp. 180–95.

INDEX OF PERSONS

INDEX OF SUBJECTS